D1255744

Mr. Scharlemann teaches at the Graduate
School of Religion at the University of
Southern California.

YALE PUBLICATIONS IN RELIGION, 7

David Horne, editor

PUBLISHED UNDER THE DIRECTION OF
THE DIVINITY SCHOOL

THOMAS AQUINAS
and JOHN GERHARD

Robert P. Scharlemann

New Haven and London, Yale University Press, 1964

McCORMICK THEOLOGICAL SEMINARY
McGAW MEMORIAL LIBRARY
800 WEST BELDEN AVENUE
CHICAGO, ILLINOIS 60614

Copyright © 1964 by Yale University.
Designed by Crimilda Pontes,
set in Garamond type,
and printed in the United States of America by
The Carl Purington Rollins Printing-Office
of the Yale University Press.
All rights reserved. This book may not be
reproduced, in whole or in part, in any form
(except by reviewers for the public press),
without written permission from the publishers.

Library of Congress catalog card number: 64–12659

MAY 14 '64 kh

BX
1749
.T6
S2 90
1964

BX
1749.T41
S311t

TO MY PARENTS

JKM Library
1100 East 55th Street
Chicago, IL 60615

Preface

One can understand the present by an analysis of its components as being simply given, or one can understand it by discerning the forces of the past which have shaped it. That I have chosen the latter way for this volume is attributable in large measure to the circumstance that my interest in the subject was first expressed in a dissertation at Heidelberg—that is to say, in a country and at a university where the past is immediately present in a way which strikes an American student quite unforgettably.

Thus I have sought to describe the confessional split in the Western church not in terms of contemporary conflicts over matters of education or politics, but in terms of classical formulations of theological differences. For it is this classical form which, in innumerable manifestations, still characterizes the division. However, since we have—with ample historical justification, I should think—passed beyond most of the vocabulary of Aristotelian scholasticism, such an analysis of classical formulations must also be an interpretation if it is to be understood in its present relevance. It is my hope that the present study accomplishes that task.

It is impossible to say how many people have directly and indirectly been helpful in the preparation of this work. I should like, however, to name those in whose debt I most consciously stand: Robert Bertram of Valparaiso University, who first made me aware that philosophy can be exciting; Arthur Carl Piepkorn

PREFACE

of Concordia Theological Seminary, St. Louis, and Peter Brunner of the University of Heidelberg, to whom I owe the beginnings of an interest in pre-Reformation theology; and Sydney Ahlstrom and George Lindbeck of the Yale Divinity School, who have been most helpful with constructive suggestions for the present publication. The opportunity to do the research on John Gerhard was provided by a research grant from Lutheran Brotherhood and a research fellowship from Yale University, to both of which I am indebted more than I can say. To the editor of Yale Publications in Religion, David Horne, and to the editor for Yale University Press, Alice Augusta Miskimin, I owe thanks for their patience and encouragement during the laborious hours spent in preparation for publication.

R. S.

Los Angeles, California
September 1963

Contents

CONTENTS

A Note on Citations and Abbreviations

CITATIONS.

Where the source of a quotation or reference is listed in the Bibliography, the footnote cites only author, short title, and page number, without publication information. Where a source is used only incidentally and therefore does not appear in the Bibliography, full bibliographical data appear in the footnote. All translations of foreign language quotations are my own, except where the source is given in its English title.

ABBREVIATIONS.

L. Th. *Loci Theologici*
S. Th. *Summa Theologiae*
CG   *Contra Gentiles*
De car.   *De caritate*
De ver.   *De veritate*
DDN   *De divinis nominibus* (of Pseudo-Dionysius)
Proœm.   the prologue (*proœmium*) which precedes the first *locus* of Gerhard's *L. Th.*

Since references to the *Summa Theologiae* of Thomas and the *Loci Theologici* of Gerhard are so frequent, *L. Th.* and *S. Th.* are omitted in such references, except where accompanied by other material. Thus a reference to Thomas' *Summa Theologiae*, Part I, question 20, article 1, appears simply as (1.20.1) after the material in the text to which it refers. A reference to Gerhard's *Loci Theologici*, Locus IV, paragraph 5, appears as (IV.5).

Introduction

One of the promising developments in recent theological work is the interconfessional discussion between Roman Catholics and Protestants, which has been carried on for some time on the European continent without much fanfare. But the commencement of the second Vatican council in the fall of 1962 has given it a publicity hitherto lacking.

Although the eventual outcome of the cross-confessional conversations is unpredictable, some agreement has been discovered already in areas where it was least expected. Thus, there are theologians on both sides who hold that there is no longer a confessional opposition in the understanding of justification by grace. This is the thesis which Hans Küng, the brilliant young Roman Catholic theologian at the University of Tübingen, has set forth regarding Karl Barth and the Council of Trent.

Not everyone agrees that Küng has succeeded in providing the kind of common ground necessary for real rapprochement. Roman Catholics have objected to his interpretation of the Tridentine council. Protestants have suggested that Karl Barth diverges too much from the Reformation tradition to be taken as representative. Barth himself raises an incredulous question in his prefatory note to Küng's book. He asks, "How do you explain the fact that all of this could remain hidden for so long from so many people on the inside as well as on the outside?"[1] The answer to that question

1. Hans Küng, *Rechtfertigung*, p. 12.

I

could, I think, be given rather easily. For one thing, only in the present century has the historical distance from the sixteenth century become great enough to make credible evaluations which are more than traditionalistic (whether by affirmation or by denial). For another, the spirit of ecumenicism has brought forth a new will to understand.

Of course, approaches toward agreement have been made repeatedly through the centuries of division, even by such prominent figures as Leibniz and Bossuet. Perhaps the present endeavors will be equally fruitless. Or perhaps they will at last bring the earlier work to completion. Who can say? For the time being, at least, prospects seem favorable, for in addition to all else, the present century has inherited analytic tools which allow a nontraditionalistic evaluation.

Whatever the outcome, it is clear that Küng's work invites further inquiry: he has compared the normative dogmatic tradition of the Roman Catholic church with a very influential contemporary Protestant theologian. What would be the result if, instead, one compared representative theologians from the classical periods of the Roman Catholic and the Protestant theological history? This is the question behind the present work. Like Küng's work, it centers upon one major question. Unlike Küng's work, its comparison is not between a dogmatic tradition and an influential theologian, but rather between two influential theologians who are central to their traditions in the same way.

A study of classical theologians will, in the nature of the case, be of less interest to people who find it possible to overleap or ignore historical development, who approach questions *de novo*. It will be of greater interest to those churches which, like the Lutheran and Presbyterian, consciously trace their roots to the European Reformation. These churches are often haunted by the fear of irresponsibly sacrificing their Reformation heritage. In most cases they do not find it possible to ignore, with an easy conscience, the sixteenth and seventeenth centuries. Thus, in grappling with the present ecumenical questions, especially those concerning the relation to the Roman church, they find it necessary as a preliminary step to examine the classical formulations of the *status controversiae.*

The classical period of Roman Catholic theology (and only secondarily its dogmatically normative period) is the thirteenth century. This fact is too well known to require documentation. It is also well known that Thomas Aquinas is the focus of that era as far as the Aristotelian direction in theology is concerned.

But what of Protestant theology? The studies in the Reformation, inaugurated at the end of the last century, have tended to obscure that, as far as its theological history is concerned, Protestantism attained its classical period not in the sixteenth but in the seventeenth century. By this I mean that the directions in theological thought which appeared in Luther and Calvin and to some degree in Zwingli, reached a synthesis only in the early seventeenth century. The man who is focal to this period, as Aquinas is to the thirteenth century, is the professor at the University of Jena on whom contemporaries bestowed the title of "the arch-theologian." Bossuet named him *"le troisième homme de la Réforme."* He is John Gerhard (1582–1637).[2]

In both cases the synthesis was made in the framework of Aristotle's philosophy shortly after a general renewal of interest in the metaphysics of this philosopher. Whether this happened by historical accident or was due to an inherent characteristic which predisposed Western theology to Aristotle is a question beyond the scope of the present book. In any event, it is true that seventeenth-century theologians are relatively unknown at the present time in this country. Consequently, it is advisable to digress in order to explain the selection of John Gerhard as a representative of classical Protestant theology.

2. In the case of Roman Catholicism, the classical period antedated the dogmatically normative one; in the case of Protestantism (if it has a dogmatically normative period at all), the reverse is the case.

The choice of the seventeenth, rather than the sixteenth, century rests on the fact that the several theological themes of the Protestant Reformation had not been merged until that time. One theme was justification by grace through faith. This was the dominant concern of Martin Luther. A second theme was the problem of Scripture as sole theological principle, the concern of the more systematic John Calvin. Thus, while the message of justification was clearly the central message of God as far as Luther was concerned, his break with the authority of the existing church raised the problem of what to substitute for the church's authority. So long as Luther's dominating personality functioned as an effective substitute for the authority of the church, this was not a pressing problem. During his lifetime, Luther could serve as the court of appeal in matters of doctrine. Calvin saw more clearly that championing the biblical message against the doctrine of the existing church implies the prior question: On what grounds can one assert the Bible (the Word of God) against the church (the kingdom of God)?[3]

Both of these themes came together and received a final formulation in John Gerhard's *Loci Theologici* (1610–21), a work of which Drummond remarks that it was "distinguished by a candor all too rare among men who traverse the hot ashes of controversy."[4] The treatise on Scripture as the *principium* of theology, with which the *Loci* begins, brought together the whole complex of questions produced by intrinsic systematic problems and by the Jesuits' criticism. Gerhard's solution was based on the claim that the Scriptures meet the Aristotelian qualifications for principles in any science. That is to say, the doctrine of the Scripture was declared to be not an article of faith but the *principium* of the articles of faith. This solution stood until historical criticism

3. For a more detailed analysis of these themes, see Rupert E. Davies, *The Problem of Authority in the Continental Reformers,* and John Reid, *The Authority of Scripture.* The latter's account of the post-Reformation period is, unfortunately, based on unreliable secondary works.

4. Andrew Drummond, *German Protestantism,* p. 26.

of the Scriptures did away with the foundation of the seventeenth-century theological synthesis. Gerhard's treatise on justification (*Loci Theologici*, XVI) is similarly definitive. In amplitude of detail upon exegetical as well as systematic questions, and in precision of expression, it has no equal in the seventeenth century.[5] Thus, in the first place, Gerhard brings together the several theological themes of the Reformation.

In the second place, he crystallizes the conception of the dual nature of theology, which originated in Luther and was given its first systematic expression by Melanchthon. On the one hand, theology is considered to be the exposition of the content of Scripture in an orderly fashion and with scholarly tools. It begins in a general way with creation and ends with eschatology. On the other hand, theology is considered to be the content of the Bible in public and private use. Public use is proclamation in the church; private use is individual Christian meditation. It is this latter aspect of theology to which Schlink refers when he says that in Luther the structure of doctrinal assertions is "determined by the act of hearing God's address"; such assertions are made "in the act of hearing, in the act of sacramentally receiving."[6]

Gerhard formulates this dual conception of theology and systematically employs it by relating the content of any given topic to its practical use. The practical use did not, in this case, mean the application of a doctrine to specific situations as a general ethical principle, but rather the employment of the doctrine *in concreto* to "strike down" and then "lift up" the hearer.

In formulating the distinction Gerhard was able to use not only

5. See O. Ritschl, *Dogmengeschichte des Protestantismus*, 4, 297–302. For an example, see below, p. 192, where the meaning of faith in Abraham's case is formulated.
6. Edmund Schlink, "Gesetz und Evangelium als kontroverstheologisches Problem," *Kerygma und Dogma*, 7 (1961), 31–35. The best account of Melanchthon's theological approach is Paul Schwarzenau, *Der Wandel im theologischen Ansatz bei Melanchthon*.

INTRODUCTION

what may have been the common Melanchthonian heritage but also studies in methodology of the Italian logician, Jacopo Zabarella (1532–89).[7]

Zabarella distinguished two kinds of science, theoretical and practical, each with its own systematic order. The theoretical sciences proceeded from principles to conclusions—the compositive or synthetic order. The practical sciences proceeded by the resolutive or analytic order.[8] In general this meant moving from effects to causes. Specifically it meant that systematic exposition in a practical science began with a "pre-cognition" of the end (*finis*) to be achieved, then followed with a description of the subject (*subjectum*), and concluded with an explication of the means (*media*) by which the end is to be induced into the subject.

The model for the practical sciences was medicine. Thus, the goal of medicine was the state of health. Its subject was man insofar as he was to be healed. The means were the medicines by which health was brought into the unhealthy man.

By analogy, theology in use (publicly or privately) was a practical science. Its goal was the state of salvation. Its subject was man insofar as he is a sinner. Its means were the proclamation of the divine Word and the administration of the sacraments. "As in medicine," Gerhard states (*Prooem.* 28), "physiology and pathology precede . . . , so in theology, which is spiritual medicine, the integral and fallen nature of man is treated first, then the means are set forth which lead to the goal of theology, namely, the restoration and salvation of man. These means are the true and saving knowledge of God, true faith in Christ, and whatever serves these means."

7. See John H. Randall, Jr., *The Career of Philosophy* (New York, Columbia University Press, 1962), pp. 284 ff., on the Padua tradition and Zabarella's role. Cf. also Neal Ward Gilbert, *Renaissance Concepts of Method* (New York, Columbia University Press, 1960).
8. It is worth noting that the term "analytic," applied to seventeenth-century method, does not mean the modern minute distinctions among concepts; it means rather the resolutive order described by Zabarella.

6

INTRODUCTION

Thus, Gerhard's *Loci Theologici* brings together various streams. His general arrangement of topics (*loci*) retains the loose *historica series* of Melanchthon. Theology as an academic discipline is exhibited in the way Gerhard sets forth the content of Scripture. He uses, in an awesomely thorough fashion, all the available tools of philology, grammar, and philosophy. Finally, he imbeds the conception of theology as a practical skill in the *usus* of each topic. He shows how doctrine, when set before a man in his situation, works as spiritual medicine. Indeed, the analogy with medicine must have been especially illuminating for Gerhard, since he had studied and briefly practiced medicine before becoming a theologian.

When A. C. McGiffert remarks[9] of this stage of Protestant scholasticism that "the importance of a particular doctrine came to depend upon its place in the system rather than upon its practical relation to life," he is attributing to seventeenth-century theology a character it did not possess. Tight, deductive systems were a product of rationalism, not of seventeenth-century scholasticism. "Truth was gained," the author goes on, "not from the religious and moral experience of individual or church but by logical deduction from the accepted system, and it was tested by its consistency with the larger whole." This is simply not true. Gerhard systematically makes use of experience as the mediator of genuine knowledge of the gospel. Indeed, even in those theologians who adopted the synthetic method for theology (as a theoretic science) the emphasis was not on how things fit into a total system, but on how they fit together with the scriptural principle. On occasion, it was even possible to maintain doctrines which appeared to contradict each other, provided both could be shown to be drawn from Scripture.

Gerhard combines the Melanchthonian topical order and the synthetic and analytic methods. After him, there was a division

9. *Protestant Thought Before Kant* (Harper Torchbook, 1962), p. 145. The original edition appeared in 1911.

between the Lutheran and the Calvinist theologians. The Lutherans on the whole chose the analytic method for theology and gave it the tripartite division of goal, subject, and means. The Calvinists employed the synthetic method, treating theology as a theoretic science which proceeded from the principle of Scripture to the conclusions which were the articles of faith.[10]

Now, the development in intellectual history which gave Gerhard an advantage over his predecessors was the renewal of Aristotelian metaphysics at the turn of the seventeenth century. The scope and significance of that revival are not yet fully known. But it is already evident that this was the beginning of the great movement in philosophical thought in Germany. It is also clear that Gerhard was an active participant in the inaugural stage of this movement, and introduced it at the University of Jena, where he later held his theological professorship.

In short, if it is asked, "Why choose the seventeenth instead of the sixteenth century as representative of the classical period of Protestantism?", the answer is that this century more fully exhibits problems and solutions which were partly explicit and partly implicit in the sixteenth-century reformers. Then, if it is asked, "Why choose John Gerhard instead of some other Protestant Aristotelian?", the answer is that he is, more than any other Lutheran or Calvinist theologian of his day, a point of convergence of the several motifs in substance and in method.[11] This form of syn-

---

10. Althaus, in *Die Prinzipien*, attributes this to the fact that the stronger emphasis on justification through faith, which was the characteristic of the Lutherans, was more easily adaptable to the practical-analytic conception; the stronger emphasis on the Scripture, which characterized the Calvinists, was more suited to the theoretic-synthetic conception.

11. Among the Calvinists, theological leadership passed from Switzerland to the Netherlands at the turn of the century. The leader of the Calvinist scholastics there was Gisbert Voetius, professor of theology at Utrecht from 1634–76 and author of the five-volume *Selectae disputationes theologicae* (1648). Since this scholasticism tended to emphasize correct living (and not only correct teaching), it was not so productive as was the German school in regard to large-scale theological construction.

thesis came to an end, as we have already noted, with the rise of historical criticism of the Bible, which made untenable the formulation of the scriptural principle which was implicit in the Reformation and explicit in the post-Reformation period. Granting Gerhard's role as the central figure of seventeenth-century theology, one has the further task of limiting the discussion of such staggeringly complex material. One may easily be caught wavering between detailed discussion of minutiae in a multitude of issues and vague verbalization of generalities.

Therefore, I have arranged this book so that Chapters II, IV, and VI (or III, V, and VII) can be read coherently by themselves and, with the concluding chapter, convey the basic theme. Such an arrangement seems desirable in view of the difficulty that any Protestant faces in appropriating enough of the categories and distinctions to do full justice to Thomistic thought and the converse difficulty that requires a Roman Catholic to restrain his impulse to classify Protestant thought according to such Thomistic categories.[12]

Furthermore, I have restricted discussion to one central issue— the theological view of man—at specific focal points, the concepts of *caritas* (Thomas) and *fides* (Gerhard), in the hope of avoiding as much as possible the miasma of generalities as well as a morass of unfamiliar details.

The larger structure of the doctrine lies in the relation of nature and grace to each other and to the Creator. The question to which the discussion may be addressed is, then, "How does one

12. Regarding the chapters on Thomas, I may observe that, while the interpretation of the Angelic Doctor given there is on the whole fairly standard today, there are items in it which, as far as one can ascertain by a limited examination of an unlimited amount of literature, do not appear in that literature; namely, (1) the exposition of the Trinitarian relation at all levels of nature, grace, and glory; (2) the interpretation of the remnant of reason in fallen man as the knowing that one must know; (3) the detailed analysis of *S. Th.* I.37.I; (4) the centralization of the whole view in *caritas*; (5) the interpretation of the rationale of *caritas* as an articulation of the relation of a free creature to a sovereign Creator at various levels.

articulate a doctrine of man, not only in psychological, sociological, or other terms of description, but rooted in the creating and saving activity of God?"

To avoid terminological prejudice of the issue, "nature" and "grace" will be used interchangeably with the terms "creation" and "new creation." The latter seem to bear, for Protestants, meanings less corrupt than the former. Whether named by the one pair of terms or the other, the underlying problem is the same. It is the problem of a theological view of man—how to understand him as he is "by grace," a new creature of God, as well as "by nature," a creature of God. In the classical terms of the thirteenth century this *is* the problem of nature and grace. In the seventeenth century it is the problem of the justification (in the Reformation sense) of the sinner.

To be sure, the nature of man is a problem no longer restricted to theologians and philosophers. To assure oneself that this is the case one need only look over the titles of recent books in biology and psychology. But its theological and philosophical aspects continue to dominate interconfessional discussions of the capacities of man.

Stating the problem does not in itself reveal a solution. The classical systems are counterfoils of the intellectual transactions of a past culture; they may record the nature of those transactions, but they are no longer negotiable themselves. Thus, we must first try to make them intelligible and then try to evaluate them without subjecting them to alien norms.

The task is difficult. In the first place, the vocabulary of Aristotelian scholasticism, of whatever century, is so far from being current that very great patience is required in reading and understanding it. In the second place, we live in an intellectual climate (and a "climate" is usually more powerful a determinant than is an argument) in which the work performed by the scholastics is even at best uncongenial and irrelevant. "Scholasticism" still carries connotations of the intellectually barren waste. Indeed, Drummond issues the warning: "The reader who explores for the first time the *terra incognita* of German Protestantism since Luther must be prepared for an initial disappointment. He starts with a vision of the world regenerated by the glorious gospel. Presently, however, he finds himself wandering in an arid theological wilderness, his nostrils assailed by the acrid smoke of harsh polemics."[13] It is easy, in such circumstances, to make judgments which are erroneous and precipitous, too generous or too deprecatory.

In the chapters which follow, I have tried to elucidate as well as to evaluate. Chapter I provides background material on the seventeenth century. Chapters II through V deal with the methodology used in apprehending the problems and formulating the answers. I shall refer to this as analysis of the rationale. Chapters VI and VII deal with the two central concepts, *caritas* and *fides,* which summarize the similarities and differences in rationale. They function virtually as proper names for two whole systems. Chapter VIII is a general evaluation, the last portion of which suggests that beyond the differences in formulation and total character, which may seem irreconcilable, there may be a unity in the basic Christian intuition, or—as I have called it—in the underlying vision. It will be helpful, I think, to state my conclusions concisely here.

First, Thomas and Gerhard vary in their mode of conceptualization. Thomas leans to a formal-objective rationale; Gerhard leans to a dialectical-personal one. Accordingly, Thomas uses paradoxical (analogical) concepts in relation to his formal-objective rationale. Gerhard uses them in relation to his dialectical-personal rationale. Where "dialectical" and "formal" are used in these chapters, the meaning is always "dialectical-personal" and "formal-objective."[14]

13. Drummond, *German Protestantism,* p. 11.
14. By "formal-objective" I mean the rationale in which one proceeds from the concrete datum to the abstract form and returns to interpret the concrete by means of that form. The form may be a class (genus or species) which

Secondly, there is a difference in the character of these whole systems as they relate to other wholes. *Caritas* is self-expanding: *fides* is self-transcending.

Thirdly, it is possible to suggest the vision of a unity underlying the two views even though it is not (or, at least, not yet) possible to articulate that unity.

"locates" the particular thing in which it is exemplified, or it may be a general rule which interprets the particular data.

By "dialectical-personal" I mean the rationale whose pattern is the Yes and No involved in the encounter of persons, of one self with another self. In the formal rationale individuals are interchangeable, since they are interesting and intelligible only to the extent that they represent the genus or the general rule. In the dialectical-personal, on the other hand, the individual is not interchangeable; he is not the particular in relation to the general (a specimen of it and a means through which to apprehend it) but the singular Other, the Thou who is the Not-I of the knower.

Thus if I say "X is honest" in a formal-objective rationale, I am placing X in that class of people who are called honest. What I am saying of X can be understood by anyone who knows what "honest" means, independently of what the subject may be. In a dialectical-personal rationale "X is honest" is the assertion in which I record an encounter, or series of encounters, between the other person and me. What I am saying then can be understood only by one who has met and responded to the person or by one to whom my words convey the person rather than the objective meaning.

By "paradoxical-analogical" I mean the mode of conceptualizing in which the limits of the rationale are overcome but still reflected. In a paradoxical concept, the affirmative and the negative may be formally united—an "impossibility" for the formal-objective rationale. The union, when accomplished without destroying the rationale, is therefore the *paradoxon,* the formally impossible and unexpectable. In relation to the dialectical rationale the paradox is a *final* Yes-No leading to no further Yes; it is the Yes in and through the No. It is total personal acceptance in and through total rejection. As such it is the dialectically unexpectable, the *paradoxon.*

Thus Thomas' conception of the movement of the free will (where total agency is ascribed both to God and to man), and Gerhard's conception of the justified man (where complete rejection means complete acceptance) illustrate the paradoxical. The former conception deals not only with a form but also with the divine Form as present in it. The latter deals not only with the continuing Yes-and-No encounter of persons but with that encounter with God-in-Christ which is the final one.

CHAPTER I

The Seventeenth Century:
Background

Protestant Aristotelianism in the continental European universities during the seventeenth century has been the subject of much less research than that concerning the sixteenth century. Indeed, the suspicion is still widespread that the seventeenth century, lacking the prophetic power of the sixteenth century and having substituted for it a rigid dogmatic orthodoxy, is an embarrassing interlude in Protestant theological history. This suspicion was, unfortunately, corroborated by the nineteenth-century attempt to restore this scholasticism, which suffered from limitations subsequently read back into the seventeenth century itself. For a more balanced view one needs interpreters with sufficient patience and *Einfühlungsvermögen* to grapple with an initially very foreign intellectual milieu until its inner dynamics become apparent; at the same time such scholars must have a perspective of the history of thought so deep and broad that they will not read limitations into the seventeenth century which were not there. Neither patience alone nor perspective alone is sufficient. There have been a few such interpreters, but they are not generally known. Moreover, there has been a continuing attempt to interpret the period, and it is possible to discern in a general way the stages in the history of that interpretation.

This chapter will set forth a brief history of interpretation and the character and development of the seventeenth century, to provide a proper introduction to John Gerhard. Without attempting to substantiate every detail, such a sketch should make it relatively clear that the seventeenth century cannot be characterized simply as a relapse from the grandeur of the theology of the Reformers. There was an intelligible development, motivated by intrinsic as well as extrinsic concerns, and it brought to full expression the theological motifs enunciated by the early Reformers. Its limitations were limitations already present, if only latent, in the sixteenth century; its greatness was due to the same quality as that of Reformation theology—the conception of *fides*.

Toward the middle of the seventeenth century, Georg Hornius (*Historia philosophica,* 1654) first advanced the theory that the introduction of Aristotelian scholasticism at the Protestant universities was a falling away from the humanism of the Renaissance as well as from the theology of the Reformation. Its introduction was necessary, to be sure, because of the vigorous polemics of the Roman opponents; and it did serve the purpose of successfully combating the theology of the Roman Counter-Reformation. It was a means of resisting the opponents with their own weapons, but beyond that it served no permanent or intrinsic purpose for Protestant theology. This pragmatic interpretation was maintained by the next generation of historians, Buddeus, Elswich, and Brucker.

In the last decade of the eighteenth century, the work of Dietrich Tiedemann (*Geist der spekulativen Philosophie,* 1791–97) began to dissolve the pragmatic interpretation. The view that neo-scholasticism was a relapse from humanism could not, he thought, be sustained; for Suarez' *Disputationes metaphysicae* (1597), which had come to be the basic textbook, exhibited as much of a humanistic strain as a scholastic one. Tiedemann made his judgment on the basis of his broad understanding of the self-developing Spirit more than on the results of detailed research, and neither he nor his immediate successors provided the supporting empirical data; but subsequent research showed the judgment itself to be correct—humanist concerns were quite alive in the seventeenth-century schoolmen.

In the middle of the nineteenth century Wilhelm Gass (*Geschichte der protestantischen Dogmatik,* 1854), who had come through the Hegelian school, maintained the thesis that seventeenth-century scholasticism was the result of an inner development of the "Protestant principle" (as he called it) itself. By its own inner vocation, Protestantism was obliged to receive the theoretic-philosophical disciplines. The appearance of Suarez and the Jesuits' polemics were antecedent temporally but not causally. Gass left unanswered the question why it was precisely Suarez' *Disputationes* which became the model for Protestant school metaphysics.

At the same time, in his research into the history of the University of Helmstedt, Ernst Henke (*Georg Calixtus und seine Zeit,* 1853) provided the supporting data for Tiedemann's judgment. He showed that at Helmstedt, Johann Caselius and Cornelius Martini, who were leaders in the new philosophical thought, were at the same time the champions of humanism against "barbarian" encroachments. But he did not completely trace the humanistic origin of this new Aristotelianism because his chief interest was in the special role of the University of Jena among the Lutheran universities about 1600.

In 1891, Ernst Troeltsch's *Vernunft und Offenbarung bei Gerhard und Melanchthon* appeared. In this work Troeltsch refutes Hornius' earlier pragmatic interpretation, showing that there was a "school" metaphysics in Altdorf, Wittenberg, and Helmstedt even before the appearance of the Spanish neo-scholastic works. He substitutes a new version of the pragmatic interpretation. The introduction of metaphysics was not due to polemical interests against the Jesuits; it was due to pedagogical interests. The memory of the Aristotelian structure had never been completely erased; now it brought back the system and categories as technical aids in organizing the curriculum. It was an "unbelievably comfortable science," a "schematizing ontologism."

More fruitful than his characterization of the school metaphysics, however, was Troeltsch's recognition of a double relation between theology and philosophy, an "official" one and an "inner" one. For this is a recognition of the important fact that since Melanchthon, theology had a double meaning, or double nature. Paul Althaus (*Die Prinzipien der deutschen reformierten Dogmatik im Zeitalter der aristotelischen Scholastik,* 1914) pursued this theme in more detail, with reference to Calvinist theology and its relation to Melanchthon. He showed that the principles which Troeltsch had found in the Lutherans were also to be found in the Calvinists, especially in Germany. Indeed, Melanchthon's influence reached beyond the German Lutheran universities to Calvinist Geneva and then, indirectly, to Leyden, Franeke, Groningen, Utrecht, and Harderwijk.

Emil Weber's *Die philosophische Scholastik des deutschen Protestantismus im Zeitalter der Orthodoxie* (1907) rejected the pragmatic interpretation of Hornius as well as that of Troeltsch, and saw in the seventeenth century harbingers of the "philosopher of Protestantism," Immanuel Kant. Moreover, Weber's detailed studies traced the origin of this scholasticism not to Spanish but to Italian influences, specifically to Zabarella, Piccolomini, and J. C. Scaliger. Finally, he showed that as a matter of fact the polemical purpose served by this metaphysics was only incidentally anti-Jesuitic. The controversial questions which it was hopefully able to resolve concerned equally intra-Protestant antagonisms—Calvinists against Lutherans, Lutherans against Socinians, Lutherans and Calvinists against the anti-Trinitarians, and so on.

In his exploration of the Italian sources, Weber leaves unclear the role of the Spanish sources, and especially Suarez. This role was clarified by Peter Petersen (*Geschichte der aristotelischen*

Philosophie im protestantischen Deutschland, 1921). Suarez became the model for one direction of Protestant scholasticism, that is, for the direction called "scholastic in the proper sense." But why was Suarez so serviceable? Petersen, adopting the older interpretation of Troeltsch, ascribes Suarez' influence to the comfortable schematism his system provided. This, however, leaves unanswered why Suarez was more fully received at some universities than at others.

In the meantime, the Roman Catholic scholar Karl Eschweiler (*Die Philosophie der spanischen Spätscholastik auf den deutschen Universitäten des 17. Jahrhunderts*) sought to show that the influence of Suarez was due not to the technical usefulness of his *Disputationes* but to the fact that this work filled the general spiritual need of the baroque era. The University of Altdorf had never adopted Suarez; it remained in a special position. Weber attributed this position to the Italian sources; Eschweiler attributed it to the existence of a Thomistic tradition there. The baroque spirit needed a practical, purposeful form of thinking, which Suarez supplied. But the Thomistic spirit, as at Altdorf, was moved by the quest for knowledge of intelligible being.

Eschweiler's thesis was opposed by Ernst Lewalter (*Spanisch-jesuitische und deutsch-lutherische Metaphysik des 17. Jahrhunderts,* 1935). Lewalter's research pointed out the fact that the alternatives available at the universities in the 1600s were not "Thomas or Suarez?" but rather "metaphysics or no metaphysics?" or, in different terms "Suarez' metaphysics or Philippo-Ramian dialectic?" Suarez' *Disputationes* became the prevailing model because it fulfilled the humanistic as well as the ontological purpose. It was a book of systematic ontology and at the same time a source book for Aristotelianism. It met the *ad fontes* cry of the humanists as well as the *ad res ipsas* of the philosophers. But Suarez was interpreted at the Protestant universities in various ways. The Wittenberg and Helmstedt philosophers, Jacob Martini and Arnisaeus, emphasized more than Suarez that ontology deals with God only under the aspect of *species entis*. In this form ontology supported no specific confessional position; there was no "Lutheran" or "Calvinist" or "Jesuit" metaphysics as such. For this ontology, Suarez was a chief resource but not a model to be followed uncritically. At other universities, especially at the Lutheran university of Giessen, Suarez' natural theology was more fully received. Here, metaphysics was confessional in the sense that it supported a given interpretation of Scripture—such as the Lutheran position regarding the mode of Christ's sacramental presence. For this metaphysics Suarez' *Disputationes* could serve not only as a chief resource but as a pattern to be copied almost in full and then supplemented. Thus, at the University of Giessen, where proximity to the Universities of Marburg and Heidelberg made the Lutheran-Calvinist dispute most intense, Suarez was most fully adopted. At the universities farther removed from the controversy, such as Wittenberg and Jena, Suarez was adopted with the critical alterations made by the Helmstedt tradition. Thus, Lewalter's research answers both questions: why Suarez' *Disputationes* was the chief textbook and why it was received in two different forms.

In summary, studies to date have shown quite conclusively that first, Protestant scholasticism was not a relapse from the humanism of the previous century to an earlier concept-splitting "school philosophy." Secondly, they have shown that the controversial purposes it may have served were not the primary motives for its introduction, but secondary motives, involving two disputes, between the Protestants and the Roman Catholics and those among the Protestants themselves. Thirdly, we may now see that the sources of the school thought are the Italian Aristotelians, the Spanish neo-scholastics, and the partially independent Helmstedt tradition. Fourthly, we have begun to see—as in Bengt Hägglund's thorough study, *Die heilige Schrift und ihre Deutung in der Theologie Johann Gerhards* (1951)—the theological continuity from the sixteenth to the seventeenth century.

THE RECEPTION OF THE NEW METAPHYSICS

The revival of metaphysics began at the University of Helmstedt and moved from there in a short time to virtually all the German universities, with the notable exception of Altdorf.

Toward the end of the sixteenth century, Solomon Gessner, in his preface to the 1594 edition of Versor's *Epitome metaphysicae aristotelicae* (first published in 1491), lamented the "barbaric" state of learning among the students who were taught from compendia rather than from sources. There was a need to go back to the sources in order to regain the depth of understanding and the humanistic elegance which the existing curriculum lacked. The reissuance of Versor, which Gessner hoped would aid in accomplishing that purpose, was at the same time the origin of a more general movement in the German universities designed to correct educational deficiencies.

Specifically, Gessner's criticism may have been in reference to the *Isagoge in metaphysicam Aristotelis* (1594, second edition 1601) of Daniel Cramer, which treated metaphysics not as ontology but as a sort of systematic logic culminating in the *primus motor* of Aristotle. Cramer's intention was basically to use a diluted Aristotle as a tool for supporting the Bible, but his book did not remain long on the scene because, in the person of Cornelius Martini at the University of Helmstedt, Gessner's challenge was beginning to be met.

At least since 1597 Cornelius Martini had been lecturing on metaphysics at the University of Helmstedt. In contrast to Cramer, Martini did not treat Aristotelian metaphysics as a kind of logical propaedeutic to a biblical physics of heaven, but as the science of being qua being. Also in contrast to Cramer, he regarded Aristotle as a classical representative of this science but not as its final authority or full actualization. Where Cramer's metaphysics tended to be a repetition of Aristotle, leading up to or corrected by the Scriptures, Martini's metaphysics was a systematic ontology, using Aristotle and the medieval schoolmen as aids, but developed according to its own universal norms.

The lectures of Martini, published in 1597, seem to have had the vivifying power and to have filled the need mentioned by Gessner. This fact would explain why Cramer's book disappeared as rapidly as it did from the academic scene. It would also explain how the Helmstedt metaphysics reached Wittenberg so soon— for Gessner was on the Wittenberg faculty. From Wittenberg it passed to Jena by means of John Gerhard.

Martini's lectures drew from Italian as well as Spanish sources, though not yet from Suarez. Suarez' *Disputationes* were published in the same year as Martini's lectures, so it is not likely that he could have used Suarez. The printed lectures refer to Fonseca of the Spanish school, but not to Suarez. Indeed, Martini's colleague, Henning Arnisaeus, disclaims any dependence on Suarez for those early lectures when he writes in a sardonic auxiliary clause, "At the time when Cornelius and I were copying from Suarez before Cornelius even knew of the existence of Suarez by so much as hearsay (*eodem tempore cum una cum Cornelio transcriberem ex Soario antequam Soarium esse ipse fando accepisset*)."[1]

These lectures are divided into three parts. First there is an introduction to metaphysics as ontology. Ontology deals with *ens* as such (potential and actual being) and as the *primum cognitum.* As in Aquinas (or Hegel), being is the immediate and universal but most imperfect concept. Following this first part there is a sketch of the contents of the coming lectures. The third part is a methodically constructed lecture on ontology, treating in order: the question of how *esse* is in *entia* (Aristotle against Parmenides) and what it means that the schools teach this to be analogical, not univocal or equivocal; the *primum transcendens,* followed by the transcendentals, *unum, verum, bonum, res, aliquid;* the modes of specialization of being (*species entis*)—substance and accident; *ens primum.*

1. Quoted by Lewalter, *Metaphysik,* p. 40.

RECEPTION OF THE NEW METAPHYSICS

The point at which philosophical and theological thought merge is the insight into the createdness of all finite things. To assert the eternity of the world is as much a philosophical error as a theological one. This axiom in Martini's ontology opened a dispute which culminated in Kant's antinomies of pure reason.

The first printed work to appear after Suarez had become known was Jacob Martini's influential *Exercitationes theorematum metaphysicorum* (Wittenberg, 1604), the printed form of lectures delivered during 1603 (at six o'clock in the morning) at the University of Wittenberg. Here Martini drew upon Suarez' *Disputationes* and J. C. Scaliger's *Exercitationes de subtilitate contra Cardanum* in about equal measure; the course was intended for teachers of philosophy rather than for students. The chief innovation was Jacob Martini's twofold division of metaphysics into a *pars generalis* and *pars specialis* (which reappear in Kant as the noumenal and the phenomenal). The division itself was not new, since Cornelius Martini and Suarez had also used it; but the emphasis and the pervasive significance attributed to it were new. In addition to the new emphasis on this duopartite division, Jacob Martini also introduced the problem of epistemology into Protestant metaphysics (following a suggestion in Suarez) and took the categorial doctrine out of logic and put it into metaphysics (this too has some precedent in Suarez).

The next work of significance was Arnisaeus' lectures of 1603 (*De constitutione et partibus metaphysicae tractatus*), which appeared in 1606. In them one finds a firm insistence that God be treated in ontology only under the aspect of the general division between *ens creatum* and *ens increatum*—in other words, as a *species entis*.

The Helmstedt metaphysics, however, did not suit the University of Giessen, which was interested in maintaining its Lutheran position against the Calvinists. Christoph Scheibler's *Opus metaphysicum* (Giessen, 1617), therefore, follows Suarez more closely than did the Helmstedtians and tends to be a positivistic approach which assigns to metaphysics the task of clarifying the meanings of terms which theology uses—such as "person," "substance," and "sign." This is the first metaphysics at a Lutheran university to hold itself strictly to Suarez' *Disputationes,* departing only occasionally to refute Calvinistic views and to take account of the Helmstedt tradition in ontology.

If then one regards the position of the University of Altdorf, which substituted commentary on Aristotle for systematic ontology, and the positions of Helmstedt and Giessen, one can understand the remark in Hartnack's *Anweisender Bibliothecarius* of 1691 that there were two philosophical directions at the universities besides the Cartesian—the scholastic and the Aristotelian. The "scholastic" refers to the direction of Giessen; the Aristotelian refers to the Altdorf school. Helmstedt and its affiliates (which would include Gerhard at Jena) fall between the two, being neither "scholastic in the proper sense" nor simply commentators on Aristotle, using Suarez, but only critically.

THE MELANCHTHONIAN HERITAGE OF THE DUAL CONCEPTION OF THEOLOGY

It is true, as Lewalter notes, that what distinguished the seventeenth from the sixteenth century was the reception of metaphysics at the universities as the superordinate "real" discipline and not (as it had been in the Melanchthonian curriculum and in Ramian dialectic) as a technical or logistic discipline. Its motto was not only *ad fontes,* with the Renaissance, but also *ad res ipsas,* with the Helmstedt philosophers and Suarez.

Concurrent with this development there is, from the more specifically theological side, a development in the conception of theology. A view which was first systematically expressed by Melanchthon reached full articulation in John Gerhard. This was made possible by the new metaphysics (as well as the studies of Zabarella mentioned earlier).

MELANCHTHONIAN HERITAGE

Melanchthon is often regarded as a theological intellectualist who did not grasp Luther's personal approach to theology. John Reid's comment[2] is representative. "Melanchthon may be said to act as the link between Luther and Orthodoxy. This is not only because he occupied a position intermediate between the two, sharing some opinions with both sides, but because in his own work it is possible to see a change coming over reformed theology." "An intellectual view," he continues, "is taking the place of the essentially religious view which Luther maintained. In other words the existential point of view has been replaced by the point of view of the spectator." As Paul Schwarzenau demonstrates, this is not a tenable judgment.[3]

Melanchthon (much like David Hume) has been, in part, the victim of his own lucidity. It is not unusual that a lucid stylist transmits his ideas without transmitting their profundity. But he has also been misunderstood because one of his basic presuppositions—namely, the double character of theology—is almost universally ignored. Without an understanding of that double conception one misses the depth and the inner dynamics of Melanchthonian theology—and also of seventeenth-century theology.

The double character of theology is not derived, as one might initially suppose, from the distinction between theory and practice. It comes from the difference between theology as academic or scientific and theology as kerygmatic (to use a current term) or personal. That is to say, theology is a discipline concerned with the exposition of the contents of the Scripture in as exact and objectively true a fashion as possible. But it is also the *use* of those contents in the concrete situation of public worship or private devotion. This distinction is contained in the difference seen between "knowledge" and "true knowledge" (*vera cognitio*) of the Scripture. Theological knowledge is the knowledge derived from

2. *Authority of Scripture,* pp. 79 f.
3. Schwarzenau's book, *Der Wandel im theologischen Ansatz,* appeared only a year earlier than Reid's and the latter seems to have made no use of it.

Scripture and objectively seen by any competent scholar to be the content of Scripture. True theological knowledge is the knowledge which comes through the Scripture when concretely proclaimed and heard as the voice of God (*vox Dei*).

There is another way of expressing the distinction which, though it is not found in any explicit formulation of Melanchthon or his successors, is more illuminating and fruitful. This way of putting it thrusts to the heart of the difference between the scholasticism of the thirteenth and seventeenth centuries, and it shows the continuity between the Reformation and post-Reformation periods. It is the difference between theology as a *theoretic* knowledge based on the intuitive recognition of the truth of its principle, and theology as an *acoustic* knowledge mediated by the word which is concretely heard as the voice of God. The pattern of the knowledge is different in each case.[4] Theoretic theology follows the pattern of a formal and objective knowledge. Acoustic theology follows the pattern of personal knowledge in a hearing-response dialectic.

Each of them has its practical side. The practical aspect of theoretic knowledge is either the prudential application of general truths to particular cases, or the actual living according to the principles known to be true. The practical side of acoustic knowledge is either the actual proclamation of something in a fashion that it is concretely heard as *vox Dei,* or the apprehension of that word heard as a voice from beyond. Theoretic knowledge in its practical side guides behavior; acoustic knowledge in its practical side transforms the person. Theoretic knowledge is tied to the interior sense of sight—intuition; acoustic knowledge is tied to the interior sense of hearing—audition.

The origin of this distinction, as far as Protestant theological history is concerned, lies in Luther's recognition of a difference

4. See below, Chapter V, on "Justification," for amplification of this conception and its significance. The term *acoustic* seems more artificial than *auditory* but it is used here because it is an exact parallel to *theoretic*.

between belief about God (*de Deo*) and faith in God (*in Deum*). "An acquired faith . . . says about Christ, 'I believe indeed that the son of God died and rose.' There it stops. But true faith says, 'I believe indeed that the son of God died and rose, but this all [happened] for me, for my sins; about that I am certain.' . . . Therefore, this 'for me' or 'for us,' if it is believed, makes faith true and distinguishes it from every other faith which hears only what things have happened (*res tantum gestas audit*)."[5]

The first systematic use of this distinction was Melanchthon's approach to the theological disputes between the Romans and the Protestants and then between the two wings of the Reformation. Melanchthon proposed the method according to which the public meaning of Scripture was to be established by a conclave of theologians with the necessary humanistic training. This form of theology occupied the same place in the public life as did any university discipline. To carry on theology publicly one needed the skills acquired through the usual humanistic education with its emphasis on philology and classical learning, which enabled one to read the Old and New Testaments in their original languages. Melanchthon believed that disputes about the meaning of any particular portion of the Scriptures could be settled by a conclave of scholars trained in letters and who could examine the Scriptures dispassionately. This view presupposes a providential concurrence of classic learning and the Christian religion.

The dispassionate, philologically correct exposition of Scripture was not, however, sufficient for the *vera cognitio* of theology.[6] True knowledge of the divine will needed something else. In Melanchthon's theology this something else came to be the afflictions and *calamitates* of history and nature. True knowledge of God was not a product of philological and grammatical study alone. It was the result of an ever renewed hearing of the promise

5. Quoted by Hägglund in *Theologie und Philosophie*, pp. 58 and 59, n. 9.
6. Paul Tillich's conception of faith as ultimate concern is a close relative of Melanchthon's conception of faith as *vera cognitio*.

of God set before the troubled conscience. "The Holy Spirit," he remarks in a letter to Spalatin, "strikes terror in consciences through the preaching of repentance and lifts them up again through . . . the proclamation of the forgiveness of sins."[7]

Thus in its theoretic character theology was a humanistic discipline. It was part of the *publicum patrimonium coeli in terras dimissum*. Its contents were taken from Scripture according to the rules of rhetoric and logic that applied everywhere. The majority of controversies, Melanchthon believed, resulted from a neglect of disciplined studies of Scripture. In resolving controversies he therefore proposed that the state select *homines sani et periti* or *judices non stulti et improbi* to make an objective and dispassionate study of the Scriptures.

The practical aspect of theoretic theology was a sort of biblical ethics, which largely coincided with Roman law in content. Theoretic theology presupposed a providential concurrence of the Christian religion, humanistic learning, and Roman law. The substantive content of all learning rested on the divine tradition. One tradition, the theological, was passed on by Moses, the prophets, the evangelists, and the apostles; the other tradition was passed on through the wise men, the *sapientes,* whom God from age to age and place to place raised up (*excitavit*). Both traditions were rooted in the original knowledge transmitted by God to Adam. Both traditions could be further transmitted by people trained in the *litterae humanae*.

Although theoretic theology provided the foundation for true knowledge of God, it was not sufficient in itself. "The truest worship of God," Melanchthon wrote in his *Epitome* of 1524, "is to call upon God in adverse fortunes (*in rebus adversis*)." These adversities provided the setting for hearing the *vox Dei* in the preached Word. As Schwarzenau[8] puts it, the reality in which man concretely finds himself "is transformed (*deutet sich*) under

7. Quoted by Schwarzenau, *Wandel,* p. 17.
8. *Wandel,* p. 39.

the preached Word into the drama which God institutes to exercise our faith." This Word interprets all personal and world history as an appropriation of justification in the concreteness of a life lived through God.

Thus, the true knowledge of God—the true theology—is acoustic rather than theoretic. Its practical side is not ethics but the use of the audible Word as the vehicle for giving and receiving the new being, the power to live from the *adesse Dei* in faith.

If the truth of theoretic theology rests upon its objective agreement with the Scripture, the truth of acoustic *vera cognitio* is the power it gives hearers to withstand the adversities of life, the power to overcome the negativity of life.

In Melanchthon, the relation between these two kinds of theology is conceived in various ways. One way relates them as the general knowledge of God (theoretic) and the special application of it *pro me* (acoustic). Another way relates them as intelligibility (the Word) is related to intelligibility-with-power (Word and Spirit). But to formulate it in a way Melanchthon did not, as the distinction between a theoretic knowledge with a "seeing" logic and an acoustic knowledge with a "hearing" logic, not only continues to do justice to Melanchthon's actual procedure but also shows the continuity with Gerhard. This is the distinction I have called the difference between the formal-objective and the dialectical-personal.

With the help of the revived Aristotle, Gerhard formulated the double conception of theology in the preface of his *Loci* as the systematic-abstractive and the habitual-concretive senses. He writes thus:

> Theology (considered systematically and abstractively) is the teaching drawn from the Word of God by which men are instructed in true faith and true piety to eternal life.
>
> Theology (considered habitually and concretively) is a divinely given habit conferred on a man by the Holy Spirit

through the Word. By it [or Him] he is not only instructed in the divine mysteries through an illumination of the mind so that, in a saving way, his intellectual knowledge also becomes the object of his heart's affection and the guide of his life (*ut quae intelligit in affectum cordis et exsecutionem operis salutariter traducat*). He is also made fit and skilled concerning those divine mysteries—both as to informing others with the way of salvation and also as to vindicating the divine truth against the corruptions of its opponents—so that men, imbued with true faith and good works, are led to the kingdom of heaven.[9]

This is still the Melanchthonian distinction, but it is a more precise statement fitted into a modified Aristotelian frame. The relationship between theoretic knowledge and acoustic knowledge is not that of the general to the specific (although Gerhard, like Melanchthon, does use that formulation) but that of the objectively ascertainable to that which comes through the living voice of a person who has the divinely bestowed *habitus*.

Theology accordingly has a double criterion. The formal and objective criterion entails that theological statements can be seen by any intelligent person (who is not prevented "by age or ignorance") to be drawn from Scripture. The dialectical and personal criterion entails that a theological statement is effective in concrete proclamation—when spoken by a person with the divinely given *habitus* it has the power to be heard as the *vox Dei*. The two are interdependent. Nothing can really be concretely effective if it is not objectively true; and everything which is objectively true (that is, drawn from the Scripture) has the latent power of being concretely effective.

FAITH AND REASON

The distinction between theoretic and acoustic knowledge was not confined, in its significance, to professional theology. Implicit-

9. *Procem.* 31.

ly it contained a new understanding of the realms of faith and reason. This understanding is, from a philosophical viewpoint, the original contribution of the seventeenth century. One part of it—the restriction of *ratio's* capacity to the finite realm of being —reached a full expression in Kant's critique of reason; another part of it—the correlation of ontological knowledge with "audition" rather than "intuition"—carries over into German existentialism as represented by Heidegger and Jaspers. Since this new viewpoint was, however, never accurately expressed, its influence on the treatises on theology and metaphysics was indirect and hidden, but nonetheless profound. The discussion of Gerhard will show one area in which that influence was at work. Briefly, the chief characteristic of this seventeenth-century thought was that *true knowledge of the transcendent was tied to the acoustic, rather than the theoretic, type of knowledge.*

The origin of this conviction seems to be in Luther again. For on this point he diverges from the nominalists. One instance will serve as illustration. Among the nominalists it was fashionable to discuss syllogisms like this:

> *Omnis essentia divina est pater*
> *Filius est essentia divina*
> *Ergo filius est pater.*

The premises of this syllogism were acknowledged to be true, its conclusion false, and its form valid, as far as reason's logic was concerned. Now, d'Ailly maintained that such a syllogism, where the premises are true and the conclusion false, contains an error either formally or materially, although that error may be known only by faith and not by reason. Luther, however, treated the whole effort as inconsequential. "That syllogism is good"—but irrelevant. What it shows, if anything, is that formal logic is irrelevant to faith.

This is more than a minor disagreement. It stems from Luther's rather consistent conviction that logical forms are restricted to the finite realm. To go beyond the finite one must leave intellective intuition and listen to the proclaimed Word. "Reason rests on, and also accepts only, that which she either feels or sees. Therefore, [in matters of faith] one must simply cling to the bare Word, close one's eyes, blind one's reason, and simply open one's ears (*die ohren hynrecken*) and take God at His Word (*auff das wort fusen*)."[10]

Luther's conviction on this point was retained in the seventeenth century—partly as a hidden presupposition (as was indeed true of Luther)—and it yielded an understanding of the realms of faith and reason which, for all its similarity in terminology, was markedly different from the medieval scholastic.

In seventeenth-century scholasticism the whole ontological realm, the realm of the knowable, was divided into two parts. One part was knowable by *ratio;* this coincided with finite being. The other part was knowable by faith; this extended to infinite being. What is knowable by *ratio* is based on principles which are intuitively certain; they are self-evident.[11] What is knowable by faith is based on what is heard. The two are merged in the *principium Scripturae*—the recognition that Scripture is the source of doctrine. That the Scripture is the source of knowledge about God is an axiom as self-evident as a geometric axiom. But the truth drawn from the Scripture is not necessarily self-evident; it is accepted on authority, not on insight. Both areas of truth are knowable, but only the finite realm of reason is comprehensible.

The whole realm of the knowable is covered by the laws of identity and non-contradiction. The truth of faith is really truth, and it cannot contradict the truths of reason. It may, and does, transcend *ratio,* but does not oppose it. The content of knowledge comes from two sources, the principles of reason and the principle of Scripture, the *liber naturae* and the *liber verbi.* "The things concerning the highest mysteries of faith which theology sets

---

10. Quoted by Hägglund, *Theologie und Philosophie,* pp. 68 f.
11. *Ratio* here refers to reason in fallen man not in pre-Fall or eschatological man.

forth from revelation the sounder and genuine philosophy knows are not to be discussed or judged from the principles of *ratio*" lest there be a confusion of distinct principles and distinct disciplines (1.475).

Gerhard uses two analogies for illustration. There is a universal conception of justice, but there are differences between the actual laws in one province and those in another province. "So too truth is one in its general conception but each discipline has its axioms which are not to be carried over into another forum but to be left in their own sphere" (1.475). Again, just as there is no conflict between cobblery and painting, there can be none between theology and philosophy. Conflicts arise only when the cobbler does not stick to his last but undertakes to judge *de omnibus pictoriae artis theorematibus* (1.476). Thus, it is true that a virgin cannot give birth to a son; it is also true that the virgin Mary gave birth to Jesus. For when reason declares that a virgin cannot bear a son, it means that within the universe of finite causes and effects it is impossible for a virgin to give birth. Theology does not deny that, for it asserts that the virgin who gave birth to Jesus did so by a power transcending finite causality (1.475). Similarly the axiom "there are as many persons as there are essences (*quot sunt personae tot essentiae*)" is true *in tota rerum universitate,* but does not apply to "uncreated and infinite essences" (III.33).

Reason knows by comprehension; faith knows by accepting the Word. In its formal aspect the scriptural principle is comprehensible. One can see the truth of the statement that truth about God is drawn from Scripture in the same way one sees the truth of any principle. When he asserts that the scriptural principle[12] is not demonstrable, Gerhard means it in the same sense that any

---

12. It is worthy of note that "principle of Scripture" is always in the singular. Scripture does not contain principles; it is the principle, the one source from which faith draws its knowledge. Thus, theological statements are always "conclusions," never "principles."

axiom is not demonstrable. It is self-evident and therefore un-
provable. He does not say that it is irrational and therefore un-
provable. Thus, in his treatise on the principle of theology
(*L. Th.* 1), which is more than 230 double-column pages long,
Gerhard wishes to accomplish only one simple aim—to show that
the principle of Scripture is self-evident, in the sense that to assert
the contrary is self-contradictory, and that the recognition of its
truth comes not by demonstration but by explication or exemplification. Quoting Aristotle, he notes in his prologue that principles
in any discipline must be "primary and basic, true, not accountable
to anything else, self-crediting, incontrovertible and indemonstra-
ble, so that when anything is opposed to them or is concluded from
things which are contrary to them, nothing appears more fallacious
than it to all sound judges, and, on the other hand, whatever
accords with them is agreed by all to be certain and sure"
(*Prooem.* 20). That these properties do apply to Scripture, and
only to it, is what he will demonstrate in the article on Scripture.

To establish that Scripture is self-evident as the principle of
theology, he proceeds as one would in showing the truth of any
axiom. He shows the self-contradiction involved in denying it
and the self-evidence apparent in asserting it. Two contrary positions were represented at the time. The Roman opponents held
that Scripture alone is not sufficient as a principle, it must be supplemented by the church's deposit of tradition. Gerhard seeks to
show how this position is self-contradictory. Begin by asserting
Scripture and tradition as the principle, and you necessarily end
by denying your assertion. How is this the case?

The Roman position commits a formal error, he maintains, because it says in effect that God, who is perfect, could not write a
perfect book. This is asserting that a perfect cause does not produce
a perfect result. But if the result is not perfect, then the cause
which failed to produce it is not perfect. Hence, the position contradicts itself. Or, if you start by saying that God, who is perfect,
might, but did not wish to, produce a perfect book, then you are

saying that a perfect God is not perfect—because His will is not perfect. Now, since the Roman opponents do not deny that Scripture is the word of God and the principle of faith—Gerhard quotes Bellarmine to substantiate this—they cannot consistently maintain that it needs supplementing by a tradition of the church. Either Scripture alone is the principle, or there is no principle but an infinite regress. If tradition must complete Scripture, then another tradition must complete that tradition, and so forth; for every argument raised about the deficiency of Scripture can *a fortiori* be raised against tradition.

From a material side, the same self-contradiction emerges. The Roman opponents held that because there were varying interpretations of Scripture, the tradition or resolutions of church councils were necessary to provide the true interpretation. Therefore Gerhard shows, by long and wide-ranging quotations from the councils, first that the councils and popes are no more consistent than the Scripture, and, second, the councils and popes themselves deny that they are the judges of Scripture. That is to say, either the position of the Roman opponents does not solve the problem of inconsistent interpretation at all, for the councils are at least as inconsistent as the interpretations of Scripture, or the position refutes itself, for if you start by accepting the Roman position that the councils are the final authority, you necessarily end at the Protestant position that Scripture is the final authority—because that is what the councils authoritatively say.

The Socinians represented another contrary position. Their position, Gerhard maintained, subjected the Scripture to the norms of intuitive *ratio*. But this is a self-contradictory position, for it asserts in effect that matters of faith (the Scripture's content) are not matters of faith, but matters of *ratio*.

The truth of a principle can be established negatively by showing that it cannot consistently be denied. It is established positively not by demonstration, but by pointing out evidences and by explication or exemplification of its meaning. Gerhard cites a number

33

of evidences of the truth of the scriptural principle. There is the inner testimony of the Holy Spirit, who testifies in the heart of the believer that "in the Scriptures the voice of the heavenly Father is contained and God alone is the fit and authentic witness" (1.36). The psychological side of this is the "lively sense" one receives from daily reading the Scripture and the *virtus consolandi et roborandi* that the Scripture provides in times of adversity and temptation.

Secondly, there are the qualities of the Scriptures—the "majesty of its contents" and the "singularity of its language." These are characteristics one would expect a divine missive to have. Thirdly, there are external testimonies, like the witness of the martyrs who gave their lives rather than deny the truth of Scripture.

These evidences indicate but do not prove the *principium Scripturae*. Beside them one can adduce arguments for the principle. These arguments are, in the nature of the case, circular; they prove only in the way that tautologies prove—by awakening intuitive assent to the truth which they exemplify. Thus, the proof that the Scripture is perfect (meaning not that it is free of all defect but that it is a sufficient means of instructing man about God's essence and will) is circular. The cause of Scripture, *Deus sapientissimus et perfectissimus,* is such that nothing could have prevented the effect from being perfect. Therefore, Scripture is perfect (1.369).

Again, the assertion that Scripture is perspicuous (that the knowledge necessary for salvation is clearly set forth to anyone who is not prevented by age or ignorance of the language from reading or hearing it) is proved by quoting the passages of Scripture which say it is perspicuous in effect, in comparisons of Scripture to a lamp or a light or an open book. Another proof is based on the nature of the author. "God, the principal author of the sacred Scripture, was able [because of His omnipotence] and willing [because of His benevolence] to speak to us in it perspicuously. Therefore, Scripture is perspicuous" (1.416). Other proofs

34

offered are of the same kind. In short, Gerhard sought to establish the truth of the scriptural principle by showing that its denial was tantamount to the self-contradiction of saying, "What God reveals is not what He reveals," and that its affirmation was like asserting, "What God reveals is what God reveals."

Theological knowledge, when it means knowledge drawn from Scripture, is accordingly as objectively certain as any rational knowledge. The difference is that in rational knowledge one not only knows but also comprehends the truth; in knowledge of faith one knows things which he does not comprehend. The truth of faith is a truth that can be heard and accepted on the word of the authority who propounds it, but it cannot be comprehended. Whatever can be comprehended is of reason; whatever can be known without comprehending is of faith. This faith is, of course, not the same as saving faith; it is faith as one medium of knowledge. The principle of faith comes to answer affirmatively the question, "Has God said?" whereas the principle of reason answers affirmatively the question, "Can I intuit its truth?" The two touch each other at one point—the point where it is possible to intuit the truth that God has said what He has said.

This relation of reason and faith seems similar to that of Thomas. The complementarity of the two modes of knowledge, the lack of contradiction between the truth of one and the other, and the truth based on authority contrasted with the truth based on insight—these are common to both. Initially there does not seem to be a recognizable difference between Thomas' assertion, for example, that reason can show the non-impossibility of the doctrine of the Trinity, and Gerhard's assertion that it cannot, except to such as have already been instructed from the Scripture (III.31).

Yet there is a fundamental difference, which came powerfully to the fore in the controversies concerning works and faith. Theological knowledge as attainable in this world bears, in Thomas, a subalternate relation to the principles which are intuitively known to the saints in heaven (and, of course, to God). Our knowledge is to heavenly knowledge as music is to mathematics. The musician applies principles which he takes from mathematics; the theologian applies principles which he takes from the saints and God. The way of deepening one's knowledge is contemplation—the attempt to reach the saints' intuitive knowledge of principles. In Gerhard's view objective knowledge becomes true knowledge not by contemplation but by hearing. Insight is restricted to the realm of the finite.

Another way of putting the difference is to say that in Thomas the gap between the finite and infinite is spanned by concepts; in Gerhard it is spanned by words. In Thomistic scholasticism, words are the bearers of concepts (the intelligible forms to which the real forms correspond); in Gerhard's scholasticism concepts are the derivatives of words. This is especially true with regard to infinite being, which (or who) can be communicated in words (for example, the language of the Trinitarian dogma) even when not in concepts. Gerhard adduces two quotations from Scaliger's *Exercitationes* in support of this point. "From the use of words we are often carried on to a perception of the thing itself" and "In treatises of disciplines one ought to use the names as starting point" (*Prœm.* 1). This was built into the schema of the topics Gerhard treated. Each *locus* begins with a section called "onomatology," in which the pertinent names or words are treated, and then it goes on to "pragmatology," in which the usual Aristotelian categories are treated—the causes, the adjuncts, the material, the form, the *finis,* the effects, the object, and finally the definition.[13]

How deeply this difference had penetrated the thinking of the Protestants was not at all clear to them, or to their opponents. In retrospect it is easier to see, especially when one examines closely Gerhard's treatment of justification. He was unable to reconcile

13. The section on pragmatology also contains the *usus,* which provides the contact with proclamation by stating how a given article is to be used in confronting a hearer with the judging and redeeming God.

the Protestant and the Roman position because, although he was only dimly aware of it, justification in the religious sense was not a formal concept but the name of a basic vocabulary. Arguing the case in formal terms alone, he met only a dead end. Why should the concept of God's moving the free human will in such a way that man and God are both totally its agents be more Pelagian than the concept of God which justifies the sinner who accepts in faith the exonerating judgment made in view of Christ's work? Or why should the Protestants object to the concept of a conditioned merit if they did not object to the concept of sanctification? There is no good answer, if one looks only at the concepts as formally conceived. The answer becomes apparent when one sees in the unresolved conflict the underlying view which restricted the domain of formal conceptualization (with its intuitive foundation) to finite being, and which allowed to the dialectical word (with its auditory foundation) a reach from, and toward, the eternal.[14]

JOHN GERHARD

In the seventeenth century, Luther's "justification by faith" was either a sectarian dogma of the faith delivered by Luther or it was one name for a radically transforming religious power. Whether it was the former or the latter in a given case seems to

14. See below, Chapter V. The connection with Kant's critical philosophy is, I think, obvious. Kant has the same restricted understanding of *ratio's* competence (elaborated in a much more detailed fashion under the forms of intuition and the categories of understanding). His illusions of the Ideas correspond to the seventeenth-century rejection of formal reason's transcendent competence. His solution, of course, is different. His critical use of Ideas is a more rigorous statement of Thomistic analogy (although contemporary Thomists do not acknowledge the similarity) rather than of the acoustic knowledge in early Protestant scholasticism, which is more easily seen in contemporary German existentialism, as represented by Heidegger ("Obedient to the voice of Being, thought seeks the word through which the truth of being may be expressed"; "Poetry and thinking are most purely alike in their care of the word. . . . The thinker utters being. The poet names what is holy"), or Jaspers, or (in theology) Bultmann.

depend upon whether the person had himself undergone the kind of experience which was paradigmatic in the Lutheran reformation—a terror-laden sense of the annihilating judgment of God. This was true of Gerhard also. The radical and universal significance of justification through faith became most real in his fifteenth year, when a severe case of dropsy not only brought him near death but aroused in him the excruciating *Anfechtungen* which were so typical of Luther. This experience, together with his native endowment, enabled him to be most receptive to the several major themes in the intellectual and spiritual life of the sixteenth and seventeenth centuries.

John Gerhard was born on October 17, 1582, at Quedlinburg in Saxony.[15] By birth he was of the nobility. His grandfather, Andreas Gerhard, was court counselor (*Hofrath*) of the abbess of Quedlinburg; his father, Bartholomaeus, was city counselor and city treasurer of Quedlinburg. His mother, Margareta Bernd, was active in work among the poor and needy. John was one of seven children.[16]

He received his early education in the humanistic school at Quedlinburg. During his critical fifteenth year, the man who provided him pastoral counsel was Johann Arnd, the author of the widely read book, tinged with mysticism, *Vom wahren Christentum;* he had fled from Anhalt in 1590 because his orthodoxy was under suspicion. The two remained in life-long contact.

In 1598 Gerhard's father died. In the same year, a plague wiped out over three thousand of Quedlinburg's inhabitants, among them the rector and co-rector of the school. Gerhard was also struck by it; but a double dose of medicine, mistakenly given because his mother did not know the physician had already administered one dose, saved his life. He continued his education

15. The anglicized form of Johann or Ioannes is used throughout this book.
16. The standard biography of Gerhard is Erdmann Fischer, *Vita Io. Gerhardi.* A popularized, but accurately abridged, version is Carl Julius Boettcher, *Das Leben Dr. Johann Gerhards.*

at Halberstadt because the Quedlinburg teachers could not be replaced immediately. At seventeen he completed his humanistic course.

The next year (1599) he entered the University of Wittenberg, to study philosophy. He attended the lectures and took part in the public disputations. He also attended the theological lectures of Leonhard Hutter, a theologian of some repute who had come to Wittenberg in 1596, and Solomon Gessner, who at the time was lecturing on the book of Daniel. Gerhard appears to have been an unusually diligent as well as gifted student. In Quedlinburg, at the age of thirteen and fourteen, he had composed a history of the Gospels in Latin verses. At Halberstadt he had done the same in Greek with the passion history. At Wittenberg he prepared for the philosophical disputations by entering into a book all the arguments he could find or construct for and against a given position.

In 1601, upon the advice of an influential relative, the jurist Andreas Rauchbar, he turned to the study of medicine. In three years he completed the course, wrote a number of articles in medical science, and briefly practiced medicine until Andreas Rauchbar hired him as a private tutor in Hemsendorf for his son, Michael.

At the death of Andreas Rauchbar in 1603, John Gerhard and Michael Rauchbar entered the University of Jena. There Gerhard decided to take up theology. In addition to attending lectures, he read and studied the Scriptures, the church Fathers, and the medieval scholastics. In working through the Fathers, he culled four volumes of quotations which undoubtedly served as one of his source books in his later work. He received his *magister's* title in the same year, 1603. Three days after receiving it, he began lecturing in philosophy and was given permission to lecture in theology also.

The lectures were soon interrupted: on Christmas day he became gravely ill with a disease that puzzled the physicians. He prepared his final testament, which began with a detailed confession of faith, on December 29; but after three weeks the disease had passed.

In May of 1604, Gerhard and Rauchbar entered the University of Marburg, attracted by the fame of the theologian and philosopher, Balthasar Mentzer. In October of that year he held his first disputation in theology. He attracted the interest and favor of Mentzer to such an extent that in the next year they took a trip together to visit the best libraries and teachers in southwestern Germany—Giessen, Friedberg, Frankfurt am Main, Darmstadt, Heidelberg, Stuttgart, Tübingen, Strassburg, Speier, and Worms.

In the meantime Marburg was converted to Calvinism under Landgraf Moritz. After a short stay in Hemsendorf, Gerhard returned to the University of Jena. By this time he had acquired enough of a reputation that calls had been directed to him from several sides while he was at Hemsendorf. Quedlinburg wanted him to head the local school; Arnd wanted him to come as deacon to Halberstadt; Mentzer wanted him to take a professorship at the new university in Giessen.

In 1606 he left academic life to become the bishop of Heldburg. Duke Johann Casimir of Coburg had heard of his reputation and wanted to call him to Heldburg as archdeacon. Before accepting the post, Gerhard went to see Casimir in person. As part of his interview he was asked to preach a sermon to the court on the text of Romans 8:14. The interview impressed Casimir so much that he changed the call. Not the office of archdeacon but that of bishop was now urged on Gerhard. He hesitated to accept for a number of reasons. For one thing he thought he was too young to be a bishop—he had not yet reached his twenty-fourth birthday. Moreover, he was accustomed to the academic life, and felt he might be accused of exchanging the rigors of academic discipline for the comfort of a bishopric. Casimir and his court replied to each of the objections in turn, and Gerhard finally consented to accept the call, with the provision that he would first finish his doctorate at Jena (at Casimir's expense). He completed that work before his twenty-fourth birthday. His public lecture on Ephesians 4, given as part of the final requirements, attracted three hundred students. The doctorate was conferred on November 13 of that year.

He was ordained in Coburg and installed as bishop of Heldburg, with twenty-six clergymen under his supervision. In addition to his bishop's duties he held weekly theological disputations at the *Gymnasium Casimirianum* in Coburg and carried on an extensive correspondence.

He received a number of other calls during this period. Jena offered him a professorship in 1610, but he declined on the grounds that he did not feel himself qualified to take a full professorship. He would have accepted a lower post at the university, but Casimir would not release him from Heldburg.

In 1615 he accepted a call as archbishop of Coburg. In the same year Jena offered him a professorship once more, this time forestalling the veto from Casimir by having Johann Georg, duke of Saxony, request Casimir to release Gerhard, should he wish to go to Jena. Casimir reluctantly agreed, but made the stipulation that twice a year Gerhard should return to take part in the examinations at the *Gymnasium Casimirianum.*

In 1616 he began his *glänzende Tätigkeit* (Heussi) at Jena. The university soon became the center of the German theological world, and Gerhard spent the rest of his life in this professorship, lecturing in exegesis and systematics; almost every theologian of note came to Jena to study. During his twenty-two years there, Gerhard received twenty-four calls to other places—to nearly every university in Germany, to Austria, to Denmark, to Sweden. He was rector of the university four times (engaged, even in those days, in fund-raising for the university) and frequently dean of the theological faculty. He was regularly the university's representative at royal affairs, such as the funeral of King Gustav Adolph of Sweden. He was the guiding figure at such theological assemblies as the Leipzig conclave in 1628, which undertook to refute the claim of the Jesuits at the Bavarian University of Dillingen that the evangelicals had long since departed from the Augsburg Confession and that there was, therefore, no further obligation to honor the religious peace. He was frequently the adviser of dukes in matters of the Thirty Years' War. With his colleague, Johann Major, he met Tilly at the city gates when that general was about to plunder Jena, and so impressed the general ("If you do not listen to me, our Lord God will") that he left the city with only a token plundering. With the theological faculty at Jena, he issued countless theological opinions on diverse matters. To the end he remained in demand also as a preacher.

The diversity of his activity and the extent of his literary output testify to his tireless energy. His colleague Johann Himmel said of him that he had written many excellent works in his life, his hand moving as fast as his thoughts, without ever revising any book once written. Troeltsch,[17] who notes that this was an astonishing accomplishment even in view of the fact that much of the content was quotation from other authors, adds the wry comment, "Dogmaticians cannot work that fast any more—*so rasch kann ein Dogmatiker heutzutage nicht mehr arbeiten.*"

Gerhard's two strictly philosophical works were *De vero* (1606), written to examine critically the view of Daniel Hoffmann that philosophy is inimical to theology, and *De necessitate et contingentia* (1607), defended as a public disputation at Jena.

In theology his most significant work, which was also the most influential work of seventeenth-century orthodoxy, was the *Loci Theologici,* written in the years 1610–21. He celebrated its completion on February 25, 1621, with a festival dinner at his house, to which he invited the Jena faculty. The first four volumes had been written at Heldburg, the remaining five in Jena.

His four-volume *Confessio catholica* appeared 1633–37. In it he attempted to confirm the teachings of the Augsburg Confession by documentation from the writings of Roman Catholic authors.

17. *Vernunft und Offenbarung,* p. 53.

It inspired a number of similar attempts by other authors like Johann Georg Dorsch, *Thomas Aquinas dictus doctor angelicus exhibitus confessor veritatis evangelicae Augustana Confessione repetitae* (1656), Paul Colomesius, *Rome protestante, ou temoignages de plusieurs catholiques Romains en faveur de la créance et de la prâtique des protestants* (1635), and Johann Pfaff, *Dogmata protestantium ex iure canonico et conciliis deducta* (1712).

The most arduous of his exegetical works was the *Harmoniae evangelicae Chemnitio-Lyserianae continuatio* (1626–27). In addition he wrote commentaries on several books of the Bible: Genesis, Deuteronomy, Psalms, Daniel, Matthew, John, Acts, I and II Timothy, Colossians, Hebrews, I and II Peter, Jude. Many of these were published posthumously, edited by Johann Ernst Gerhard, his eldest son.

His most popular work was the *Meditationes sacrae,* a devotional book written when Gerhard was a twenty-two year old student and published in 1606. These meditations were translated into many languages (English, French, Swedish, Finnish, Welsh, Greek, Arabic, Polish, Russian), and at one time had a circulation next in order to the Bible and Thomas a Kempis' *Imitatio Christi.*

He was the author of the first *Patrologia,* published posthumously in 1653. His other writings (among them over ten thousand letters) are too numerous to be listed.

He was married twice, in 1608 and 1614. His first wife (who was fourteen years old when they were married) died in 1611, leaving no children. The second marriage lasted until Gerhard's death on August 17, 1637. Ten children were born of this union, six of them outliving their father. The four sons were named—with some lack of imagination—Johann Ernst, Johann, Johann Friedrich, and Johann Andreas Gerhard.

CHAPTER II

Freedom in Form:
Thomas' Rationale of Creation

The formation of a theological view of man is one of the perennial tasks of the Christian philosopher and theologian.[1] Thomas Aquinas developed such a view in a detailed, formal rationale of nature and grace. The forms of creation and new creation are, as it were, the guarantors of the reality. Consequently, when one intellectually apprehends those forms, one understands the reality.

The present chapter deals with Thomas' rationale of God's relation to His creation. In this context the latter term embraces both the universe and man, but refers especially to man. The human creature cannot, of course, be treated completely in isolation from the world of nature, for he belongs to it and mirrors it. Yet the concern here is chiefly the rationale of the human creation, man as man—his character as human, his common native endowment, his goals, his activities to the extent that they proceed from

1. I shall use the words "theology" and "philosophy" in these chapters interchangeably to mean a system of thought which is a philosophical-theological whole. Where a distinction between theological and philosophical elements is called for, I shall indicate the referent by phrasings such as "the properly theological (philosophical)."

44

native potentialities.[2] The word stands in a twofold relation; on the one hand to "Creator" and, on the other hand, to "new creation." The new creature is, in the Christian sense, redeemed man, or Christian man in contrast to natural man. "New creation," or "grace," thus refers to that character of man which is the result of the restoring, saving creativity of God. In a broad sense, creation itself results from grace, inasmuch as the world was created by God out of His freedom and not from necessity (1.28.1 *ad* 3). He does not need the creature in order to be God. But in the narrow sense, grace applies to the free activity of God which constitutes man as *new* or restored. It is the gift of God freely given and making man acceptable to Him. *Gratia est donum a Deo gratis datum gratum faciens habentem.*

Fundamentally the problem of theological anthropology involves no more and no less than an elaboration of the meaning of creaturely freedom. For this phrase points both to the anthropological and to the theological element. Freedom is that which characterizes man in his independence, his autonomy, his self-sufficiency. "Creaturely" qualifies him and his freedom in relation to the sovereign freedom of God. As Thomas expresses it, God's relation to the world is rational (*rationis*), not real, because He is free to create or not to create, whereas the creature's relation to God is *realis* because, without Him, the creature would not be at all. Man is self-realizing, autoplastic, but he is not self-creating nor absolutely self-sustaining. Though the range of his potentialities, individual and collective, be limitless, that limitlessness is not eternity.

What, then, is his freedom? It is this problem and these creature-to-Creator relations which permeate Thomas' discussion of the creaturely love, now as *amor,* now as *caritas.* In the rationale of this account, creation appears as a huge enclosed circle, highly complex in the details which it includes. Yet it has one point at which

2. Where "creation" refers only to the extra-human realm I shall use phrases like "the world of nature."

it touches the divine. That point is, in the case of man, the movement of the free will, the form of the *liberum arbitrium*—a movement which by its very character is capable of a unique perfection, an instantaneousness not possible in other movements. Creation is autonomous but only under God's preserving grace. He has called it into being and He upholds it in its self-sufficiency. Should He withdraw His support, it would relapse into the nothing out of which it came. Though reason might not of itself know it, the world has not existed from eternity; it has been called into being out of nothing. But in His creating activity, God is not niggardly. He posits the world as a real effect of His causality. It is not just an attribute of His being or the matter of which He is the form. Like all effects in relation to their causes it stands over against its Creator in relative independence. It is His *Gegenüber,* His *vis-à-vis.* His *gratia conservans,* the continuance of His divine generosity, upholds the creation precisely in its relative self-sufficiency and freedom, and it does so through the created forms.

This vast rondure is, moreover, an analogue of the Trinitarian life of God (1.45.6 and 7). Man is made in the "image of God" and the world of nature shows His traces (*vestigia*). The concept of the image of God points to both sides in the relation, the character of the creating God and that of the created reality. Man is the image of God: this Augustinian vision, hovering always in the background of the Thomistic view, comes occasionally into the foreground of discussion. It provides, for example, the rubric for transition from a consideration of God to a consideration of man who is made in His image, as Thomas moves from Part I to Part II of the *Summa.* All of what Aquinas says with regard to the details of man's being could be subsumed under the "image of God." Nevertheless, it is well to bear in mind that this conception is perhaps more often a part of the background than of the foreground. Thus, in the prolix discussion concerning Thomas' resolution of the apparent conflict between self-love and the love of

God, D'Arcy[3] is technically correct in his hesitation to accept Gilson's interpretation. D'Arcy objects to the solution, which Gilson makes hinge on the conception of man as the image of God, because Thomas makes no definite reference to image or analogue but only to the relation of part to whole. Man loves God, Thomas can say, more than himself because he is like the hand of a body, or a single soldier in an army, or the part of a whole. And as there is no ultimate conflict between the good of the part and the good of the whole, so there is no conflict between man's self-love and his love of God. But Gilson is also correct inasmuch as the vision of man as made in the image of God never completely fades from view and even colors the part-whole relation. Indeed, the cogency of the argument from the relation of the part to the whole greatly depends upon that vision in which a "part" is not just a section but an analogue.[4] The extent to which this image-relationship is reflected in Thomas' thought, its fragments and its whole, will at least be indicated if not substantiated by the form and content of the present and following chapters.

Natural man—the image of God. Here we confront a distinction which is paramount for understanding Aquinas. "Natural," when applied to creation, has two meanings. It can refer to man in the "state of integrity," and it can refer to man in the "state of corruption." Pure man and fallen man are both "natural." This is a distinction which is easily overlooked if one only uses certain portions of Thomas' writing to find single answers to specific questions. It has consequently been the source of grievous misunderstandings—for the Protestant Reformers as well as for later theologians. To be sure, Thomas is quite conscious of the

3. *The Mind and Heart of Love*, pp. 92 f.
4. Cf., for example, *In DDN*, C. IV, lec. ix, par. 406: "Totum est bonum partis," Thomas has said. Now he goes on: "Quod enim est superius in entibus, comparatur ad inferius sicut totum ad partem, inquantum superius perfecte et totaliter habet quod ab inferiori imperfecte et particulariter habetur et inquantum supremum continet in se inferiora multa."

distinction and makes explicit use of it on a number of occasions in answering questions about man's "natural" potentialities. But when he makes passing references to "nature" and "natural man" in the contexts of other questions, he uses the word without qualification. It is imperative, therefore, to be alert to this ambiguity of meaning. Because of the importance of the distinction and of the fatal facility with which it may be overlooked, the remarks in the following sections are separated: the first section deals with man in his essential and unspoiled nature, and the second with man in his fallen nature.

PURE NATURE: ITS CHARACTER

Pure man is an abstraction. To treat of man in his natural purity is to abstract him from his total actual situation. Man in history, empirical man, is not pure. Thus a discussion of man's pure state, the *status naturae integrae,* concerns a state which in Thomas' view was never actual. Not even Adam was ever in that state; at his creation he was immediately endowed with the gift of grace. There never was and never will be—apart from Jesus the Christ— a pure specimen of man in history. In actuality no man is natural, and that on two counts. Either he is, as R. Guardini notes,[5] the man who has been called into God's grace—in which case, if he obeys he becomes more than natural man, and if he declines he becomes less than natural. Or he is, as H. R. Niebuhr points out,[6] to be conceived of as always conditioned by his culture—"in human existence we do not know a nature apart from culture."

Neither of these two qualifications, however, denies the validity of an abstract theoretical concept of human nature in its essential purity. They both alert us to the fact that we must be alive to the kind of concepts with which we deal and that we must handle them accordingly, conscious of their functions and their limits.

5. *Freiheit, Gnade, Schicksal,* p. 165, n. 1.
6. *Christ and Culture,* p. 39.

According to the Angelic Doctor, creation in its purity and without the endowment of grace is good—but incomplete. It is, as it were, "good as far as it goes—but it cannot go far enough." It is good because it is created by God and because it is capable of being ordered to the supernatural. Creatureliness is not in itself reprehensible. Death is not in itself a consequence of sin, but is implied in the fact of being finite; it is a consequence of sin only in the sense that sin robs man of the primeval endowment of grace which was to preserve him from decay and enable him to live forever. The creature's works are good, and the ends he achieves are good. His acts, as Bouillard phrases it,

> are not perfectly good because they lack the ordering to the final end which is theirs. Yet they are veritably good, for they can of themselves be ordered to the principal good which is the ultimate end, the enjoyment of God. If they could in no way be so ordered, they would be evil. Inasmuch as they can, they constitute a veritable virtue, but an imperfect one to the extent that it is not related to the final and perfect good.[7]

Thus creation is, though good, yet in a sense incomplete. It has an opening into which God must enter anew in order to complete it, to bring it beyond its natural *telos,* or beatitude, which does not include a participation in eternal life. This incompleteness comes to the fore in a number of areas. With regard to his *knowledge of God,* man can know that God is, he can know the *an est* of God; but he cannot know Him as the "object of beatitude," he cannot know the *quod est* (or *quis est*) of God (II.i.113.4 *ad* 2). He can know Him as the first cause and universal good but not in His *tota virtus* as Himself being man's eternal beatitude. The natural intellect catches sight of God only from afar. It cannot see the eternal character of God except according to its "irradiation" (II.i.93.2). Like a person who sees someone

---

7. *Conversion et grâce,* p. 191.

in the distance walking along the road, the intellect can tell that someone is walking there but not *who* it is. Natural knowledge binds man to a stranger, an unknown (I.12.13 *ad* 1), and "this is the ultimate of human knowledge of God: to know that one does not know Him."[8]

With regard to his *love of God,* his "natural *amor* which is only natural," man is similarly incomplete, though good (II.i.60.1 *ad* 1). He can love God as the source of all good, as the origin and general goal of all natural striving; but he cannot love Him as the special good and the ultimate beatitude. He can love Him as the giver of good things in nature; he cannot love Him for Himself, as the ultimate good. He can love Him with *amor* but not with *caritas.* For God in His fullness eludes natural love and happiness. No more than he can love an unknown stranger can man naturally love God in His eternal qualities as the Friend, the Thou, in conversation with whom man finds the fulfillment of his deepest longings.

With regard to his *faith in God,* there is a parallel incompleteness in man's endowment. The potentiality to believe is there, but the impulse and content of faith must come from without. Eternal truth is not in reason, not even latently, even though when revealed it does not contradict reason. The things of faith exceed and supplement human reason.[9] Furthermore, there is nothing in his natural endowment which enables man to assent to the truth of these contents (II.ii.2.3 *ad* 1; 5.2 *ad* 1; 6.1). Miracles, persuasion, the inner power of the free will—none of these is sufficient, at least in Thomas' later writings, to evoke assent to the content of faith. True, they can nourish it when it is present and so they do not contradict it, but they cannot give birth to it. To create faith a new inner impulse from God is needed.

In short, with regard to his total creaturely endowment and striving, man is able by his acts to attain a kind of *natural beatitude*

8. *De potentia* 7.5 *ad* 14.
9. *CG* I.4–8.

which is good but not eternal. God has implanted in creation certain goods as ends of certain operations. All of them constitute man's happiness. But to no activity or sum of activities has He ordained eternal life as a *finis*. It is a good which is beyond the natural good, just as God in His eternity is outside the created order of things, *extra ordinem naturae* (1.28.1 *ad* 3). However curious this may sound, Thomas had his good reason for saying it, as will become clear later on.

Moreover, creation's goodness is rooted in the Word of God in much the same way that an artifact is rooted in the idea in the mind of the artificer. Creation, as a real expression of God's goodness, is an analogue of the eternal *Verbum Dei,* the second Person of the Trinity. Ultimately it is only from the perspective of the Trinitarian *Verbum* that pure nature is fully intelligible. For the Word is the adequate representation (*sufficienter repraesentat*) both of God and of creation. It (or He) expresses what God is. It expresses and creates what the creature is. It expresses and reveals even the things that are yet to be (1.34.3 *ad* 5). The eternal Word expresses the vis-à-vis within the divine nature itself. As such He is also the exemplar of the goodness which is in creation.

A full account of nature in its integrity must, therefore, include its imbedding in the *Verbum Dei increatum,* the eternal Word. "Things," says Thomas, "can be considered in two ways; namely, as they are in themselves and as they are in the Word."[10] Considered in the first way, nothing has life. Considered in the second way, everything is "living" and "life." Look at creation as something self-constituted and self-explanatory, and it is dead. Look at it as an analogue of the Word of God, and it is living. Creation in its isolation remains a puzzle; in its cradling in the eternal Word it discloses its mystery. The illustration which Thomas uses in this connection is that of a work of art in relation to its artist. If it is viewed in itself it is relatively meaningless, dead. If it is, on the contrary, viewed in connection with the idea of it in the mind

10. *In Jn.* 1.2.

of the artist, then it has life. In other words, if one tries to understand the creation as something in and for itself, its full meaning remains hidden. But if one understands it as the expression of the Trinity, it discloses its meaning. For the *Verbum Dei* is the "creative reason of things which God makes" (1.34.3).

If man is made in the image of God, then creation stands over against the Creator in a way analogous to that in which the eternal Son stands over against the eternal Father as an expression of the Reason, the Word, in the Trinitarian nature. For the Son, Thomas reminds us (1.35.2), is Himself the eternal Image of God because He is the *Verbum*.[11] Creation is not a peripheral part of God any more than a word is a part of the speaker. It comes forth from God, at the initiative of God, but it is an independent reality. The word *proceeds* from the speaker and is not simply an excised section of his being. Amplify all the capacities of man to infinity and he still is not God. The difference between God and man is not a quantitative one but qualitative. God is not simply more of what man is. Man's creaturely freedom is an analogue of the divine freedom, his creaturely sufficiency analogous to the divine Word. And like every analogue he has his own order of being. To pass from God's Being to man's being involves a leap. God's infinity, His absolute aseity, is different from that of all creatures, as Thomas says, just as whiteness-itself, if it were self-subsistent, would differ from every whiteness which exists in things.[12] Add together an infinity of white things and you would still not reach whiteness itself.

11. One of the best technical discussions of Thomistic analogy is that of Gallus Manser, *Das Wesen des Thomismus,* pp. 393–490 ("Die analoge Erkenntnis Gottes"), which also contains bibliographical references. What tends to be neglected in the literature on analogy, as far as I have been able to examine it, is the discussion of the analogy not just between man and God but between man as image and Christ as Image—a point which did receive some attention in the theological controversies of the seventeenth century.

12. I.7.1. Thomas conceives "infinite" primarily as "unlimited in any way," whether by form or matter or unrealized potentialities. Yet the other meaning of aseity or eternalness is often admixed.

The double characteristic of this rooting in the *Verbum Dei*—
independence and relatedness—emerges forcefully in the discussion of the potentially explosive question of man's ability to perform meritorious works (II.i.114.1). If one does not immediately boggle at the words, "merit" and "work," one finds that they do not involve in Thomas' thought the crassly selfish superficiality and self-reliance which interpreters of the Protestant theological tradition tend to attribute to them. Can man deserve anything from God? Thomas replies first in the negative. Certainly, if "deserve" is taken in an absolute sense (*simpliciter*), a creature cannot be said to deserve or merit anything from the Creator. For God and man belong to two different realms. There is an infinite distance, a *maxima inaequalitas*, between them, and "every good of man is from God." Yet in a qualified sense (*secundum quid*) there is, indeed, an area of merit and reward. God has appointed certain goods as the reward for certain deeds. That is His divine ordering, rooted in the eternal Son of whom man is the analogue. On the basis of that ordering—but only then—can one speak of the merit of the creature before God.

This conception gives to the Christological foundation in Thomas a dual role which is also reflected in the conception of *amor* and *caritas* and which is not fully synthesized. On the one hand, the Christological relation is expressed in the principle of analogy—as God is to His Being, so man is to his being—which is nothing more nor less than man made in the image of Him who is the eternal Image of God. Concerning man's merit, Thomas can then say that man works according to *his* power and God rewards according to "the excellence of *His* power" (II.i.114.3). On the other hand, because Christ is the creative reason in all things, the paradoxical rationale of Christ's merit (III.49.6) applies also to man's merit; namely, the attainment of good comes not through laying claim to what is one's due but through giving up *coram Deo* any claim to what is one's natural due. In this dual conception of the function of the Christological basis one finds Thomas' use of the formal mode as well as his awareness of its limits.[13] For nowhere in the created correlation of activities and rewards is there a place for merited eternal life. It is an end which radically "exceeds the proportion of human nature" (II.i.109.5) and as such is unattainable by any act or series of acts of natural man. Nevertheless, this exclusion of eternal life from the naturally attainable ends is not simply a matter of divine caprice. On the contrary, it was "impossible" to give man an inner principle by which to attain eternal beatitude (II.i.5.5 *ad* 1). Impossible to do so: the word is to be taken strictly. The idea of a man with an innate principle of eternal life would be formally self-contradictory. If of himself he could attain eternal life, he would not be man; if he is man then he cannot be the author of eternity. By formal definition God alone is eternal; by formal definition man is finite.

The conception of man as capable nonetheless of participating in eternity breaks through as well as upholds the formal rationale. That is the brunt of the notion of natural beatitude, as we met it earlier. Non-eternal happiness which natural man can attain in principle is real happiness—until it is faced with eternity. If C. Friethoff[14] is correct in his comparison of the doctrine of predestination in Thomas and Calvin, then that doctrine offers confirmation of the consistency with which Aquinas held to the view of the natural goodness of creation in spite of its lack of eternalness. Reprobation to him means simply that to *some* creatures God has not antecedently willed *that* good which is eternal life. Instead He has willed only that which is natural beatitude, whatever it may or may not include. This reprobation, or non-election, is not the consequence of foreseen sin. In Calvin's view, on the other hand, reprobation is the consequence of sin: it is punishment.

13. Cf. also Chapter VIII.
14. "Die Praedestinationslehre bei Thomas von Aquin und Calvin," *Divus Thomas* (1926). Cf. also Bouillard, *Conversion et grâce*, pp. 7–16, for an account of the controversy on this problem generated by Stufler's *De Deo operante*, and pp. 77 ff., for an exposition of Thomas' conception of natural beatitude.

Punishment here; incompleteness there. Figuratively expressed, to Calvin the non-elect are like prisoners who are punished for their crimes—in contrast to the elect who are not punished because the penalty for their crimes has already been paid. To Thomas, the non-elect are more like people who have had the joys of attending two great universities—in comparison with the elect who have had the same joys *and also* the joy of attending the University of Paris. Or the non-elect are like citizens who know, perhaps even in detail, all the formal characteristics of their ruler —in comparison with the elect who also have a dialectical-personal knowledge of him.

The natural incompleteness in man's cognitive and volitional endowment is, in other words, conceived partly as a formal-objective knowledge and love of God alone, without the additional dialectical-personal acquaintance, and partly as formal knowledge and love without the additional (but still formally conceived) knowledge imparted through revelation. Indeed, Thomas' scientific apparatus allows for a conscious explication only of this latter conception; but in the distinction between man's natural relation to God (in which he knows that God is) and his supernatural relation (in which he knows God Himself as the "object of beatitude") he at least adumbrates the former conception; for in this contrast the phrase, "knowing God as the object of beatitude," becomes virtually synonymous with the personal knowledge of Him.[15]

The Aristotelian doctrine in which this view is scientifically expounded is that doctrine of form which Thomas wrested from Aristotle and used as a foundation stone in his own intellectual edifice. In the wake of early Barthianism this doctrine has tended to become a summary designation of scholastic sterility and its

15. Bouillard, *Conversion et grâce*, pp. 138 and 140, notes the fact that when Thomas comments on Scripture he tends to conceive grace as the "impulsion divine" rather than as a permanent form: that is to say, as the influence from an Other rather than as the effectiveness of a new principle or form.

perversion of the *kerygma* into what F. H. Bradley would have called a ghostly ballet of bloodless categories. But the doctrine of form, as Thomas employs it in its broadest sense, articulates the reality of a thing in the sight of God. Its rationale is predominantly formal, but it has its dialectical overtones. The problem involved in this doctrine is no other than the relation of the creature's real freedom to the Creator's sovereign freedom. In Thomas' language, one must ask the question thus: "How is one to conceive the relation between God as the cause (or principle) and the form as the cause (or principle) of all the creature is or does? How does one avoid conceiving man as a dead instrument?" The answer in brief is this: "God, as the causal agent of creation, informs it not with His substance but by means of the form which He causes in matter" (II.i.110.1 *ad* 2).

In the notion of form are contained the two elements of creaturely freedom and of the divine prevenience. The form is that by which a thing is a definite, distinct reality and by which it can act as a unitary being (I.42.2; II.ii.179.1). It is God who moves the creature; but He moves it as the definite creature which it is. He moves man as man, animals as animals, plants as plants. The causality of God does not denature the creature. This is the whole point of the doctrine of form in its specifically theological perspective. Once the form has been given, the creature acts out of his own freedom, for the form is the inherent principle of his acts at the same time as it is the contact with God. Through the form God is continuously operative in the actions of the creature. The form gives a thing its nature, which cannot be violated without a destruction of the thing itself, but it is at the same time directly tied to the Creator.

In upholding creation, God respects all things in their proper forms; therein is the mystery of His creative power. He also deals with man according to man's peculiar form, the *anima intellectiva,* the capacity to know and freely choose the good. It is the peculiarity of man that he is such a creature of free will. When God moves him, therefore, He moves his will *precisely as free will*. Thus human love, as an act of the will, is the expression of man's freedom. In his capacity to love the good, man is most autonomous and yet most directly moved by God.

How is this possible? Only because God is the Creator of all forms. Only He can so move the will who is also the cause of it. He who made the will to be will can move it without destroying its voluntary character: "that a voluntary movement should be brought about by an extrinsic principle which is not the cause of the will is impossible" (II.i.9.6). Only the agent can move through the form. The same is true of the whole world, of stones as well as of men. A brute can move a stone upwards by pushing it; but that movement is not natural to the stone, it is not a movement of the stone as stone which by nature (in Thomas' view) moves only downward. If the human will were similarly impelled by something extrinsic to it, the movement would not be natural or voluntary. Only if the extrinsic mover is at the same time the Creator of the will can the movement be at once extrinsic and intrinsic, extra-human and human.

Dynamics

Creation has been posited by God. But it is not static; it has its own inner movement. This takes place not as the dialectic of Yes and No but within the limits prescribed in the conceptions of "form" and "end." Each thing has, as it were, its space. In that space it moves from potentiality to actuality, and beyond that space it moves to the space occupied by a reality with a higher form. The universal striving of every form for its perfection, its *finis,* is the dynamics of creation. It applies to creatures on all levels, the striving of the form of plants to the perfection of planthood as well as of the form of man to its own perfection. Everything strives to attain its own good. But—a caution—this is not to be interpreted as selfish intention. Thomas reserves the term, *"inordinate* self-love," for that kind of seeking of one's own good (II.i.77.4). To say that every creature seeks its own good is tantamount to saying that every creature seeks to be its real self rather than to atrophy. Just as one who is hungry naturally seeks food instead of stones, so man as man desires naturally whatever in general fulfills his manhood. That desire is inherent and in itself ethically neutral.

The universal striving of things for their own good is, in other words, not an ethical but a metaphysical conception. Thomas does not hold that every man, if he is confronted with the choice of doing something for himself at the expense of another or of doing something for another at his own expense, will necessarily choose his own convenience over the help for another person. That would, indeed, be selfishness. To be sure, one may raise the question, as R. Voelkl does,[16] whether this metaphysical ego-relatedness does not lead to an ethical selfishness. (Thomas does, for example, seem to hold that a man ought not to choose to sacrifice his own eternal beatitude in the interest of his friends or countrymen because that contradicts the order of *caritas*.[17]) But there is little doubt about Thomas' primary intention. Thus Nygren's general use of the adjective "acquisitive" to modify natural love is misleading because of its connotations of selfish endeavor. Self-seeking in the sense of self-affirmation is a drive inherent in creation. Its opposite is not altruism but self-destruction. A thing in seeking its own good is following the pattern established by God's order. Viewed logically or grammatically, "good" is an internal accusative to "seeking." *Whatever* a creature naturally seeks is by definition its own good.

The name of that universal striving, that seeking of the good as good, in all realms and at all levels, is *amor*.[18] Love is the im-

---

16. *Die Selbstliebe in der Heiligen Schrift und bei Thomas von Aquin*, p. 286.

17. *In Rom.* IX.I.

18. Cf. *In DDN*, C. IV, lec. ix, 401 ff.

planted dynamics in the creature. It is analogous to the divine *Amor* with which God loves Himself and the world. The restlessness of love is not a vagrant rushing hither and yon. Rather it is a "wishing well to someone" *(velle bonum alicui)*. To will what is good for oneself is self-love. That is not in itself selfish love but simply the directedness of the self to what is its *finis*. The good of man includes, for example, altruism and self-sacrifice. Nor does Thomas understand self-love individualistically as the creature's realization of its potentialities or the following of its whims in disregard of everyone and everything else. On the contrary, he understands it as the creature's movement toward self-realization according to its respective standing in the hierarchy of beings. Perfection *in that status* is the first good. Man does not naturally wish for himself that good which is proper to the angels, nor do angels desire godhood. Each strives for his own perfection. That this notion of love does not immediately resolve practical ethical problems may be granted, but that objection is not to the point in places where Thomas characterizes nature in its abstract purity, driven as it is by love for its good, a love given with creation by the source of all good.

Since God is the source of all good, creation can be said to be in movement toward God. He is the universal good, the good in general. Wherever the creature seeks good it is seeking God; wherever it seeks God it is seeking good. Where the creature seeks particular goods like food to satisfy hunger, that seeking is but an instance of seeking good in general, not just the good which fills this or that special need but the good as good and because it is good. This is creation's movement upwards.

But the good, even God as the Good, moves the creature by attraction and not as an efficient cause. It moves as *finis* rather than as *causa agens*. Thus it does not violate the autonomy of the creature. Even that word of Pseudo-Dionysius, "Good is diffusive of itself," Thomas interprets to mean not the "operation of an efficient cause" but rather the "habitude of a final cause."[19] The good attracts all things to itself. In that sense it "diffuses" itself.

The Trinitarian Image

This, then, is creation in the image of God: nature in movement toward its good, rooted in the Trinitarian *Verbum* and *Amor*. Into this framework are placed the Augustinian formulations of the Trinitarian image in the rational and non-rational world. There are two levels at which God's inner nature is reflected in creation. The non-rational world is the *representatio vestigii* and humanity is the *representatio imaginis.* That is to say, the world, by the strength of the fact that it exists at all, shows a "trace" of the Trinity. It points to its cause in the same way that the existence of a building is a trace which points to a builder and exhibits something of the mind of the maker. But on a higher level the rational creature points to his Maker in the way that a statue of Mercury points to Mercury himself (1.45.7). It not only shows that it has been made but bears a likeness to its exemplar.

In more precise terms it is to be described in the following way: Man is the image of the Trinity because in his intellect and will the Trinitarian processions are reflected. The manner of procession of the Son from the Father is that of the "word of the intellect," and of the Holy Spirit that of the "love in the will" (*amor voluntatis*). In man's intellectual and volitional activities, his knowing and speaking and loving, we find the pattern of the divine life. These capacities have not been arbitrarily placed into man; they stem from the fact that he has been created by the Trinitarian God. He reflects the processions of the Trinity "because the processions of the Persons too are the cause and reason of creation" (1.45.7). "Mind" is the principle of all mental activity and thus represents the Father; "knowledge" is the intellectual activity which, working with word and concept, represents the

19. *De ver.* 21.1 *ad* 4.

Son, the Word; "love" is the volitional activity which, uniting knowledge and mind, is the representative of the ordered love of the Holy Spirit in whom God loves Himself and the world.

The lower creatures, however, do not possess intellect and will. They do not, therefore, represent the Trinitarian processions as an image does. How then are the processions represented in these creatures? In all of them one finds, Thomas declares (1.45.7), those characteristics which are reducible to the Trinitarian processions as their cause. Consider: every creature has a certain power of subsistence, otherwise it would not be there; it also has a form which makes it a definite being, placing it into one species or genus and not another; and it is "ordered" toward something else as its end. To the extent that a created thing is *substance*— the principle of its own being—it reflects the Father who is the cause and principle of all; to the extent that it has *form* it represents the Word, or the Conception of its Maker; to the extent that it has *relatedness* it represents the Holy Spirit who is the bond of unity in God. These general characteristics are pointed up also in the other Augustinian ternaries of *mensura-numerus-pondus, modus-species-ordo,* and *quod constat-quod discernitur-quod congruit.*

Thus the picture of the goodness of creation includes the perspective of it as the representation of the divine life in finite form. If the creation reflected only the Father and the Son it would consist of innumerable relatively self-sufficient things in isolation from each other and from their Creator. There would be fragments but no cosmos. If, on the other hand, it reflected the Father and the Holy Spirit but not the Son it would be chaos. Indeed, to speak of relatedness in love is meaningless without the presupposition that there is something to love and be loved. As the Holy Spirit presupposes the Son and the Father in the Trinity, so the striving and interrelatedness of creaturely beings presuppose their existence as definite and relatively self-sustaining things.

At the same time, however, this conception includes the incompleteness of the good creation. Man can know what is his natural good and he can love it but he cannot know nor love his ultimate good. The image of the Trinity remains at the creaturely level, good because it is of God but incomplete because it cannot attain to that ultimate Good which alone satisfies its longing and fully sustains the image. Of the "divine things" man has no knowledge, he must rest on faith, accepting as true what has been revealed though unable to have insight into that truth. Furthermore, this natural faith remains unformed, unordered by *caritas*. It is coupled with a general love for the good but not with the special love of God as the ultimate good. Man's knowledge of and love of ultimate truth and good remain largely aptitudes, not acts. Man is open to the new knowledge and new love but he does not possess them.

FALLEN NATURE: ITS CHARACTER

The foregoing description of man in the image of God does not apply directly to man in history or in present actuality, but rather to his abstract essence. For as we find him in his concrete situation he is not integral but fallen. He is still man, to be sure; he has fallen from his essential purity but not from his manhood. Corruption is essentially a defection from good and not an absolute privation of all goodness. Creation never falls totally from under the guidance of God since the fall was anticipated by His providence. "If God permitted no evil, many good things would be lost" (1.48.2). However corrupt the sinner be, he is still sinful *man* and not a brute beast or a fallen angel, and it is the greater manifestation of God's power that He can overcome evil rather than simply exclude it from the start. Beyond the distortions seen in actual man, the picture of his pristine state is still visible. Add sin upon sin to infinity, says Thomas (1.48.4), each sin in its turn diminishing a little more man's openness to God's gracious activity (*habilitas animae ad gratiam*), still the power to respond is never lost. Sin may corrupt man's created visage but never so distort it that it cannot be recognized as the handiwork of God.

If the fall means a defection from original goodness, then it must bring "wounds" to all realms of nature, to the *modus-species-ordo* of the vestige and to the psychic functions which are the image of God in man.

The *modus-species-ordo* of the created world is the vestige of the Trinitarian processions universally present but corrupted in the whole circle of creation. Whatever exists is what it is by virtue of its form. But the fact that anything has a form presupposes a previous determination or "commensuration to that form: either of principles, or of materials, or of the things effecting the form itself" (1.5.5). A form cannot rudely impose itself on unprepared matter. If there is an oak tree standing in the yard, then in its very existence as a species (oak tree) the genus (tree) is presupposed. There could be no oak trees if there were no trees, logically and metaphysically speaking. The genus is the father of the species. Moreover, merely random material will not suffice for the making of an oak tree. The form cannot unite with, say, the material with which the form of a stone unites to make actual stones. It can unite only with predisposed material. This predisposition of the material is, again, the "father" of the material which is actually constitutive of the oak tree. Finally, forms are not virgin born. The form of the tree originates in the more general forms of plant life; every form has an ancestry. Now, the term which is applied to these various kinds of predetermination is *modus*. Thus whatever is has a form, and whatever has a form has a presupposed *modus* as its father. This is the universal vestige of Father and Son.

Furthermore, if anything has a form it is also inclined to its correlative end. This inclination toward a certain end is called its *ordo,* its "relatedness" or "order." The *ordo* of an acorn is its inclination to become an oak tree. Acorns do not become apple trees because their *ordo* does not allow it. But any such inclination to an end is love. It is, therefore, the vestige of the Trinitarian

Ordo which is the Holy Spirit. Finally, it is the form which "constitutes" a thing as a *species* and makes it a definite being. So here in the *modus, species,* and *ordo* which are present by implication in all things, we have the vestige of the Father, Son, and Holy Spirit.

Perhaps an analysis of the meaning of the vestige and image of the Trinity is the clearest illustration of the fact that such conceptions as "form" in the Thomistic frame had a lively quality which they lack in modern thought, and that the dialectical element is implicit even in this predominantly formal order of thinking. In Thomas' Aristotelianism (one might say even in Aristotle himself, though that is beyond the point here) to speak of the *modus* simply as that which precedes or prepares for the form; or to speak of the "form" in an objective and static way would miss the dynamics as well as the dialectical flavor of those terms. The *modus* is the father of the form, the form is the son of the *modus* —this kind of metaphor would better catch the flavor Thomas himself seems to have found in the rationale of the vestige.

It should be noted, therefore, that Aquinas' use of this scheme of dispositions, forms, and orders was not due to a slavish imitation of the Philosopher. There was a happy coincidence—if not, indeed, a natural relatedness—between the Trinitarian understanding of reality as received from Augustine, biblical and dialectical in its rationale, and the formal-Aristotelian way of understanding it. The biblical served to make audible the dialectical overtones of the doctrine of form; the doctrine of form endowed the Augustinian-biblical dialectic with scientific, objective exactitude.

In man, the fallenness of creation manifests itself specifically in his rational nature. In his *intellect* is the "wound of ignorance," which deprives reason of its direction toward the true (II.i.85.3; 74.5; 76.2). Ignorance is more than an absence of knowledge, more than not-knowing (*nescientia*). It is rather a privation of knowledge, a culpable not-knowing of what should be known.

There are two ways in which this ignorance reveals itself. First, reason may err concerning the cognition of the true. This is a sin if it has to do with things which all men should know, namely, "matters of faith and universal precepts of right (*jus*)" in addition to whatever specially pertains to the individual's status or office. Even those who lack the leisure or ability to arrive independently at a knowledge of these fundamentals are obliged to know them because they can be found in revelation. Not everyone, on the other hand, would be required to have a knowledge of, for example, geometric theorems. Ignorance concerning the necessary things is the mark of the fallen world, and that ignorance is itself sin.

The second way in which the corruption is exhibited in the *ratio* is through its commanding the lower parts to do "inordinate acts" or through its negligence in restraining them from those acts. The drunkard who knows that drunkenness is ruinous of his health, immoral and irrational, yet who cannot use his *ratio* to restrain his inferior appetites is an example of this second kind of corruption in reason. According to his integral nature, no man would so act, for essentially reason has power to hold the inferior appetites in control unless it has been stupefied by sin's narcotic effects.

Corruption is irrational, and yet a trace of reason always remains—inasmuch as man can always *know that he should know* the fundamentals of faith and nature. And if he is ignorant of them, he can nevertheless know certainly that he should find them out from someone who is not ignorant. The truth about God in His inner life and in His dealings with man, together with the natural principles that guide the world; these are what everyone knows he should know. Even in his fallen state, man remains aware of his origin in God and of his essential manhood. Though Thomas never formulates the remnant of reason in this way, it is an obvious presupposition. This makes understandable his interpretations of non-Christian religions (e.g. Islam) as the result of deliberate fraud.[20] For, if it is true that all men can know that they ought to know the things of faith, and can also know where those things are to be found—namely, in the writings of those men whom God has attested by miracles and prophecy and martyrdom—then one must account for the *origin* of a religion like Islam by reference to the exploitative intentions of its founder, and for its *continuation* by reference to the carnal satisfactions which it affords in present fact and future promise to its adherents. The result of such an interpretation is a curious twist. Thomas' principle of the remnant of natural goodness in concrete man leads him by consistent logic to a more deprecatory estimate of those religions than if he had been less certain of that remaining rationality or if, at least, he had placed it differently. Had Thomas not been convinced that man can always know the *that* and the *where* of the truth of faith, there would have been available more sympathetic interpretations of the origin and continued existence of non-Christian religions. The same comment would fit the sanction which Thomas could give to the use of physical force to bring back the infidels who had forsaken the faith they had once accepted (II.ii.10.8). For this too proceeds on the assumption that the apostate is willfully disobedient to what he knows to be the truth, that he holds to his crotchets knowingly and perhaps willingly.

As the corruption in the intellect is ignorance, so in the *will* it is disordered desire. In the state of pure nature, the will was in harmony with the other functions of the mind as well as with itself; in the state of corruption there are varying degrees and varying areas of disharmony.

First, the defection of man's will from its original goodness may result in a conflict between the private good and the general good. Ideally there is no opposition between the private and the general; actually, in the present life, there is. Where the individual good does not find its genuine fulfillment in the common good, there

20. Cf. *CG* I.6.

the fallenness of actual good is manifest. It is true that Thomas, in the case of such conflicts, tends to solve the problem in theory uncritically, by a sacrifice of the individual in the interest of the whole, rather than the converse; yet he does recognize that it is a conflict which may arise in actuality but which is not implicit ideally in man's creatureliness, only in his corruption.

Secondly, the opposition between private and general good may be reflected in the individual person himself when he seeks temporary goods that in the long run will negate his general good. The fact that man can, for instance, actually choose immediate satisfactions in preference to the long-term ones of a rationally moderated life is the manifestation of the corruption of an essentially good will which, in its purity, desires things only in their proper order. The present disorder in which the sensual appetite may predominate over the rational one is what Thomas calls the "wound of concupiscence" (II.i.85.3). It is the desire for things unmoderated by a rational account of their intrinsic worth; or it is passion overcoming reason's control.[21]

Both of these oppositions, between the private and the communal and between the immediate and the long-term, reflect clearly Thomas' method of formal conceptualization. For the *bonum in communi* has three distinct, though formally related, meanings. It can mean first the "generically good," the good qua good, that which makes anything which is good to be good. As such the *bonum in communi* is prior to the *bonum in specie,* metaphysically, logically, and ethically. It is that by which the special good is classified as good and by which it has its metaphysical status. Secondly, the *bonum in communi* then comes

21. Though "concupiscence" and "irascibility" belong properly to the "inferior" part of the soul, and are not strictly on the level of the intellect and will, still Thomas does recognize a form of concupiscence and irascibility also in the will, which in Thomistic psychology means the rational appetite in contradistinction to the inferior, sensitive appetite (cf. I.81.3 and 82.5). In other words, "reason," which consists of intellect and will, is capable of its own concupiscence and irascibility.

derivatively to have a social application, and the "common good" is identified with the good of the whole community in contrast to that of the individual member. For the individual is related to the community in the way in which a specimen is related to its species or the species to the genus. Therefore the notion of a private but not public good is nearly as self-contradictory as would be the notion of a special good which is not, generically classed, good. Thirdly, the *bonum in communi* comes to be applied to the whole span of life in contrast to a part of it, the individual moment or a short series of moments. The temporal is here interpreted also according to the formal rationale. The good of a single moment is dependent upon the good of the whole span in the same way that any special good is dependent upon the general notion of good. Therefore in this application of the term also the notion of an immediate, or short-term, but not long-term good is nearly self-contradictory. The good of the moment is what appears as good, but whether it is really good is decided only over the complete phase of time.

The only important exception to this view of the relation between the short-term and the long-term good, as far as I have ascertained, occurs in the ambiguity of the notion of natural beatitude in its relation to supernatural beatitude, for there Thomas apparently holds to both sides of this contradiction: that the natural beatitude is a real and not just an apparent good but at the same time, in contrast to supernatural beatitude, it is only an apparent good.

In the third place, the defection from purity may result in man's actually willing evil instead of good. This is the "wound of malice," which results when the will is deprived of its directedness toward the good. Here it is not a case of willing something which is mistaken as good but turns out to be evil, as would be true if in particular cases the use of certain medicines should not cure but actually complicate a disease; for this latter is not a matter of universal knowledge, ignorance of which is culpable. What is at issue here is the plain fact of experience that many people do act contrary to their own better knowledge. "Experience shows (*experimento patet*) that many act contrary to what they have knowledge of (*ea quorum scientiam habent*)" (II.i.77.2). Even though every rational being by nature wills the good, yet it is possible that this natural *habitus* does not become actual in concrete cases. The agent may be distracted or be hampered by some impediment, like the overwhelming power of passion, or by his physical states, like sleep or drunkenness, so that the habitual knowledge does not become actual knowledge.

Finally, if one regards man not from the standpoint of his psychical functions of reason and appetite but rather from the viewpoint of the four cardinal virtues which characterize the good man, then the fourth defect is the "wound of infirmity," according to which the "irascible part" is weakened. Instead of making him courageously face arduous tasks, it allows him to lapse into doing what is easy and at hand. This wound is a defect in his *courage*, as the wound of ignorance is a defect in the virtue of *prudence*, the wound of malice a defect of *justice*, and the wound of concupiscence a defect in *temperance*. The corruption of the psychical functions leads to a disorder which can be classed either according to its relation to pure intellect and will or according to its relation to the four cardinal virtues (II.i.85.3).[22]

The corruption affects the intellect and will individually, as the foregoing argument shows. It also affects their interworking so that there is a disharmony not only within each of them but also in their interaction. In this aspect, the defection might be described by a phrase more dialectical, and of more recent vintage, than scholastic terminology: the lack of personal centeredness. The term is new, but the method of interpreting man's fallenness is foreshadowed in Thomas' Aristotelianism, though it is tied, of

22. The theological virtues of faith, hope, and love were, of course, not a part of man's natural equipage. Instead they were the additional gift of grace, also lost through the fall.

course, to the "faculty–psychology" in which intellect and will are
the two parts of man's higher psychical capacities. The lack of
centeredness, in this interpretation, amounts to a clash between
the parts of the psyche. The intellect may be ordered to the true,
but the will not to the good, or the will to the good, but the intellect not to the true. Wherever something appears to be true but
not to be good, or to be good but not to be true, the latent split
displays itself. For in essence the good and the true are one; essentially what is true is *eo ipso* good, and conversely. Truth is
dyed in goodness. But where there is no knowledge of the good
or no love of the true the centeredness or unity of the human soul
is lost. In a telling passage, Miguel de Unamuno gives account of
that situation of conflict in these words:

> Intellectual love! intellectual love! what is this intellectual
> love? Something of the nature of a red flavor, or a bitter
> sound, or an aromatic color, or rather something of the same
> sort as a love-stricken triangle or an enraged ellipse—a pure
> metaphor, but a tragic metaphor corresponding tragically
> with that saying that the heart also has its reasons. Reasons
> of the heart! loves of the head! intellectual delight! delicious
> intellection!—tragedy, tragedy, tragedy![23]

This passage blazons forth both sides of the corruption: the
tragic loss of unity and the dim remembrance of it. When it comes
to believing the things of God, the impulse to do so may come
from either of the two parts, the intellect or the will. That is to
say, man can believe them because he has insight into their truth,
even though he may have no particular love for God Himself; or
he may believe them because he loves God and therefore accepts
whatever He says, whether or not the truth of His sayings is
patent. Certainly, Unamuno's strong sense of the tragedy is not
immediately at the surface in Thomas' description, but it does
lurk beneath and is later made explicit by John Gerhard (XI. 118),

23. *Tragic Sense of Life,* pp. 234 f.

precisely in relation to the observation in Aristotle's ethics that many people do what they know to be wrong.

These are the ways in which the corruption of nature, the defection from good, manifests itself in the actual world. Not all of them are universally present in equal degree. The universal element is the sheer fact of corruption, in whatever degree and whatever domain of life, the loss of natural integrity (and of the first endowment of grace, it may be remembered) which erupts in disorder.

Dynamics

As there is an inner drive which prevents nature, in its pure state, from remaining fixed and aloof from its Maker, so too is there one which impels fallen nature in a way adapted to its condition. The rationale of the impulse in the fallen creation follows from the nature of the defection. If there is blindness of the intellect, then that blindness must be counterbalanced by sight; if there is disorder in the will, or a clash between the will and intellect, then the disorder and clash must be prevented by a counterpoise of external restraint.

Because corrupt man lacks insight not only into the principles of divine truth which exceed his natural reason but even into the natural principles accessible to the pure intellect, he is led in the *realm of intellectual things* to an acceptance of truth on *authority*. The need for authority arises not only from God's sovereignty, which leaves to Him the initiative in all revelation, but also from the "obscurity of the intellect" which befogs man's knowledge even of the things which he should naturally know concerning God. And there *are* things he should know, things for which he is held responsible. If he does not know them he is guilty; ignorance does not excuse him. Since he knows that he must know, he is driven to finding out the truth. But if he cannot, out of his own impoverished resources, find this knowledge, his recourse is to ask those who have it and to receive it on their word. If one cannot grasp the inner truth of what he is told, he must take it on the strength of their trustworthiness. For to reject it is to risk the punishment which follows on ignorance.

From the viewpoint of authority this need of all men for knowledge justifies transmitting "in the manner of a faith" (*per modum fidei*) even things which could be shown to be true by demonstration, if one took the time and if one had students capable of following the argument (II.ii.2.4). Authority is the counterweight to culpable ignorance, a device making it impossible that there should be anyone who cannot find the truth. Thus it is that one finds in the Word which God has transmitted in the Scriptures many things which are in principle accessible to reason. For though they are in *principle* naturally knowable, yet in *fact* so many errors creep in (as is evidenced by the many ghosts of falsehood which haunt the systems of the philosophers, Thomas observes) that the truths are directly revealed by God. He makes them known in order to make it possible that everyone has the opportunity to learn them regardless of the degree of *obscuritas* in the intellect.

Furthermore, the same need calls for the dogmatic formulation of the truths of faith even though they are already contained in the biblical writings. Since even the fastest reader must take a good deal of time to read the Scriptures and since, moreover, the truths are contained in them diffusely and in various ways rather than in systematic form, it is understandable—even necessary—that the symbols of faith, the creeds, should be compiled. They compress into small scope the things which everyone is held accountable to know but which take long study and exercise to discover in the Scriptures. "Necessarium fuit veritatem fidei in unum colligi, ut facilius omnibus proponi, ne aliquis per ignorantiam a fidei veritate deficeret" (II.ii.1.9). Now, Aquinas does not state, in his amplifications of this subject, whether this kind of collection of the truths of faith into symbols would be necessary for man in his essential purity, but it seems clear that the necessity is due more to the corruption of the intellect than to its natural limitations.

But why—if such a collation of truths is so indispensable—do not the biblical writings themselves collect them and so present them? Thomas has two ways of accounting for their diffuseness. First, it may be traceable to the darkness of man's intellect which cannot apprehend truth unless it comes in many different guises. Secondly, in accord with an Augustinian view, it may be accounted for as a counterpoise to the form of human corruption which is pride. For if access to the divine mysteries were too easy, man might become too readily proud of his accomplishment.

But however it be interpreted, the quest for truth on authority is one of the dominating characteristics of the fallen world. Authority remains largely external to man in his fallen condition. The obscured intellect accepts things as true even though it cannot see their truth and even though, in fact, they may contradict what the intellect holds as true. Where the choice must be made between what the intellect apprehends as true and what authority guarantees as true, the latter shall be chosen—that much fallen man can know.

In the same fashion, the hierarchy of authorities with a single magisterial office at its pinnacle is correlated with the corruption in nature. In matters of faith everyone is held to know those things which are necessary to salvation (II.ii.2.6; 1.10; 6.1). Yet since it is an obvious fact of experience that not all people have the same degree of insight or critical judgment, revelation comes through an established order of transmission: from God by way of the superior angels to the inferior angels, from them in turn to the seniors (*majores*), and from them to the subordinates (*minores*). Faith's truth is transmitted from the top to the bottom. The hierarchical order is in itself a part of creation and not the result of defection from created goodness. Corruption, however, manifests itself in the disturbance of this order, as when the *majores* use their critical understanding not to promote but to distort the truth of faith. The dynamics of fallen creation mean that in such situations the lowliest members act in the knowledge that they are reliant on the *majores*. If some of the *majores* do in fact distort the truth, it is not held against the simple believers, who are gulled by it, unless it is stubbornly held in plain opposition to the universal faith of the church. It, the faith of the church, Thomas maintains (II.ii.2.6 *ad* 3)—citing Luke 22:32, "I have prayed for you, Peter, that your faith fail not"—cannot be corrupted. Thus at all events the truth of faith can be found at least in the highest among the *majores,* the teaching of the single head of the temporal church.

Hence the papal authority must be exempt from the corruption which may infect the lesser believers and even some of the *majores*. For his part, the simple believer is immediately dependent upon the faithfulness of his superiors in transmission of the truth. Whether he comprehends what they tell him or not, he confesses the faith they teach because he is aware that he is held responsible for knowing the truth of his salvation. Yet there is a possibility that some of the immediate *majores* defect from the universal faith of the church. Hence they in turn must be measured by the authority above them. Though the judging itself cannot be done from below by the simple believer (for he is utterly dependent upon his superiors), yet it can be done from above by the superiors of the superiors and finally by the papal office itself. That office is the incorruptible area in creation. Corruption suffuses everything between, but not including, two fixed points: at the top, the incorruptibility of the highest teaching office, and at the bottom the incorruptibility of man's awareness that there are things he must know.

These two limits stand and fall together. The awareness of the need to know is the universal and unambiguous "question"; the *magisterium,* the equally universal and unambiguous "answer." The positing of the incorruptibility of the magisterium makes sense in the light of the universal responsibility to know certain things. That universal responsibility in turn, if it is not to become an expression of demonic caprice, makes understandable why there must be a single highest authority, able to be located unambiguously and the judge of all the lesser authorities to which recourse may otherwise be had, but which in plain fact sometimes are mutually contradictory. Skepticism can never become absolute; the teaching of the highest magisterium can never become impure. To deny either of these two correlated assertions would make of the Creator, Thomas would be convinced, a demonic tyrant.

With regard to its mode, the rationale of the creature's freedom and relatedness to his Creator, as given in the preceding pages, is formal with dialectical coloring. However, Thomas does employ, though less extensively and deliberately, a dialectical rationale at the same time. This emerges in connection with the question of the sending of the Son into the world, the *missio temporalis* (III.1.3). Thomas asks whether, if man had not sinned, the Word would have become incarnate. He replies that, although it were not impossible for God to become incarnate if man had not sinned, yet it is more appropriate to say that He became incarnate in order to remedy sin. Had man retained his integrity, he would have been permeated with the light of divine wisdom and the integrity of divine righteousness; he would have known all things necessary for him to know. But now, in his fallen state, he has turned away to material things. "Homo, deserto Deo, ad corporalia collapsus erat" (III.1.3). On that account it was expedient that God, in order to save man, take on a human body. Because his intellect is no longer purely receptive to the divine impartation, man readily misunderstands God. As a kind of visual aid, then, God Himself takes on human form in order to convey what He cannot convey otherwise. "It is as though a teacher, noting that his meaning is not understood by the hearers in the words that he has used, seeks to use other words to make clear what he has in his heart."[24] Flesh has blinded man; by flesh shall he be saved. Thomas grants that it is not necessary to save man in exactly this way (III.1.2), but it is the method most adapted to the condition of the fallen world, the world as driven toward the flesh. Now it is possible to see, even in flesh, the truth of salvation. This method of reaching man corresponds to the nature of man's corruption much in the way that a teacher's method of reaching the student is adapted to the present concerns and intellectual development of the student. Man's intellect, turned toward the concrete, the bodily, can now find in a concrete personal life the truth which God wants to convey to him.

Thus far the need for the *missio temporalis* is formally reasoned. The incarnate Word is that concrete reality which best exemplifies the divine meaning. The corruption of man's intellect is interpreted as the dulling of its power to abstract the form of divine meaning from the concrete world. Thus a better, clearer specimen is required; namely, the incarnate *Verbum* in whom the abstract and the concrete are uniquely joined. But a teacher uses all devices of teaching as early as possible, and a formal rationale cannot account for the fact that this supreme manifestation of God's Word came at a certain point in history. Why did God wait so many millennia before sending the Son? Again, it is partly due to the corruption of man. For, Aquinas explains (III.5.5), since the root of all sin is pride, it follows that man would have to be set free from sin in such a way that he would be brought to the knowledge of his need for divine help. This could not occur until man had passed through generations alone, exhausting his own resources in trying to save himself. Then at least he would be able to see the depth and breadth of his need for a divine Savior. Pride makes him desire a knowledge which is beyond his assigned measure, the knowledge to determine out of his own resources what is the good or evil to be done, rather than to hear it from

24. *Super ep. S. Pauli* (*I Cor.*) 1.55.

God. And under pride's domination, the blinding of the intellect is such that its utter inability to know the ultimate good or evil can be shown only in the course of history, history interpreted as the resistance of man to God and God's chastizing of man. The "proof" of man's fallenness is provided thus not by a logical formal demonstration but by the course of history understood as God's dealing with man. Man does not know the real depth of corruption until he has seen it in his historical development, as one by one all of his attempts to save himself have shattered and continue to shatter. This is the purpose of the history of Israel: to show the impossibility of mankind's saving itself out of its own resources. The history of Israel provides the dialectical-personal rationale (the meta-history) of the human situation, just as the Aristotelian metaphysics provide the formal rationale of the same situation. But the dialectic of history convinces where the logic of demonstration fails.

While integral man is ordained for revelation and is immediately able to receive it, fallen man is driven to it; but he receives it only slowly and he distorts it with error. In pure nature the hierarchy of teacher-student or superior-inferior is a vehicle of transmission of undistorted truth; in corrupt nature the truth may be distorted by the superiors and it may be rejected by rebellious inferiors. Hence there is call for an external authority to prevent the entrance of error and the rebellion of pride. Even the additional visual aid, the incarnation of God in the personal life of Jesus Christ, remains somewhat extrinsic to the intellect of fallen man. For the truth which he finds there may not penetrate his own being but reside objectively "without," in Jesus Christ as the perfect example of the divine Word (even though unintelligible to a man's intellect), or in the history of Israel as a history in which the Gentile does not participate, the story of a people similar to stories of all other peoples.

The same externality appears in the regulation of the movement of *the fallen will*. Because man in his fallenness lacks ordered

77

love, he must be guided by external *discipline* in doing what the will internally is not able to do because of its condition.

One kind of external discipline is the persuasive action of intellect on the unordered will. It may happen that the will is not ready to receive the things of faith. In such a situation, reason sometimes works to convince the will—"when someone either has no will or has a will not ready to believe" (II.ii.2.10). The intellect in this case acts as a gentle discipline, a persuasion, on the will which has lost its orderedness. (This is, of course, not to say that reason always exercises that kind of function, for it is also employed to reflect on the things which are already believed and which the will already loves.) The recalcitrant will which says, "I do not want to hear or see the truth of God," is reprimanded by the rational faculty, which replies, "But there are reasons why it is more sensible to believe than not to believe." A perverse will which refuses obedience to God can partly be brought around by the *ratio humana inducta,* to which it may be subject as to an external discipline, a demonstration that faith is not preposterous. A faith so aroused is preferable to no faith at all. However, where the will must be thus persuaded, the merit of its faith is diminished because the truth is accepted, not out of devotion to the Him who reveals it, but because reason has shown that what the revelation asserts is at least not impossible to believe. For the merit of faith lies in the will's readiness to accept the truth on the basis of its love for the Author, rather than on the basis of the reasonableness of what He says. The lack of meritorious faith, that is, faith which is in true accord with God's ordering of creation, results from defection from original goodness. Where it is lacking, the will can be gently coerced by the intellect.

But the disciplining power of reason is limited. There remain those who have never accepted the Christian faith, such as the Jews and the pagans. Thomas asks whether they are to be coerced by physical force to accept it (II.ii.10.8). He replies in the negative

78

because even those who are vanquished in war or taken captive must still be left to accept or reject the faith in their own liberty. The will retains an ultimate freedom which leaves it incoercible by physical force or rational argument. However, such discipline as can be exercised externally should be used to prevent the unbelievers from trammeling the faith by "blasphemies or evil persuasions or even open persecutions." This is why Christians have waged wars against unbelievers, not in order to compel them to accept the faith, for that is impossible, but in order to prevent them from hindering the profession and practice of faith by others. In other words, like rational persuasion, physical coercion remains extrinsic to the will. What can move the will is alone the will. But the truant will, too weak or too perverse to accept the truth from God or too zealous in waging war against the true faith, can be held within bounds by reasoning and compulsion. Whereas the pure will is open to receive God, the corrupt will tends to rebellion and must be trained.

Compulsion is also to be used against heretics or apostates (those who once accepted the faith and then fell from it), but more sternly than against pagans. For though the faith is accepted only by a free choice, once it has been accepted, its continued practice must if necessary be physically compelled (II.ii.10.8). Acceptance of the faith is voluntary but maintaining it is necessary. Here again the peculiarity of the fallen creation emerges. It is not the case that once it has chosen its good in God the fallen will is necessarily able to follow through and carry out its initial intention. The threat of relapse is omnipresent until the inner strength of the will is confirmed in the state of glory. Consequently, an external restraint is always a potential demand: bodily compulsion if necessary, but at least strong persuasion. One cannot be compelled externally to accept the faith and its obligations, but one can and should be compelled to carry out the obligations of faith once they are accepted.

The task, therefore, of the disciplining agent is twofold: first, to maintain social and political conditions which allow for the free course of the gospel in order that all may hear and in their own liberty accept or reject it. This is the task of the church against the world. Secondly, those who are in the church must be prevented from relapsing. Indeed, this latter power of restraint, in cases of repeated and persistent relapses permits the church to deprive the unfaithful of his material possessions, even of his life, in the interest of his eternal good. For the inability of the will to support its intentions is obvious in the case of continually relapsing Christians. To counter this internal weakness, all of the weapons of persuasion and compulsion can be enlisted for the sake of the lapsed one as well as for the sake of others. The good of the many (as being the more general good) is preferred to the good of the single one if there is a conflict, and the eternal good (as being again the more general) of any man is preferred to his temporal good (II.ii.11.4). If the alternative is to save a man's soul by stripping him of his physical possessions—money and office and fame—or, on the other hand, to preserve these possessions and thus endanger his soul, the choice must clearly be for the former, because in the formal order the general occupies a higher status than the particular good.

Moreover, the exercise of discipline comes from the top rather than from the bottom. The simple believer does not deprive the ecclesiastical official in order to save the latter's soul. As Thomas notes in another context (II.i.2.1), "the judgment concerning human goods should come not from fools but from the wise." Thus the two polar points appear in the discipline of the will in a fashion similar to that they had in the authority for the intellect. At the top is the supreme disciplining agency which in its turn is not disciplined because it is not subject to distortion. At the bottom is the ultimate freedom of the individual will to accept the faith, an ultimate incoercibility. The disorder of the will never becomes so chaotic that all freedom vanishes and only compulsion remains—for then man would no longer be man. And, on the other hand, the highest office of discipline, the very incorporation of the will of God, remains incorruptible. Both of these two points are unambiguously present in temporal reality. The directedness of the will which is weakened by the fall must be strengthened by external forces, just as the "obscurity of ignorance" in the intellectual domain must be counterbalanced by external authority.

The Corrupted Image

In the state of integrity man is in the image of God. In thinking and willing according to his own order of being he bears the Trinitarian processions. But the purity is lost and the image is corrupted. This corruption is a universal characteristic of temporal reality, introduced, according to Thomas' view, by the sin of Adam who, as a kind of supra-historical figure, stands in a unique relation to the whole human race. He "moves" all people "by the motion of generation" in the way that any man's will moves all his members to action. The human race is the body of Adam, and in that way it can be said that in Adam all sinned. The solidarity of sin is, in any case, the incontrovertible fact.

Corruption does not affect the substance of humanity, but it does affect his inclination. He cannot will or accomplish his natural ends. The Trinitarian processions are distorted in much the same way that rough waters distort an image reflected in them. The word as proceeding from a speaker and love as proceeding from both of them: this would be the pure reflection of the Trinity. But the harmony is broken; the will loves not the word (truth) but something else. The mind can form the idea (the word) but the will does not carry it out. Thus every artist who forms ideas for works of art but never executes them; every person who, knowing something to be true, yet works against it; everyone who works for what he believes to be good and true but who is mistaken; all are distorted representations of the Trinity.

Instead of a centered life, man displays the fragments without a center. The will and the intellect are not held together by their inner power and the "supernatural *donum*" attending creation, but, having lost their directedness, they must be held together by external authority and discipline replacing the original natural and supernatural powers. What is left of the image is like the pieces of a picture puzzle which, because they no longer interlock as they ought, are held together—the church's authority and discipline as the unbroken frame of the puzzle.

CHAPTER III

The Dialectic of Obedience: Gerhard's Rationale of Creation

Nowhere in his *Loci Theologici* does John Gerhard undertake a systematic exposition of the nature of man. Indeed, even his picture of the physical universe can be derived only from an assemblage of scattered remarks, such as Troeltsch has done.[1] The same is true of his doctrine of the nature of man. Moreover, he is not completely consistent in what he does say.[2]

Nevertheless, there is every indication of almost full agreement between his view and that of Thomas. In part this agreement can be accounted for by the renewal of the study of Aristotle in the early seventeenth century. In part it can be accounted for by Gerhard's study of the medieval scholastics. To what extent his knowledge of Thomas came from a direct study and to what extent it was drawn from compendia is difficult, if not impossible, to determine in every instance. That he used both methods of

1. *Vernunft und Offenbarung,* pp. 41 ff.
2. Cf., for example, the primacy of the will in the first paradise (VIII.38) and the coordinate status of will and intellect in beatitude (XXXI.*Tract.* VI.119); or the inconsistency in use of the term "image of God," below, pp. 90 f. The inconsistency is, however, not too remarkable in view of the fact that the *Loci* were written over a period of ten years.

study is, however, fairly clear; one finds, for example, that he occasionally quotes Aquinas on both sides of one question without attempting a reconciliation. This would suggest the use of compendia. On the other hand, one finds him adducing and analyzing extensive passages from the Angelic Doctor. This, in addition to the general availability of Aquinas' works and Gerhard's own conscientiousness, would suggest a direct use of sources.

Naturally, Gerhard does not treat every question that Thomas does. Indeed, had he attempted to do so he would often have found no way of judging alternative answers. The issues behind the questions and the implications of the several answers, as well as the principles on which they were based, were no longer alive in the seventeenth century.

With few reservations, then, it can be said that Gerhard's doctrine of the character and dynamics of creation, in its pure and its spoiled state, is a consistent Aristotelian-Thomistic one; namely, that man is by nature a rational animal, a creature of free will, whose final end is the beatific vision in which the mind knows and the will loves God—a vision to which man attains only by the grace of God.

Thus, the exposition of Thomas' conception of natural man as given in the preceding chapter would en gros be equally valid for Gerhard. It is, therefore, all the more significant that he does not systematically articulate that conception. Something new had entered as a theological principle—the Reformation conception of justification—which in part displaced even some items that belonged to a discussion of natural man. This displacement is reflected in a number of points on which he takes issue with the Thomistic view, specifically as represented by Bellarmine, but by implication also by Thomas himself.

This present chapter will accordingly be devoted to an examination of those points in order to expose the nature and extent of the divergence and its methodological significance. There are areas of disagreement in the conception both of the character and of the dynamics of creation. The disagreement with regard to the former emerges in the network of questions relating to the *imago Dei*, the *donum supernaturale,* and the immortality of original man. With regard to the dynamics, the disagreement comes forth in the conception of the function of the *lex Dei,* the law of God.

THE CHARACTER OF CREATION: THE *IMAGO DEI*

Two views could hardly appear more flatly contradictory of each other than those of Thomas and Gerhard on the question of the image of God in man and the way in which it is related to the state of integrity, the *justitia originalis.* Speaking of the perfection of that first state, Thomas maintains that it followed not from nature but from a supernatural gift of grace (a *donum supernaturale*) (1.95.1; 97.1). That is to say, what preserved man from corruption and disorder was not a natural power but a supernatural one. Gerhard maintains equally pointedly the opposite. He asserts, "We deny that that original perfection was a supernatural *donum*" (VIII.79).

Moreover, in apparent contradistinction to Thomas, in whose view the image of the Trinity is found in all creation at the three levels of nature, grace, and glory, Gerhard holds that the image of God "is not to be sought . . . in the soul insofar as it is spiritual, incorporeal, immortal, and endowed with the faculty of knowing and willing" (VIII.34).

Thus, we seem to have this contradiction: Thomas maintains that the image is found in the soul's functions of knowing and willing as analogous to the Trinitarian processions; Gerhard denies it. Thomas asserts, even though with some caution, that the purity of the original state was due to the supernatural *donum* as the power preventing corruption; Gerhard denies it.

However, this contradiction is only at the surface. The disagreement between the two views is not what the foregoing juxtaposed quotations would lead one to believe. Indeed, were one otherwise too careless to do so, one would be impelled to a closer scrutiny of Gerhard's position by the fact that he does in another place (VIII.79) remark that prelapsarian Adam *did* have, as part of his pristine state, the indwelling Holy Spirit and Trinity. This *inhabitatio,* he says, was not a part of the natural condition but was a *donum supernaturale!*

What then is the disagreement? In brief it comes to this: part of it is semantic, due to a different application of the term, "image of God"; and part of it is due to a conceptualizing of man's relation to God in dialectical-personal terms rather than in formal-objective ones. In other words, the disagreement is partly terminological and partly methodological.

First let us examine the application of the term, "image of God." Gerhard does not deny that there is an analogy of the Trinity in the faculties of knowing and willing, and in such ternaries as the mode, species, and directedness of beings. But these are taken as illustrations rather than demonstrations of God's Trinitarian being. They can be a source of delight to the believer but no proof to the unbeliever. Nor does he object unreservedly to calling this analogy the image of God in man. Indeed, in the *locus* on the Trinity he lists (III.28) from the theological tradition, one after another, all the characteristics of three-in-oneness that can be found in the created world. "In rational creatures one finds not only a vestige but also a certain image of the Trinity." He does not, therefore, simply deny the Thomistic position. The image is, to be sure, distorted, and most of the ternaries one finds have as much of dissimilitude in them as of similitude; and, while they do not lead to a demonstrated science of the Trinity, they can be adduced to make the concept of Trinity more intelligible. But in spite of the distortion, the image is there and a Christian can find a kind of playful delight in scouting the sciences for ternaries wherever they may be found.

Indeed, Gerhard does not even disavow the more general use

of analogy in giving substance to theological assertions, for he can write (*Prœm.* 18) that, as there is an internal and external word in man, "*so* God, in whose image man is made," likewise has an internal (eternal) and external word.

However, Gerhard can also reject entirely the presence of an image of God in the creation. When he does so, he uses the term differently. For in *Locus* VIII, in the discussion of the *imago Dei* in man, he is concerned with the question of how the biblical authors use the word rather than with the question of whether man as a rational creature exhibits analogies of the Trinitarian processions. In this discussion he is concerned first of all with a philological and not a theological issue. Three times in the paragraphs 31 to 40 he inserts the qualifying clause, "if we desire to follow the usage of Scripture (*Scripturae phrasin imitari*)." This is a clear indication that he does no more than carry out what he states in the introductory paragraphs of the *locus;* he adjudicates among the many interpretations of the *imago Dei* by an inspection of the biblical usage itself. After citing many opinions from ancient and contemporary theologians concerning the constitution of the image, he rejects as "too bold" (VIII.27) Bellarmine's contention that there is a unanimity among them; and he concludes that in view of the diversity "we ought to discuss the meaning of the divine image on the basis of Scripture and to follow its lead."[3] It is in the light of such scriptural usage that Gerhard rejects a distinction between the "similitude" and the "image" (VIII.14–21), made by those who referred "image" to the essence of the soul and "similitude" to the holiness, justice, perfect knowledge, etc., of created man. "We state that both words express the same thing and that the word, 'similitude,' is to be taken as an

---

3. Cf. also III.20: "Quia enim non omnis imago est similis prototypo, et ipsa ratio imaginis Dei in homine varia ac multiplex excogitari potest, ut divortia sententiarum in patribus testantur, ideo Deus ipse investigationem verae sententiae ostendit, atque addita voce similitudinis (Gen. 1:26) docuit, talem fuisse hominem primo conditum, ut in ipso imago per omnia similis creatori cerneretur."

interpretation [of 'image'] (exēgētikōs)" (VIII.18). A similitude is a more perfect image. A coin, for example, bears the image of a ruler but not his similitude because it does not show all the details (*lineamenta*).

If this explanation is set next to Thomas' answer to the question, whether the image of the Trinity can be seen only when the psychical functions have God as their object (1.93.8 *ad* 1, and *ad* 2), the difference between the doctrine of Gerhard and of Thomas virtually vanishes. Indeed, Gerhard quotes that very answer of Aquinas in support of his own position (VIII.80). Thomas too maintains that it is only the knowledge and love *of God* which can be called the image of God in man; "the image of God is in the soul according as it is drawn, or is born to be drawn (*ferri*), toward God." Not simply the capacity and act of knowing and loving but those of knowing and loving *God* constitute in a complete sense the image of God in man. Behind the terminological difference there is then the agreement that man bears a three-foldness in his being which is an analogy of the Trinitarian processions, and that in the pristine state this threefoldness, manifested in the knowledge and love of God, had a perfection and transparency to the Creator which is now obscured.

The appearance of disagreement is increased by the fact that what the doctor of Paris holds together the doctor of Jena splits asunder. Gerhard can nearly separate the two considerations of the psychical faculties and their perfect functioning. He can, therefore, make of the *imago Dei* in *Locus* VIII a virtual synonym for the original perfection, the *justitia originalis,* a quality which man presently lacks. That is to say, it is the God-relatedness of the image which he considers essential rather than the analogy of the processions. The cause of this shift of emphasis was partly the alembic of pre-Reformation nominalism and voluntarism.[4] But partly it was Gerhard's exegesis of the two primary texts, Ephesians 4:23, and Colossians 3:10, which bear on the meaning

4. Cf. Paul Vignaux, *Justification et prédestination au xiv⁰ siècle.*

of "image of God."[5] From these and related texts he formulates three "theorems" with two corollaries:

1. The image is something bestowed in the renovation of man —that is, the renewal or the set of "new qualities" which follows upon the "gift of regeneration." Therefore, it cannot be interpreted as a quality transmitted by "carnal generation." It is an accompaniment not of natural birth but of spiritual rebirth. The corollary of this theorem is that, if one is to follow the biblical usage, the term, "image of God," cannot refer to the substance of the rational soul itself, for the rational soul can be found in any human being whether or not he is reborn.

2. The new nature is "renewed in knowledge after the image of its creator,"[6] a knowledge which is given through the renewing work of the Holy Spirit. Therefore, the image cannot be defined by those things which are essential even to the non-regenerate, for the knowledge is not an accompaniment of creation but "a light from elsewhere" (*lux aliunde*). The corollary of this second theorem is that the image cannot be situated in any of the soul's characteristics, such as that it is spiritual, incorporeal, or immortal, or that it is endowed with the faculties of knowing and willing, or that it has the freedom to choose among things external and civil, or that it has the power to command the body; for all of these characteristics apply to the *non renati* as well as to the *renati*.

3. If one adds to these considerations the evidence of II Corinthians 3:18, the theorems are further confirmed.[7] For the restitution of the divine image is accomplished in such a way "that we put on a new form after discarding the old one." The image cannot, therefore, be in the essence of the soul. Furthermore

5. Eph. 4:23: "Renovamini autem spiritu mentis vestrae et induite novum hominem, qui juxta Deum conditus est in justitia et sanctitate veritatis." Col. 3:10: "Induistis novum hominem, qui renovatur ad agnitionem juxta imaginem ejus, qui condidit illum."

6. Col. 3:10 (*RSV*).

7. "Nos omnes revelata facie gloriam Domini velut in speculo intuentes in eandem imaginem transformamur, a claritate in claritatem, tanquam a Domini Spiritu."

since it is worked by the Spirit of the Lord, it cannot be constituted by any of those things which are found in the soul of even the non-regenerate man.

In short, the *imago Dei,* whatever it be positively, is negatively, at least, not a universal and essential characteristic of man in history. It is something that was *lost* in the fall and which must be *restored* through the working of the Holy Spirit, for it can no longer be transmitted by natural generation. After saying all this, Gerhard seems to execute a *volte-face.* His later paragraphs seem to be a direct contradiction of these earlier ones. He writes subsequently that, although the image has been lost, there are still fragments (*reliquiae*) of it remaining in every man (VIII.57 ff.), which are a part of the whole of the image. Surely this is an inconsistency? If the image is something that has been lost and can be found only in those renewed by the Holy Spirit (which was the substance of Gerhard's theorems), how is it possible to maintain that relics of it, or a part of it, can still be found universally in fallen man?

There is, to be sure, an inconsistency, occasioned by the different framework of the problems in the earlier paragraphs, and perhaps also by a lapse of time between them and the later ones. Yet there is a consistent underlying view. It is expressed in the conception of the image as the original *perfection* of the state of integrity (the *justitia originalis*). It is not the psychical faculties which constitute the image, but their full perfection, their *justitia et sanctitas vera.*

"Image of God" and "original perfection" are in this way interchangeable terms. Thus the loss of the image, that is, the loss of the *perfection* of faculties, is not the removal of the faculties in which the perfection was realized.

For example, in the realm of the intellect, the image of God included a perfect knowledge of God. The loss of the image does not annihilate the cognitive faculty. It does not even remove all knowledge of God. Fallen man still has the power to know things and to know partial truth about God. This power is "a natural power of the soul and a small part of the divine wisdom (*judicium*) in the minds of men" (VIII.59).

Gerhard can, therefore, maintain at one and the same time these two positions: the image of God (meaning the perfection of all faculties) *cannot* be found at all in natural man and only germinally in the new man; the image of God (meaning those faculties themselves) *can* be found to some degree in all men, the naturally born as well as the spiritually reborn. The extent to which this is, in spite of the misleading ambiguity of the terms, a homogeneous view cannot be fully answered until we have examined Gerhard's Lutheran understanding of the "article of justification" as the final theological criterion. In that article one finds the answer to the question, how is it possible that a partial knowledge and love of God can be interpreted, specifically in the article of justification, as the negation of all knowledge of God? By anticipation we can formulate the answer briefly thus: partial knowledge is the negation of knowledge when perfection is the single and absolute criterion. That absolute criterion appears when man faces God as nothing more than a sinner.

The Donum Supernaturale

Up to this point there seems to be no substantial disagreement between Gerhard's conception of the *justitia originalis* (which he can also call the image of God) and that of Aquinas. There is a second apparent clash regarding the related question of the *donum supernaturale*. Is the original perfection to be considered as natural to man or is it due to a supernatural gift? Thomas holds the latter, Gerhard the former view. Again we are met with an apparent contradiction. How deep is the opposition?

Thomas' rationale proceeds as follows: With some caution he concludes that man was *created in grace* because "the very rectitude of the first state seems to require this" (1.95.1). The uprightness of that state included the subjection of reason to God, the inferior powers to reason, and the body to the soul. Now, it is clear that such an ordered state of powers was not natural, otherwise it would have remained even after the fall. That is to say, since it was a condition that no longer characterizes man as man, it cannot be called "natural." If it was, however, not the result of anything natural, the only alternative is that it was a supernatural gift of grace. Even though this original perfection would have been transmitted by Adam to his offspring, had he not fallen, it would have been transmitted as a gift of grace and not as part of his nature; children would have been born in grace as Adam had been created in grace (1.100.1, and *ad* 2). The word "natural" is here synonymous with "generic": nothing can be natural which is not present as an essential in every specimen of humanity, as long as it is a specimen of that genus. Since fallen man is still generically man, his *justitia originalis* cannot have been an essential part of his manhood.

This train of reasoning sounds like an exact counterpart of Gerhard's argument, that the image cannot be located in the substance of man or in the psychic faculties that are present in every member of the genus. Gerhard had reasoned thus: since the image of God is, according to the Apostle Paul, a quality in the regenerate but not the non-regenerate, it cannot be generically essential. Thomas had reasoned thus: since the perfect orderedness of man is not generically essential, it must be something else (and that something else can only be a supernatural gift). The starting point of the two is different but the content is the same.[8] One would fully expect Gerhard to conclude, with Thomas, that the perfection of the original state was not a natural condition but a supernatural gift. Yet he asserts the very opposite: that the perfection was natural.

What grounds might Gerhard have for *rejecting* the conception of the original perfection as a supernatural gift? Thomas

8. Cf. also VIII.94: the *imago* was "intrinsic" but not "substantial."

had concluded that it must be supernatural because it is obviously not natural; Gerhard, starting with certain Scripture texts, concludes that it must be natural because it is obviously, i.e., according to the statements of Scripture, not supernatural (VIII.58–63). Why can it not be interpreted as a supernatural gift? First, because according to Paul in Romans 2:15, the Gentiles still have in their conscience a knowledge of the divine law. Since knowledge of God is part of the image of God, in that partial knowledge there is still a fraction of the image of God (and of the *justitia originalis*) in the non-Christian. But it would be absurd, in Gerhard's mind, to maintain that there is a *supernatural* gift in the *heathen.* So he is forced to the conclusion that the righteousness of the first man was natural to him.

Secondly, in agreement with Thomas, Gerhard believes that, if man had not fallen, he would have transmitted to his offspring the original perfection. But to say that he would have transmitted anything to his offspring is in Gerhard's view the same as saying that he would transmit it naturally. The *imago Dei* would have been propagated naturally, and those things which are propagated naturally are, of course, natural: *quae naturaliter propagantur, naturalia sunt.* Again one is led to the conclusion that the original righteousness was natural.

Finally—after a third argument which is not apropos here—Gerhard adduces as evidence the radical terms (*tragica verba*) in which the Scriptures describe the corruption of the whole human nature by original sin. One could hardly speak of the corruption of *nature* if it were only an extrinsic and supernaturally added gift, lost through the original sin. Gerhard concludes, therefore, that the Scriptures, in speaking of the corruption brought in by the *peccatum originale,* do not make reference to the privation of supernatural gifts but to the destruction of natural powers.

A comparison of this line of reasoning with the reasons he had given earlier for the contention that the image of God could not be located in the essence of man first seems to yield the conclusion that Gerhard argues from two incompatible axioms. In the one case, where he was concerned with the meaning of the term, he had argued: the image of God cannot be in man's generic essence because it is *not* universal; it is not found in the unregenerate but only in the regenerate (and that would seem to make of it something supernatural). In the present case, where he is discussing the issue of the *donum supernaturale,* he seems to be arguing thus: because the image of God *is* in part still universally present in men, it cannot be something supernatural. There is certainly an inconsistency in the use of the word, "natural," in these two arguments. But I do not think there is an ultimate inconsistency in the underlying view. In the one case "what is natural" means "what is given in all men at birth"; in the other case "what is natural" means "what is given with the creation (concreated)." Gerhard himself later recognizes this distinction (XI.18). In one sense the image is not natural; in another it is. It is *not* natural (but spiritual) because it is bestowed not by physical propagation but only by a rebirth in the Holy Spirit. It *is* natural (rather than supernatural) because it is an intrinsic characteristic of the original creation. Thus Gerhard can speak of the partial knowledge of the law of God as being "naturally written in the heart" and of the perfect knowledge as being "natural in men before the fall" (VIII.58). He does not add, as one should for completeness, that partial knowledge is not natural to prelapsarian man and perfect knowledge is not natural to postlapsarian man.

In other words, by maintaining that the *justitia originalis* was *not* a supernatural gift, Gerhard sought to safeguard the view that it was not additional and extrinsic to man's created endowment but simply the perfect state of that endowment. Perfection was natural to man before the fall; imperfection is natural after the fall. Thomas, on the other hand, had maintained that because the original state of perfection is not natural in the sense of applying to man as man in whatever state it must have been supernatural—supernatural, but concreated. What Gerhard called "natural," meaning "given with creation," Thomas called "natural and concreatedly supernatural." Thomas' *donum supernaturale* was neither extrinsic nor temporally additional to nature as created.

The comparison can be stated in the following syllogism:

1) Major Premise (Thomas and Gerhard):
   The original righteousness was either natural or super-natural.

2) Minor Premise:
   (Thomas): It was not natural (because man is man even when imperfect).
   (Gerhard): It was not supernatural (because a partial knowledge of God is found even in the un-godly).

3) Conclusion:
   (Thomas): Therefore, it was supernatural.
   (Gerhard): Therefore, it was natural.

This much of the disagreement between the theologians can be resolved by terminological clarification. Still a question remains. Gerhard does not maintain that everything about the original state was natural. Indeed, in reply to an allegation of Bellarmine, he asserts (VIII.79) unequivocally if only *en passant* that it is a false charge to accuse the Protestants of not recognizing any *dona supernaturalia* in the first man.

What Gerhard objects to is the false conclusion he believes his opponents to have drawn from a true premise. Bellarmine has committed the fallacy of the undistributed middle term when he concludes: "Man was at first adorned with supernatural *dona*. Therefore, the image and similitude of God, in which man was created, was a supernatural gift" (VIII.84). In the Protestant view, the image of God was not a supernatural gift, yet there were supernatural elements in the original state, specifically the in-dwelling Holy Spirit. Thus, whereas Gerhard denies that the image of God was a supernatural gift, he affirms that "the inhabitation of the Holy Spirit, indeed of the whole Trinity," in Adam was supernatural.

In Gerhard's as well as Thomas' theology, the first state of man included both natural and supernatural elements, even though the former gives comparatively slight attention to a discussion of the supernatural elements. In what he does say, however, the difference in mode of conceptualization is reflected. Whereas Thomas interprets the supernatural element in formal terms, Gerhard interprets it in dialectical-personal terms. To Gerhard the supernatural is the person of the Holy Spirit; to Thomas it is the gift in which and through which the Holy Spirit dwells as a new enabling form or set of forms.

Immortality

The third question involved in the consideration of man's original state is that of his natural mortality or immortality. That Adam, in his state of perfection, would not die, both Thomas and Gerhard acknowledge. But the issue is whether the immortality is the result of natural perfection or of supernatural power. The position of each of the theologians on this question is in accord with the foregoing account of their understanding of the image of God. However, their answers in this case appear more similar than they did with regard to the supernatural gift in the *justitia originalis*. Not only do both of them answer affirmatively the question whether man in the first state was immortal, they also hold that immortality was a part of that original righteousness. Yet they diverge in interpreting the reason for the immortality. Gerhard believed man was *naturally* immortal; Thomas that he was immortal by virtue of the supernatural *donum*.

Thomas (1.97.1; 11.i.85.6) cannot immediately assert that pristine man was immortal, for the characteristic of mortality did belong, after all, to the definition—the nature—of man. Man is a mortal being. Had Adam been by nature immortal, man would still be immortal—but he obviously is not. If Adam was nonetheless immortal, he would seem not to have been a man. An angel, or a celestial body, or a saint perhaps; but not a man. Thomas shows this by an analysis of the possibilities of incorruptibility. To be incorruptible by nature might mean being incorruptible from the side of the constituent matter, either that no matter is admixed with the form at all, as in angels, or that it is in potentiality to one form only, as in the celestial bodies. Or it might mean being incorruptible from the side of the form, if there is inherent in a thing which is corruptible by nature a disposition which totally shields it from corruption. Neither of the possibilities was, however, true of the original state. Furthermore, one cannot understand mortality as merely an imperfect immortality. At first it would seem that if man's present intellectual power is an obscure version of his original intellect, his present mortality might be similarly a diminution of his immortality. Yet the two are not similar. The corruptible and the incorruptible belong, as Thomas holds with Aristotle, to two different *genera.* There can be no reciprocity, no *transmutatio in invicem,* between the two.

On the other hand, however, Thomas cannot simply assert that man in his original state was mortal. For if it was true that mortality belonged to the definition of man, it was also true that Paul and the Christian theological tradition maintained that death entered the world through sin. Thus, while he could not maintain that man was by nature immortal, he still had to maintain that in his original rectitude he was. He concludes, therefore, that the incorruptibility of man in his original state lay "on the side of the efficient cause," namely, God, whose *donum* counterbalanced the defectiveness of the *materia* which of itself was corruptible. "There was in Adam's soul a supernaturally and divinely given power through which the soul could preserve the body from every corruption as long as it remained in subjection to God." And this, Thomas notes, was "done reasonably." The power had to reside in the soul and only through the soul could the body be sustained from its natural corruption. Otherwise the condition of immortality would have violated man's nature.

The problem that had been set for Aquinas by the definition of man as by nature mortal did not greatly trouble Gerhard, for as we have seen, he worked with two concepts of nature, one meaning "universally true of every man in whatever state," and the other meaning "given with or in the original creation." Indeed, this dual use of "nature" emerges most clearly in the discussion of the question of Adam's natural immortality. To hold that man's original immortality was natural, he must defend the view on two fronts. In the theological tradition he meets the Pelagians (represented in the sixteenth and seventeenth centuries, according to Gerhard, by Bellarmine and the Photinians), and in the philosophical tradition he meets the Aristotelian view of the corruptibility of all matter.

Against the Pelagians, who according to Augustine taught that man would have died even if he had not sinned, Gerhard maintains that death is the punishment of sin and not a condition of nature. His reason for holding this view is no different from the Thomistic; according to the Scriptures man was created "in incorruption" and "in the image of God"—Gerhard asks, how could a mortal creature be the image of the Creator who is immortal? Bellarmine joins them in that view. Yet Gerhard opposes Bellarmine (and, indirectly, Thomas) for his too close alliance with the Pelagian view. For although Thomism did not question the fact that Adam in the original state was immortal, it was concerned to demonstrate that such immortality was due to a supernatural gift. Gerhard finds such a view close to Pelagianism because "it asserts that death was natural to man in the state of integrity" (VIII.102). He maintains rather that immortality was natural because it came as a part or at least a consequence of the divine image (VIII.99); the divine image was natural because it was given to Adam immediately *with creation* as something *in-*

trinsic even though not "substantial." However, since neither Thomas nor Bellarmine rejected the idea that immortality, as part of the original righteousness, was given together with creation and that it was intrinsic rather than extrinsic, Gerhard does not actually speak to their position except as a question of the meaning of the term "natural."

A second difficulty is posed by the axiom that terrestrial matter, as composed of contraries (the four elements), is essentially corruptible. Gerhard solves the problem not by positing the *donum supernaturale* as a power which prevented the corruption of matter but rather by positing a perfect balance of the contrary elements in the material part of man. "God was able to find the means of reducing those contrary qualities to a most exact harmony so that the necessity of dying would not have to be feared" (VIII.102). God simply created man in such a way (VIII.103) that, as long as no guilt intervened, the body would remain in subjection to the soul, there would be no separation of the soul from the body, and the bodily material would not be corrupted. "Keeping the body from every stain of corruption was natural to the soul as long as it was itself subject to God and the body too was itself equipped with an exactly proportioned mixture of elements" (VIII.103). For Gerhard, in other words, the harmony of elements which results in incorruptibility was natural *because Adam was created with it;* for Thomas it was the result of supernatural power *because man is still man* even without it. The opposing terms in Gerhard are here, as before, "what is natural" and "what is the result of sin." In Thomas they are "what is natural" and "what is original" or "what is in the state of glory." "Death and mortality," writes Gerhard (VIII.82), "are the punishment of sin and therefore not a necessary part of nature as it was before the fall." That God *could* find the means of reducing the contraries of matter into an *exactissima harmonia* Gerhard proves by a rhetorical question (VIII.102): "Or shall we say that the bodies of Christ and the elect are not true bodies, even though spiritual and glorified? Shall we attribute to them a necessity of dying?" Thomas, of course, does not deny that the glorified bodies are that; he does however reserve the term, *"secundum gloriam,"* for that condition and distinguishes it from the condition "according to nature." The philosophical axiom of the corruptibility of matter posed a problem for Gerhard as well as for Thomas. Both of them resolved the problem by preserving the axiom—but also its opposite. Thomas did so in his conception of the supernatural gift, Gerhard by his dual conception of nature.

In summary, the agreement and disagreement between Gerhard and Thomas on the question of man's essential perfection (for which Gerhard also uses the term, "image of God," when he follows the usage of Scripture) could be stated thus: both of them are agreed that the original state included both natural and supernatural elements. The perfect harmony and orderedness of that state Gerhard calls "natural" (meaning "created so") and Thomas calls, as it were, "natural-in-grace." They are further agreed that the original harmony would endure as long as man remained in subjection to God. Gerhard conceives the supernatural element as the indwelling of the Trinity in a personal way. Thomas conceives it as the *donum* which is at one and the same time the Holy Spirit and a form in man. The difference on this latter point is not an irreconcilable opposition. It is the difference between taking the biblical material and expressing it in formal concepts (that is to say, putting the Genesis account of creation into Aristotelian terms)—Thomas' procedure, and taking the Aristotelian-Thomistic expression and putting it into dialectical-personal terms—Gerhard's procedure. Precisely in this difference is the foreshadowing of future developments in the history of philosophy and theology: the preoccupation with the historical and the personal in preference to the general and the formal, and the conviction that it is not language in the formal mode but language in the dialectical-personal, which has a transcendental reference. Accordingly, Gerhard takes what is to him a formal term, the supernatural gift, and interprets it in a dialectical-personal way; Thomas takes the personal term and interprets it formally. This is, to be sure, a difference in emphasis and not an exclusive alternative, for there are dialectical elements in the *donum* as Thomas conceives it and there are formal elements in the *inhabitatio* as Gerhard conceives it. Yet Gerhard's inability to allow—or even to understand correctly—the Thomistic view manifests the strength of his distrust of formal language even when he uses it. Further documentation for this assertion will be provided in the following chapters. Here it is worthy of note that because of the difference in rational mode, Gerhard's Lutheran axiom, "man is by nature corrupt," is not a formal generalization about the characteristics of all men but is primarily the expression of man's self-condemnation, either on the empirico-historical level (where he condemns himself in the dialogue with himself) or on the transhistorical level (where God condemns him).

THE DYNAMICS OF CREATION

In Thomas' scheme the dynamics of creation were understood as the tending of forms to their ends and as the modifications due to the intrusion of corruption. Thomas had before him, as it were, the whole picture of everything in the universe. The movement which took place there was from the bottom to the top. An advance in movement meant that a thing had reached a higher *place* in the whole picture. The difference between this view and that of Gerhard is noticeable in the general outline of their systematic works.

In his *Summa Theologiae* Thomas describes (1.2.Prol.) his purpose as the imparting of the knowledge of God, not only as He is in Himself but also as He is the principle and end of all things and especially of the rational creature. Thus in Part I he treats of God, in Part II he treats of the "movement of the rational creature toward God," and in Part III of the Christ who, as man, is the way to God. In the first part he treats the exemplar; in the second, the image (by analogy); in the third, the way by which that creature who is made in the image of God can attain his due end. These are the separate parts of the whole picture of the universe.

In the *Loci Theologici* Gerhard's scheme seems at first glance quite similar, beginning with a treatment of God in Himself,[9] then moving to a discussion of man, and concluding with the things that belong to and will secure man's ultimate end. Yet a closer inspection discloses that the difference between the two is once again the difference between a rational mode which is chiefly formal and one which is mainly dialectical. When Thomas moves from a discussion of God to a discussion of man, the connection is provided by the relation of one part to another part of the whole picture; and the progression of topics (where it is not determined by casuistic considerations) is according to the logical interrelation of those parts. If God is the exemplar and man the image, then in logical order one treats first the exemplar and next the image.[10]

When Gerhard moves from one part to the other it is usually by means of a temporal *then* (implied, if not expressed)—*first* this and *then* that happened. First God was alone in His Trinitarian life; *then* He created man; *then* man fell; *then* God gave His promise of a Savior; *then* He sent the Savior. The connections between the major divisions of the *Loci Theologici* can, in that sense, be called *heilsgeschichtlich* or meta-historical, rather than (formally) logical or metaphysical. It is, of course, true that some of the connections between the *loci* are made according to a consideration of their formal relation, but the grand scheme is the

9. I am omitting in both cases the prolegomena: in Aquinas the question on "sacred doctrine"; in Gerhard the *locus* on the Scriptures as the *principium cognoscendi* of theology.

10. "Postquam praedictum est de exemplari, sc. de Deo, et de his quae processerunt ex divina potestate secundum ejus voluntatem, restat ut consideremus de ejus imagine, id est de homine, secundum quod et ipse est suorum operum principium, quasi liberum arbitrium habens et suorum operum potestatem" (II.i.Prolog.).

dialectic between God and His creature. Moreover, it is fully in accord with this mode of rationalizing that emphasis is placed not on what God's nature is but on what He *does* and *says,* for it is through actions (initiative and response) and words (address and reply) that we meet the person of the Other. This kind of rationale is endowed in the intellectual world of Gerhard and his Protestant contemporaries with a greater power than is the formal. Thus the dynamics of creation are understood not as those of forms seeking their ends but of the interaction between the personal God and the personal creature.[11]

Thus, after treating of God in His essence—His *natura,* the Trinity, and the person and work of Christ—in *Loci* II to IV and of God's will as expressed in the fact that He created the world (*Locus* V), Gerhard introduces the sixth *locus* with the words, "God the Creator of all did not withdraw from His handiwork but to this day still conserves it with His power and rules in it and governs it with His wisdom." After the seventh *locus* concerning God's election and reprobation, *Locus* VIII on the image of God in prelapsarian man is introduced thus: "The decree of predestination, made in God's eternal counsel before the world's foundations were laid, was followed in time by the creation of man." But the original perfection of creation did not endure. So the next *loci* tell how man afterwards sinned, and the eleventh *locus* (on the free will) unfolds the question of what still remained after man had fallen. *Loci* XII to XVII treat of God's subsequent dealing with man through His law and His gospel. If man had not sinned, the law would have been enough. But *after* the sin, God issued the promise of the gospel (XIV.2). "After he has by his lapse into sin fallen into complete impotence with regard to fulfilling

11. Protestant theology has been dogged by this methodological fact from the start down to the present, and has wavered between, on the one side, attempts to make constructive use of this fact and, on the other side, a despair of any possibility of theological construction. A recent constructive work is that of Richard R. Niebuhr, *Resurrection and Historical Reason* (Scribners, 1957).

the law, man needs another means of attaining salvation, namely, the promises of the gospel—as is clear from the fact that the merciful God of Adam and of all of us, coming forth from the silent throne of His majesty, immediately after the fall revealed the protoevangel of the seed of the woman . . . ; from that time on the preaching of the law and the gospel have always gone together. . . ." *Locus* XVIII takes up the sacraments. After summarizing the sequence of events to that point, Gerhard states, "God the most compassionate, looking both to the salvation of men and to the weakness of our faith, did not stop at manifesting His fatherly will by the word of the gospel's promise but gave confirmation of it in addition by external tokens. . . ."[12] From a consideration of the sacraments he proceeds to an exposition of God's provision for the continuing maintenance of the world through the various vocations: the ecclesiastical, through which the Word and Sacraments continue to be publicly provided; the political, through which the conditions of external discipline, peace, and tranquillity are maintained; and the domestic, through which the personnel for the other *status* are provided (XXII–XXV). To some degree latent in the present life, fully revealed only later, are the "last things." These Gerhard treats in *Loci* XXVI to XXXI: death, resurrection, the last judgment, the consummation of the world, damnation or life, eternal life.

In other words, the transitional remarks between the major parts of the systems themselves suggest the difference in conception of the dynamics of creation. The movement of the rational creature toward God is expressed by Thomas in terms of the relation of every form to its end, which is ultimately God. In

12. It may be noted in passing that the role of the sacraments in Thomistic and Gerhardian theology is marked by the same distinction in rationale. To Gerhard the sacraments are outward tokens of the faithfulness of the person who makes the promise of salvation, the signs that the person is trustworthy, and the means to increase trust in that person. To Thomas they infuse grace, that is, new principles of action by which higher ends are obtained, rather than simply increasing confidence in the faithfulness of the One who has made promises about saving man.

Gerhard's rationale the same movement is expressed not in terms of form and end but of the dialectic of God's Yes and man's No (or vice versa) in its movement through time. More specifically, Gerhard has, in place of Thomas' relatedness through form–end, the relation of "obedience" or "obedience-in-law." In both cases the intent of the formulation is the same—to give a rationale to the freedom and relatedness of man to the God who is sovereignly free and man's Creator. For Thomas, that requires the creature's acting toward its end, the end to which the implanted form directs it. For Gerhard, on the other hand, the creaturely freedom and relatedness must be understood not so much as acting toward an end but as acting in obedience to the law which expresses the will of the Creator.[13] The creature's directedness toward God is expressed as the confidence he exhibits by the obedience that he shows his Maker. The law is that which man in his perfect state can fulfill; and, by fulfilling it in freedom, he retains his relatedness to God.

If, for Thomas, God is that end to which the form is ordered, for Gerhard He is that person in whom perfect confidence is expressed by the fulfilling of His law. Conversely, if in Gerhard the form is that which makes a thing what it is and separates it from other things by giving it its nature and place, for Thomas it is the very principle by which a thing not only is what it is but is directed to God as its end.

The function and understanding of "law" are accordingly different in the two theologians. In Gerhard, the law places a man into the relationship of obedience in freedom to God; it is the

13. A difference is to be noted in passing: in the voluntarism of late medieval nominalism, the "will" designated the one psychic faculty to which primacy was given over the intellect as the other psychic faculty. In Gerhard (probably already in the Renaissance and Reformation) the "will" in such contexts as the present one designates not so much a psychic faculty as the *person* of the Creator, His character as the Thou over against man. Because of the similarity in terminology, it is not surprising that early Protestant theology often appears to Roman Catholic theology as nothing more than a variation of late medieval voluntarism.

bond of unity between man and God as between personal subject and personal ruler. In Thomas it is, on the other hand, that guide for actions by which the form can attain its end, a "rule" or "measure" for practical reason (II.i.90.1; 91.3). This is true of the law in all forms, whether as "natural" (that is, showing the general principles of action) or as "human" (containing the "particular dispositions" to those general principles) or as "divine" (ordering to the supernatural end of eternal beatitude). In all cases it provides the means of attaining the given end. First, the divine law is necessary in addition to the natural and human, as we are told (II.i.91.4), because it supplies some deficiencies. Secondly, especially with regard to particular applications or particular and contingent acts, the reason's judgment is not always clear; therefore "in order that . . . man could know without any hesitation what he ought to do and avoid, it was necessary that in his own acts (*in actibus propriis*) he be directed by a law divinely given." Thirdly, reason can give judgment concerning outward aspects of acts, but not concerning the interior motives. The divine law supplies the judgment of interior motives. Fourthly, human law cannot condemn *all* sin—because it would condemn some good with it—so the divine law supplies the missing totality of judgment. The intention of the law is to place man into friendship with God *by making him good* (II.i.99.2; 99.3); its content is the description or prescription of the ways through which that intention is realized. What actions should man do in order to attain the end? The answer is given in the law in its various forms. The question of man's inability to do those actions will be taken up later in connection with the relation of the old and new law. Here the point to observe is simply the conception of law as the rule showing the pattern of actions by which the form attains the end, since it is in this conception of form that the creature's freedom and dependence are both expressed.

In Gerhard's theology the question regarding law is not, what shall man do to attain his end? but rather, what shall man do to express his obedience to God? It is in this obedience that his freedom and relatedness are contained. In the state of integrity, obedience would have been expressed by the fulfillment of the law in all its points. "If the first parent of the human race had remained in his created integrity, one kind of divine teaching [namely, the law] would have been most sufficient to salvation; that is to say, man could have won the prize of eternal life by showing perfect and in all points absolute obedience to the law" (XIV.2). This sounds much like Thomas—as though the law were there to show the means of reaching beatitude. However, Gerhard's emphasis is new, as a few further references make clear.

In answering why the prohibition concerning the tree of the knowledge of good and evil in Paradise was given, Gerhard explains:

> By this command God wanted to declare: 1) that He was man's Creator and Lord, whom man as subject and creature is held to serve and obey; 2) that man was endowed with perfect powers of reason and integrity of his whole nature and in addition with the faculty of free will in order that he might serve God; 3) indeed He set forth in this special command an opportunity to exercise (*gymnasion*) obedience which would have been most pleasing to God and most useful to man. For if man had persevered in holy obedience to this precept, he would have, after a certain time, been translated without death or sorrow from the earthly paradise into the heavenly. . . . This is in fact the answer given by those who debate why God gave man a command which He knew would be disobeyed—He commanded it in order to have it obeyed; He gave man powers to be able to obey it; and He added the threat of death to prevent his declining to obey it. (IX.5 and 6)

The special command regarding the tree put into *krisis* the law as law: the opportunity for man to express his relation of absolute confidence in the Creator. By obedience-in-freedom to this law, man would attest his independence as well as his relatedness. Indeed, God allowed the temptation "because He wanted man to show Him free obedience" (IX.18). The law is a "rule of justice and righteousness," a *regula justitiae* (XII.1), not because it shows what acts attain an end but because it shows what acts are the expression of perfect obedience to the Creator, "most pleasing to God."

The relation between these two views of law is not one of mutual exclusion. Gerhard can say that *if* man had kept the law in all its points perfectly, he would have attained the status of "confirmation in the good." In that sense, his keeping the law was a means to the end of beatitude. Conversely, even in Thomas' view the carrying out of the actions set forth in the law is a matter of obedience to God. In other words, Gerhard's dialectical rationale contains formal elements and Thomas' formal rationale contains dialectical elements.

FALLEN CREATION

The same differentiating characteristic marks the account of the dynamics of the fallen creation in the two theologians. Whereas for Thomas those dynamics are determined by the loss of the *donum supernaturale* and the consequent need for something to replace it—namely, the teaching and discipline of the church—in Gerhard, the relationship of fallen man to God is still described in terms of his response to the law of God. In the original state man was able to obey in freedom. In the fallen state he can only disobey, in the sense that he cannot ever *fully* keep the law; for a *partial obedience is tantamount to disobedience when the purpose* of obedience is not the carrying out of commands in and for themselves but rather the expression of the *confidence of the doer with respect to the law-giver,* and when "law," "obedience," and "disobedience" are functioning as primary terms in a dialectical rationale. Thomas' fallen man still knows that he must know and love God, and he is led to seek that which can supply his deficiency; Gerhard's fallen man still has a partial knowledge of the law of God, but this partial knowledge discloses only that the relationship to God has been disrupted—that, far from being man's opportunity to express his confidence in God, the law becomes man's accuser.

The lawful relation of the original state was that of filial obedience, of the *servus* (without its derogatory connotations) or creature or son. In fallen creation the lawful relation is that of the courtroom, where God is the judge and man the accused, and where the condemnation by the judge is only corroborated by the self-condemnation of the man who knows he has not fulfilled the moral law, the law which is normative for the actions of all people at all times and in all places. "Since through sin his whole nature and all his works are miserably contaminated, man finds nothing that he can set against the judgment of God. The law therefore hurls the lightning of curse and condemnation against the man convicted of sin. . . ." (xvi.6). Where the logic of Thomas' view leads him to articulate the difference between man in the state of integrity and in the state of corruption in terms of the presence and absence of the supernatural gift, Gerhard is led rather to *shift the scene* of the law-relationship from that of paradisiac and filial obedience *to that of the courtroom* and accusation. What carries over from one state to the other in Thomas' rationale is the formal interpretation of the relationship; what carries over in Gerhard's is the dialectical interpretation of the lawful relation.

Thus, in the fallen state there is no question for Gerhard as to whether or not all men are still so related to God through His law; they are. The only question is how they may view that relationship. There are two possibilities. On the one hand are those who underestimate the gravity of the unfulfilled law, the "Epicureans" who take their sin too lightly because they think

God takes it lightly, and the pharisees, who underestimate the gravity of their sin because they have not grasped its full import or demand. On the other hand are the despairing men who take the law-relation of fallen man as absolute and therefore as ultimately damning.

Because the law-relation is still the determinative one, Gerhard concludes that the counter to the false optimism of the Epicurean and pharisee is the proper setting of that relation, namely, the courtroom:

> Epicureans are of the opinion that justification from sin is an easy matter, so they are not sufficiently concerned about sin; pharisees persuade themselves of their own goodness by which they can face God. But when the doctrine of justification is set forth *under the image of a trial (sub imagine judicialis processus)* before the court of God, those Epicurean and pharisaic notions easily fade. (XVI.6)

This courtroom setting, as we shall see later, is also the only genuine counter to the man of despair who is allowed to see not only the judge but the mediator-advocate.

Gerhard thus interprets man's fallen condition in terms of his *dialogue with himself* (self-approbation or self-condemnation), rather than as intellect against will or in some other formal manner. This is, in the transcendental domain, the dialogue *between man and God,* in which God as the Other condemns man: "as man resists his enemy (*voluntas hominis inimico suo repugnat*) so does he also, before his conversion, flee from God." Or it is the contest[14] between God and Satan as two opposing personal powers active behind the scenes of world and individual history.

But while this view of the relation between God and man carries the greater theological weight for him, Gerhard has not altogether given up the formal description of man in terms of his faculties of knowing and loving. This implies, first of all, that

14. Cf. e.g. I.304.

the "partial knowledge of the law" which remains in man after his fall is not only the knowledge that his relation to God has been shifted from that of the son in Paradise to that of the accused in the courtroom, as we have seen, but is also the knowledge of *some* of the universal moral principles. Some of those principles are still inscribed in every sound mind (XXV.301)[15] which is not "completely reprobate." Dialectically, partial knowledge would mean that the law-relationship is still valid but that instead of providing the opportunity for the expression of filial obedience it now provides the occasion of God's condemnation of man and of man's self-condemnation in the sight of God. Formally, partial knowledge would mean a knowledge of *some* of those things of which the mind in its pure state knows *all.*

The fact that Gerhard still retains the formal elements implies, secondly, that a partial love of the good replaces a total love of it. In his purity man loves and can accomplish things which are good in both civic and spiritual senses; fallen man has the capacity only to do civic good and spiritual evil. Therefore, what Gerhard as a Lutheran calls the corruption of the total nature of man must not be confused with something like "absolute" corruption. That is to say, corruption infects *every* part and is therefore total; but it does not infect the parts *absolutely* (if such a conception were even possible). All of the faculties, infected through the fall, can do only in part what originally they could do in full. The good things (XI.109–11) which pertain to his animal life, man can still will and do; the good things which pertain to his specifically human life (creating works of art, performing moral virtues, acquiring scientific knowledge, etc.) he can still do, at least in respect of their external aspects. It lies within his power to do such things as listening to the words of the gospel or carrying out the external exercise of religion. What does not, however, lie within the power of fallen man is to assent with his heart to the gospel, to know

15. The discussion in this *locus* concerns the legitimacy or moral propriety of marriage between close relatives.

God "truly," or to live according to the Spirit—in short to give an external and internal obedience to the law.

In other words, the "spiritual" good is an addition of the part which is missing in the civic good, the internal motivation and purity of heart. The general (formal) term is "the good"; its parts are the "civic, or external (good)" and "the spiritual (good)." With regard to the spiritual part, man has the capacity only to reject it, either by failure to do it or by doing the opposite of it.

Thirdly, this formal interpretation of man's fallen and partial knowledge leads Gerhard, as it did Thomas, to posit a place where the intellect can find God's truth unambiguously and an order where the will can be externally constrained. In place of Thomas' authority of the hierarchically structured church, Gerhard (as a result of the Reformation controversies, and not in opposition directly to Thomas) places the unambiguous truth more specifically in the clear message of the Scriptures. Indeed he draws the parallel between man as the center of the *universe and nature* and Christ as the summary and center of the whole *Scripture* (1.53). Thus nature (or the universe) is virtually identified with creation and the Scriptures with new creation. Man is never completely ignorant of God; he can always know that his relation to the Creator is determined by the law. But this very knowledge leads him to ask what that means for his ultimate state since he cannot (as his experience plainly attests) fully keep that law. Are his imperfections simply overlooked, as the "Epicureans" would hold? Or are they taken absolutely seriously, and do they therefore condemn him? When he is brought before these questions there is only one place where he can find the clear answer: in the Scriptures.

True, the Scriptures are not separate from the church; for, as Gerhard puts it, "in the interpretation of Scripture we ought to acknowledge with reverence the gifts of God in [the doctors of the church both old and recent] and to use their service with gratitude" (1.537). But if the place of unambiguous authority is sought, it is to be found not in the temporal church (which may teach falsely) but only in the Scriptures, which have their authority as the "pure and uncorrupted . . . , unique and highest principle of our faith," regardless of whether bishops or councils recognize it (1.323; 317).[16] They are God's *"cathedra,* from which He speaks to us," His "school in which He educates and informs us," His "medical and spiritual laboratory," His "armor with which He protects and arms us against enemies of all kinds," His "hand by which He leads us through the narrow paths of faith and righteousness to eternal life" (1.364).[17] There alone you find that which can be set against the universal testimony of the law. And it can be found by anyone who looks. "The articles of faith . . . the knowledge of which is necessary for anyone's salvation are transmitted in Scripture with clear and lucid words; their summary is repeated in the apostolic symbol, which the fathers frequently call the rule of faith, in brief form" (1.532).[18]

Moreover, to hold in check the recalcitrant will of man who, in breaking the law, knows that he is doing so but cannot restrain himself, the political magistracy has been constituted by God to keep external order; the ecclesiastical ministry to take care of the public order in the church and to guard against heresies; and the family, the domestic order, to control inordinate passions.[19]

16. Cf. Friedrich Schenke's *Der Kirchengedanke Johann Gerhards und seiner Zeit.*

17. The fact of theological divergence among the Protestants themselves even on such capital matters as baptism and the Lord's Supper, which would seem to challenge the clarity of Scripture, was apparently of small concern, for it was customary to be satisfied with an oversimplification: Gerhard admits (1.431) that the Calvinists hold this same position concerning the clarity of Scripture and he is quite convinced that the Protestant divergence in doctrines of baptism and the Lord's Supper is due to the fact that the opponents depart from their own principles and deny what are the clear passages of Scripture; the Calvinists, of course, could and did reply in kind.

18. Cf. 1.414 and 418, on the meaning of "perspicuity."

19. Cf. Schenke, *Kirchengedanke,* p. 52.

CHAPTER IV

The Forms of Grace:
Thomas' Rationale of the New Creation

Neither Thomas nor Gerhard commonly uses the term, "new creation," to refer to the restoration and fulfillment of creation. They are both, of course, acquainted with it, since it is a Pauline term.

Thomas gives a definition in his commentary on Second Corinthians. We may ask: "In what sense can it be said that the restoration in grace and completion in glory of the created world is a new creation? Why is it a creation and why is it new?" Thomas replies:[1] To create is to bring something into being out of nothing. The original creation brought the world into the "being of nature" (*esse naturae*). The second creation, which is the infusion of grace, brings the already existing nature into the being of grace (*esse gratiae*). This latter is a creation in the sense that those who lack grace, as does everyone by nature, are as nothing before God—*qui gratia carent nihil sunt*. As Augustine had said, sin is nothing and so those who sin are also nothing. Thus, the infusion of grace into the natural creature is an act of creation.

1. *II ad Cor.* v.4 (v. 17).

The parallel or the contrast between the nothing out of which the original creation emerges and the nothing which is sin in relation to grace is not a subject that Thomas pursues at length. He does, however, observe that the reason why creation is nothing if viewed by itself is that it does not have its own principle of life. And he explains why the infusion of grace is a *new* creation. It is new because the original creation had been made old through sin (*inveterata est*). "New creation" must mean, then, "renewing creation (out of nothing)" rather than "second (or novel) creation." The fallen world is like an aging person losing his health and strength; and time, which in Shakespeare's words

> doth transfix the flourish set on youth
> And delves the parallels in beauty's brow,

is but the agent of sin. Out of his own resources, the aged is not able to regain health; his restoration comes, therefore, out of "nothing."

When Thomas actually deals with the subject here called "new creation," implying not only a renewal of nature but a new act of God in history, the more customary terms are "grace" and "glory." The state of grace refers to the initial stage of new creation and the state of glory to its consummation beyond this temporal life. Whereas the line from grace to glory is continuous (though, of course, its development may be interrupted before reaching its fulfillment), the line from nature to grace is discontinuous. That is to say, grace introduces something in principle new into nature, whereas glory simply is the completion of the process begun by grace. Although nature may become old and corrupted by the intrusion of sin, grace is both incorruptible and losable. The contrast, therefore, between creation and new creation is not at all foreign to Thomas' thinking. Yet, were we using his terms, it would be more usual to speak of the contrast between nature on the one hand and grace and glory on the other. The

THE FORMS OF GRACE

state of glory is, in principle, nothing new in relation to grace, but the state of grace and glory is precisely that in relation to nature—new *in principle*.

Now, the question that presents itself with regard to the man of grace in relation to God as the New Creator is the same as that which concerns the man of nature and the Creator; namely, how to preserve simultaneously in one frame of thought the absolute prevenience of God and the real freedom of the new creature. The increased attention which, from about the middle of the twelfth century, was devoted to the development of a theological doctrine of virtue, was symptomatic of the fact that this specific question was receiving more attention during Thomas' time. The notion of virtue, of course, was at least as old as Greek thought, but new refinements and applications of it appeared in the high Middle Ages, in the deepened consciousness of the complexity of the "supernatural" side of man's relation to God—the limits as well as the positive content of the natural virtues.

Augustine had attempted to settle the question of man's *natural* relationship to God, as he worked out the concepts of creatureliness, the love of God, and the love of self or the world (*amor sui, mundi*), together with the distinction between *uti* ("using" the world) and *frui* ("enjoying" God). But the specific problems arising from the attempt to set *new* man in place with relation to God on the one hand and to natural man on the other, remained to be labored over in the Middle Ages, especially in connection with a positive evaluation of Aristotle. The problem and the specific issue was the question of man's relative autonomy and God's sovereign freedom with reference directly to the Christian man.

Thus, at the level of the new creation, Thomas is concerned to hold in balance and proper relationship the reality of the creature and the sovereign initiative of the Creator. He emphasizes the latter element repeatedly, explicitly, and clearly. In his *Sentences* he could speak of the natural ability to prepare oneself; yet in his later writings, after he had become acquainted with the danger of semi-Pelagianism, he placed "into greater relief, even in the preparation for grace, the divine initiative and the close (*intime*) dependence of the will on the divine aid."[2] Man cannot save himself, the initiative is solely God's. But correlative with this emphasis is also the doctrine of the free will by which man responds to God's first act. These unite in the notion that even in man's response there is always the element of divine aid (*auxilium*). It is not as if God, out of His sovereign freedom, makes the proposal, and then man, on equal footing, accepts or rejects, both in the manner of diplomats from equally powerful countries.

Thomas preserves the absolute initiative of God, both in the preparation for grace and also in the reception of it and perseverance in it. If the question should arise—as indeed it did in the theological controversies of the Reformation and post-Reformation periods—why it is necessary to speak of a preparation for grace in addition to the reception of it or why it is necessary to distinguish, as Thomas does in the *Summa Theologiae,* between the *infusio* and the *consecutio* of grace, since indeed both stages depend upon God's act, the answer lies partly in the Aristotelian notion that unprepared matter cannot receive a form, and partly in the Trinitarian view of creation.[3] And it should be remembered that preparation is logically prior to reception but not necessarily prior temporally. Man is utterly unable to prepare himself to receive the gift of grace, the *donum habitualis gratiae,* for sin has robbed him of everything. It has stripped him of the original "beauty of grace" by which he should have been able to preserve himself from corruption; it has deprived him of the natural good

---

2. Bouillard, *Conversion et grâce,* p. 92. Cf. also pp. 85 ff., 103 f., 190.
3. Cf. above, pp. 60 f. Bouillard, *Conversion et grâce,* pp. 24, 30, 166–71, et passim, brings out the self-evidence of a stage of preparation for an Aristotelian ("on ne vois plus que, dans un système de pensée aristotélicienne, elle allait de soi" p. 215), but he neglects to consider that preparation is also the creaturely analogy to the person of the Father in the Trinity.

in which he could at least have enjoyed his natural happiness; it has lost him his innocence before God.

Since even the original grace was a gift given at the spontaneous generosity of God above and beyond the natural endowment, it follows that man in his present fallen state can certainly not re-acquire its *politesse.* But neither can he acquire his natural good, for he lacks both the will and the means to do so. No purpose is served by telling him to reacquire his lost good, for he does not *want* to do so. The root problem is that in his present state his will itself is misdirected. Or if, in particular cases, it is indeed directed toward a genuine good, it still lacks the tenacity to follow through to the final end. Moreover, if man has lost his innocence, his guilt can be removed only by Him in whose sight he became guilty (II.i.109.7). The conclusion is that man needs the *auxilium Dei,* the aid which moves his soul from within or "inspires" the good set before him, even in order to *prepare* himself to receive the gift.

The fact that he cannot prepare himself to receive it does not excuse him of responsibility for his corruption and lack of grace. Rather, that inability is itself a defect in his nature for which he is accountable (II.i.109.8 *ad* 1). He would not be responsible if the deficiency were inherent in his nature, for then its removal would demand from the start that he step outside of his essential self in order to accomplish what is required. Thus, had Adam remained without grace, he should not have been guilty on that account. But when by sin he has lost the gift of grace and incurred a weakening of nature, he is indeed responsible for corruption, and withdrawal of grace is a punishment. He is held guilty not for failure to be an angel, but for not being man.

As the "gift of habitual grace" presupposes God's preparation of the man who prepares himself, it is at least indirectly dependent upon initiative from above. Yet even directly its character shows that divine initiative; it is a gift and not a reward. This gift is the basis of any merit man has before God. If eternal life is given as a "reward" for man's good works, then it is only on the basis of the fact that the good works have proceeded from the antecedent habit of grace as their principle of action. Reward is, in Augustine's phrase, God's crown on His own gift. It is due to man only according to God's ordering and not as an unequivocal ground of human claim. Thomas' maxim is: man works according to his ability but God rewards according to His grace.

Moreover, it is not as though God grants the gift and then retreats deistically to His corner of the universe to let man work out his own salvation. The *donum* itself has a dimension of continuing divine activity. Thomas brings this out when he asks the question whether the man who is constituted in grace needs the aid (*auxilium*) of grace for persevering to the end of life (II.i.109.10). He answers affirmatively. Whereas the gift carries with itself a certain power of standing firm and avoiding the unvirtuous, as well as of intending to persevere to the end, in Thomas' terms the habit is endowed as the *principle* of those actions—yet for the actual "continuation in good up to the end" the divine aid is needed. Nothing apart from God's continuing presence can uphold the new creation. Just as creation, even in its integral state, always presupposes the aid of a first mover, as a continuously present force in all things, so new creation, both in the state of grace and in the state of glory, always presupposes an element of help in and beyond the habits of grace (II.i.109.9 *ad* 1).

So the circle of nature is not completely closed. There is a point at which God steps in to endow the creature with the principles of actions leading to supernatural felicity. Those principles are the infused "habits." No natural habit, whether innate or acquired, is able to serve as the principle of actions that will attain the ultimate end. This incompleteness of nature is the first reason for the infusion of new habits. One could call this infusion, figuratively, God's entering the circle of nature. A second reason, one which points to God's freedom from His own ordinances

(II.i.51.4), is that He occasionally works without secondary causes, as when He brings about the cure of a disease without medicine. "In order to show His power" He may infuse habits which serve as principles for attaining otherwise natural ends and which could have been acquired with natural powers. For this kind of new activity on the part of God, one could use the metaphor of breaking into the circle of nature. For it refers to cases where He interrupts His own established natural order in a way that is not only supernatural but also unnatural.

Apart from the occasional breaking in which may occur at any point in the circle of nature, the question arises, where is the point at which God enters in order to endow the creature with the principles of salvation? The answer, with regard to the human creature, is, the free will (*liberum arbitrium*), that is, will acting in conjunction with reason. For this is the open point in the circle of man's natural life.

"Nature is not lacking in the necessities." This maxim, which Thomas accepts (II.i.5.5), indicates the character of creation as a closed circle. The open point becomes visible when that maxim is applied to man. For just as God did not make him to be born clothed, but gave him intelligence and hands, so also He did not implant in him principles of actions which lead to supernatural beatitude—indeed that would have been a contradiction of his humanity—but implanted in him the free will "by which he can be turned to God who makes him blessed" (II.i.5.5). Thus, the free will is the point at which he is open to receive the new act of God and, in receiving it, to find fulfillment. In the use of his free will man is at once perfect and not perfect. It is the free will, Thomas tells us (II.i.109.6 *ad* 1), by which man is converted to God—and yet the free will cannot be converted to God unless God converts it to Himself. The free will is that distinctively human function through which God acts in order to bring man to his eternal goal, that goal which is not man's by nature—and yet in a way *is* his by nature. This openness to a goal which exceeds the natural but is somehow present in the natural is what Hugo Lang[4] has called the "Sehnsucht nach einem Glück, das namenlos ist, uns noch unbekannt, an dem wir aber rätselhafterweise alles bekannte Glück messen und unzulänglich finden müssen."

In using his natural capacity of free will in its most "natural" way, man discovers that precisely this natural capacity is the point at which God enters his life anew in order to lift him beyond nature. Acceptance of the new act of God fulfills the freedom; rejection of it is in principle an annulment of the freedom. For the free will is not simply the capacity to choose between equally valid alternatives (although Aquinas does often make it sound so[5]), but is in a more profound sense the capacity of the whole self to respond affirmatively to God's acts, which means, finally, the capacity to transcend all natural limitations. If man uses his freedom to reject God, he loses his freedom and becomes less than man. To use an image which Aquinas adopts from the Augustinian-Platonic tradition—if, in relation to God he is conceived as analogous to a person standing in the light of the sun with his back toward the sun itself, then his freedom is his ability to turn toward the sun. The turning, however, is at once his free act and God's turning of him. True, even when he is turned he might insist on keeping his eyes closed. Should he do so, his choice does not mean that he lives by his own light rather than the light of the sun; it means simply that he does not then live freely because he refuses to recognize the real source of his life.

The initiative in the new creation is *cap-à-pie* God's, and the response is man's with the aid of God. The new creation, how-

---

4. *Gottes gute Welt*, p. 87.
5. Contrast, for example, II.ii.24.1 and II.i.113.3. As a general description one could say that the understanding of freedom as choice between alternatives appears where Thomas is explicating the meaning of the term *liberum arbitrium* in the context of the human faculties in themselves. The more profound meaning of freedom appears in the function of the free will in conversion as expressing the relation of man to God.

ever, bears a twofold relationship to nature in present actuality.
It is related both to corrupt nature and to nature restored (in
principle) to its purity. The relation to corrupt nature is that of
healing. Grace heals the wounds of nature. It is *gratia sanans*.
This healing begins in the "mind"—the *mens*, that part of man
which includes his intellect and will but not his sensual or carnal
appetites (II.i.109.8 ff.; 74.4). The healing in the mind is the
restoration of order, the removal of the disorder and misdirected-
ness that characterize fallen man. As the essence of physical disease is the disorder which corrupts the principle of biological
life, so the essence of spiritual disease is the disorder which results from sin. As a disorder which corrupts the principle of life,
sin is like a disease which needs curing. Thus, the first stage of
the work of grace is the restoration of that principle. God's new-
creating activity in this respect is like the new-creating activity
of the physician. But since the principle of man's spiritual life
lies in his mind and not in his body, it follows that the healing
occurs primarily there rather than in the body, where it takes
place only secondarily. Specifically, the restoration of life's principle means a reordering of the intellect and will toward the true
and the good. Grace is thus primarily the restoration of the natural
disposition. It cures the mind of its self-destructive chaos and
gives it the principles of an ordered intellect and will.

Although it takes place first in the mind, the healing is even
there not complete. A certain "obscurity of ignorance" and inclination to sin hangs on. Even though the new man may will to
do the good, he is not always able to calculate the effects of his
actions. What he does may in fact lead to an evil when he has
wanted it to bring about good. As we are accustomed to saying,
sincerity is not a guarantee of truth. That maxim fits Thomas'
view also. In order to preserve the new man from doing uninten-
tionally evil acts, the continual direction and protection of God
is necessary as a counterbalance to the intellect's ignorance. Moreover, the healing of the will remains similarly incomplete. For

the pattern which purging the mind follows is that of a dialectic between the reason and the will. The mind is not always disposed indifferently to two alternatives; it may actually lean to one. Now, if it should happen that the leaning is toward the evil rather than the good, the mind will choose it unless it is led away from it by the "discussion of the reason."[6] There must be, as it were, a conference between the reason and will in order to clear the mind and direct it rightly. Thus, Thomas analyzes the inner dialectic of the self as between the intelligence and the will. In Gerhard's conception, as we have seen, it is in *spiritual* matters a dialogue of the self with the self, and only secondarily and in "civil" matters a dialogue between intelligence and will, or between the mind and the passions.

It is impossible, Thomas knows, that every single thing which is done or willed can first be discussed between the intellect and will. Time is not sufficient. The cleansing of the inclination requires at least a great deal of time before all traces of evil are removed, more time indeed than is available to mortal man. Therefore, in regard to both the intellect and will, grace heals but leaves scars. Secondarily, and even less completely, the healing work of grace has to do with the inferior appetites. These appetites of themselves still serve the "law of sin," in the Pauline phrase. In the present life corruption remains in these appetites; they continue to be inordinate, chaotic, and destructive. If they are brought to order at all, it is through the control of the mind whose disease has in principle been cured. And yet even the healed mind is not able to be vigilant over all of the carnal impulses. While it undertakes to restrain certain ones, others crop up in their place.

This fact—that grace begins its healing in the mind rather than in the lower parts—leads to the distinction between mortal sin and venial sin. In contrast to fallen man, who may avoid single mortal sins at particular times but who could not continue to do so indefinitely, restored man is able to avoid mortal sin com-

6. *CG* III.160.

pletely. Yet even he is not able to avoid venial sins because they originate in the sensual parts. Unhealed sensuality is the remnant of original sin, the tinder for acts of sin in the new creature. This residue of sin is not fatal because it does not reside in the principal part of man, his mind. It dwells in an appurtenance, his body, and tries in fact to contravene the order of the healed mind. It affects his carnal appetites but not his essential manhood.

Whereas the relation of grace to corrupt nature is one of *healing,* its relation to restored nature is one of *elevating.* Grace heals corrupt nature, but it elevates pure or healed nature to supernatural felicity. In that sense it is *gratia elevans.* True, the question of its relationship to pure nature is one which concretely concerns no one except Adam, as the first man before the fall, and Jesus Christ, as the true man appearing after the fall. Still inasmuch as both Adam and Jesus Christ are more than individual men in that they preside over and represent the whole human race, there is a purpose in speaking of the relationship of grace to pure nature. For what is restored to all men is what was integral to the prelapsarian Adam and to the humanity of Jesus Christ.

Whether one speaks of restored or pure nature, the relation of grace to it is elevation. Grace lifts man to a level of attainment which he cannot reach by his natural powers. It raises him to a status of participation in the eternal beatitude of God. Without the gift of grace man passes his time subject to Him as Lord and Master; with the gift of grace he can, on the grounds of the gracious communication from God, converse with Him as friend. From the status of inferiority he is raised to the status of donated equality with God. From subjection to decay, he is raised to participation in the power of life. Man's natural principles sustain him only a certain number of years, after which they have dissipated their power. Grace rescues him from that natural destruction and raises him to new power.

Logically or metaphysically described, the relation of grace to healed nature is that of the special to the general. To a general directedness toward God, grace adds special elements: to the intellect which knows general truth, it adds the special truth of God's inner life and intentions; to the will which has a general love of God as the common good, it adds the special element of a love for Him as the "object of beatitude." Viewed from the side of the Giver, nature's existence is the result of His general love. Elevated nature, as a new creation, is the result of His special love in which He wills to the creature not alone temporal existence but participation in His own eternal life. This formal way of conceiving the relation between grace and nature transfuses virtually all of Thomas' theology: grace is specialized nature as an elm is a specialized tree, or a Caucasian a specialized man; grace is nature-plus as any species is the genus-plus-differences.

This characteristic applies to all forms of grace. It applies not only to saving grace (*gratia gratum faciens*), but also to the "grace freely given" (*gratia gratis data*), for which the term *charisma* is today more common. *Gratia gratum faciens* is the grace which makes man new. *Gratia gratis data* is an irregular gift given to some individuals, as the power of prophecy or eloquence in preaching. It is bestowed not for the purpose of saving the one to whom it is given, but to bring others to be disposed for the reception of saving grace themselves. Furthermore—and this is a rather incidental function of grace, although it too exhibits the same trait—grace is sometimes given in order to facilitate the performance of what are otherwise natural operations. Where natural ends are usually attained with some drudgery, grace can facilitate the attainment. Thus, some people can acquire facility at mathematics by long practice, whereas to others the special "habit" of mathematical skill is given all at once. That special habit is given in addition to natural capacities by which a similar skill could be acquired but only with time and effort. It too is, therefore, a natural aptitude plus specific difference.

Both of these relationships, that of elevation and that of logical specialization, express in formal terms the discontinuity between creation and new creation, the underivability of grace from nature. Although it is possible to move from species to genus without a break, to move from genus to species requires a "leap," a positing anew. The species implies the genus, but not the converse. Similarly, one could say (although I believe Thomas nowhere says it in precisely this way) that nature can move "downward" continuously; but to move upward, to be elevated, a new impulse from outside is needed. This is important to bear in mind when we cite the two maxims which characterize Thomas' viewpoint *en gros: Gratia praesupponit naturam* and *gratia non tollit sed perficit naturam*. "Grace presupposes nature." This means that the logical or metaphysical movement "backward" from grace to nature is continuous, but not the forward movement. From the fact that there is a creation, it does not immediately follow logically or *realiter* that there must be a new creation, or grace. From the fact that man is a creature of God it does not immediately follow that he must receive the grace of God to eternal life. Nature does not essentially and without interruption develop into grace. On the contrary, nature alone perishes. Negatively speaking, then, grace presupposes nature not primarily in the way that an oak tree presupposes an acorn or an adult presupposes a child (even though Thomas does use such analogies), but in the way that the reality of an elm tree presupposes the reality of trees in general. For the movement from acorn to oak tree is continuous, direct, predictable, and spontaneous; whereas the movement from nature to grace, as Thomas says over and over again, is only by way of a new positing on the part of God, a new creation.

Again, "grace does not destroy but perfects nature." This is not to be understood primarily as analogous to the perfection which adulthood brings to childhood but rather in the sense that grace adds to nature something which is otherwise not there. In principle the adult is inherent in the child; but grace is not in nature, not even in principle. To be sure, nature even at its completest has an open point at which to receive grace. Nevertheless, for that point to be closed and the circle completed, a new act of God is required. There is thus a leap between nature and grace which is not present in the relation of child and adult. One of the ramifications of this fact is that grace can be bestowed upon individual creatures directly as they share in Christ's benefits. It does not need, as it were, to be filtered through the whole universe first. Whereas a child must pass through adolescence before reaching adulthood, nature does not need to have developed all its potentialities first before the individual can receive grace.

THE CHARACTER OF NEW CREATION

Creation as pure or restored is, as we have seen in the previous chapters, good but incomplete. In similar fashion the new creation can equally well be labeled as good and completed. Whereas the creature is left by nature with an open end, an unfulfilled longing for an eternal beatitude which is his but at the same time not his, the new creature is endowed with the capacity to reach his eternal goal. The new creature is ordered to his *ultimus finis*, to God Himself. In a word, the new creation is not merely good, but "holy," for holiness is a quality attributed to those things which are directed immediately and intimately to God (1.36.1).

Furthermore, as creation has a special carrier in the eternal Word of the Trinity, so new creation is specially related to the eternal Love which is the Holy Spirit. Nature marches under the banner of "Word," grace under the banner of "Love." There are a number of ways in which this fact comes to expression. Thus, man is made in the image of God and the Word is the eternal Image. New man is lifted to a union with God in love and the Holy Spirit is the eternal Love, the bond of unity in God Himself. Creation exhibits the character of the divine life by vestige or image; new creation brings the power of that life into the creature. For as "spirit" is that power (*vis motiva*) which moves the will

of the lover toward the loved one, the Holy Spirit is the Love
with which the Father and the Son love each other and which
turns the will of the creature to God. Or, the new creation is in
a special sense the gift of God. But gifts of God are attributed
properly to the Holy Spirit rather than the Son or Father. The
Holy Spirit's name and person is Gift. Again, just as the Holy
Spirit is related to the Father not directly but through the Son,
so new creation is related to its principle not directly but through
creation (cf. 1.35.2). Creation's reality rests on the Word-relation
to God, new creation's on the Love-relation.

This description of the special rooting of new creation in the
Holy Spirit is valid even though the incarnate Son is the one who
is the author of the new creation. For apart from the work of the
Holy Spirit, the mission of the Son remains extrinsic to man's
life and understanding—like a visual aid whose truth the world
cannot appropriate. The intent of the Son's *missio temporalis*
must be found in the Love of the Holy Spirit. The Son is sent,
Thomas informs us (1.43.5 *ad* 2), according to such an "instruction" of the intellect which makes it issue in an "affect of love."
As love is the terminal of the work of the Word, the Son works
in view of the Holy Spirit. The Holy Spirit interprets and makes
effective the Son's work. Conversely, grace presupposes nature
just as the Holy Spirit's Love presupposes the Word: the Holy
Spirit proceeds from Father and Son, His work as Gift is based
on the work of the Son, who "authorizes" the gift.

The dual relationship of the Son and the Holy Spirit to the new
creation, together with the special relation of the Holy Spirit, is
brought to a focus in the question whether it was seemly for the
Spirit to be sent visibly (1.43.7). In response, Thomas points out
that both the Son and the Holy Spirit became visible because
man's natural way of knowing is to proceed from the visible to
the invisible, from sense perception to abstract concepts. Therefore "God demonstrated Himself and the eternal processions of
the Persons, as it were, through visible creatures as pointers

(*indicia*)." The why of the visible sending is traceable to the peculiarity of man's formal way of knowing, in which the concrete provides the sense data for the abstraction. However, the Son and the Holy Spirit are not sent visibly in the same way. The Son is the Author of sanctification, the Holy Spirit is its Index. New creation is, in other words, the work of the whole Trinity but the Persons have special functions. The Son brings it about in principle, but the Holy Spirit is its power to take effect, to be appropriated, to be known. There is, then, a certain formal parallelism and Trinitarian progression between creation and new creation. In the work of creation the Father is the author, the principle, while the Son is the expression, the sufficient representation of it. In the work of the new creation, the Son is its author and the Holy Spirit is its expression. Thus, whereas the Son appears visibly only in the form of one man, taking on the whole "rational nature," the Holy Spirit appears in the form of any creature. Since it is man who is to be saved only Man can bring about salvation. But any creature can be the concrete datum which displays the character of the new creation as gift in its various and manifold aspects.

"Author–Index": these two terms express the relation, respectively, of the visible Son and the visible Holy Spirit to the new creation. Add these remarks to the first ones concerning their relation to new creation and the whole picture takes the following shape. With regard to the *bringing about* of new creation, the Son is the initiating power and the Holy Spirit the effective power; the Son makes renewal possible, the Holy Spirit makes it actual in the believer. With regard to the *character* of new creation, the Son is the author, the Holy Spirit is the index. If one asks how one comes to know *what* it is, the answer is in the visible manifestations of the Holy Spirit; if one asks for the *whence,* the answer is contained in the human form which the eternal Son assumed. That is why in the era of the Old Testament the Holy Spirit never appeared visibly: the new creation, of which

His visible appearance is the indication, had not yet been inaugurated.

But now a question arises, in the domain of new creation, parallel to one in creation: if the Holy Spirit is the indwelling motive power of the new life, what concepts can be employed to house in the same rationale not only that motive power but also the real freedom of the restored humanity? How does the Holy Spirit move the creature so as not to annul the creature's humanity? It is in the context of this kind of question that the doctrine of virtues, especially the theological virtues, must be understood. The concept of virtue or gift (*donum*)[7] serves the same function here as that of form at the previous level. It expresses the way in which man is able to participate in the eternal life of God without being consumed by it. For Thomas can say (1.43.3 *ad* 1) that in and with the use of the *donum creatum,* the gift in man, the creature enjoys also the divine person, the Holy Spirit Himself, who is the "uncreated Gift." By the gift of grace the "rational creature is perfected, to the end that he not only use the gift freely, but also that he enjoy the divine Person Himself." Like the natural "form," the virtue or *donum* has a double function. On one hand it enables the creature to act out of his own power and on the other hand it retains an intimate connection with its divine ground. Like the form, it is the concept which embodies the two maxims that guided Thomas in these matters: "God works nothing which is against nature's interest" and "God works in all things according to their own manner" (II.i.51.4 *ad* 2).

7. "Virtue" in the narrow sense and *"donum"* are objectively the same. The difference between them is that the latter looks backward to the origin, the Giver, whereas the former looks forward to the act which proceeds from the virtue. Or, to put it differently, the theological virtues of faith, hope, and love are like the roots out of which the specific gifts (wisdom, counsel, knowledge, etc.) grow. I shall accordingly use the two words more or less interchangeably in this section. For further distinctions see II.i.68.1, and also O. Lottin, "Les dons du Saint-Esprit chez les théologiens depuis P. Lombard jusqu'à s. Thomas d'Aquin." See also below, pp. 209 ff.

The roots of the doctrine of virtues in general go back to Aristotle and the Platonic tradition of Plotinus, but the specific Christian contribution was the addition of the infused virtues as an expression of the reality of a new creation. This was accompanied by a more detailed elaboration of them in the light of the solutions that had been formulated in the theological controversies over such central problems as those of Christology. Thomas takes over the definition of virtue from Peter the Lombard: "Virtue is that good quality of the mind by which one lives rightly . . . and which God works in us without our aid" (II.i.55.4). In spite of this agreement in definition with the Lombard the disagreement on the question of the relation of the virtue of love to the Love which is the Holy Spirit makes clear what Thomas' concern is: to preserve God's sovereign initiative as well as the humanity of man's response. Thomas maintains that the Lombardian solution denies what it attempts to affirm.[8] Were one to follow this solution one would deny precisely the unique character of *caritas* in relation to the other virtues. For Thomas saw, on the basis of an insight drawn from Aristotle's *Liber de bona fortuna,* that the movement of God on the will must be *interior* if the will's integrity is to be preserved. If the impulse of theological love were, as the Lombard maintained, a direct and extrinsic movement on the will by the Holy Spirit without a mediating virtue, then the uniqueness of the movement of the will would be annulled. It is in the nature of the will that it is never simply moved but also self-moving at the same time; there is no such thing as a voluntary movement whose cause is purely external. An act of the will uniquely has its principle in itself. An external movement might conceivably be a movement by the Holy Ghost, but it would not be a movement of love unless it were also an act of the will, that is, intrinsic and voluntary. "For Thomas, as for Aristotle, the action of the mover in the *mobile* is nothing else than the movement itself of the *mobile* since this

8. See below, Chapter VI.

movement is, from opposed points of view, the common act of motor and *mobile*."[9] Thomas does not thereby remove every conceptual difficulty—he does not resolve the paradox—but he locates the point at which divine activity and human activity coincide. The *donum creatum*, like the "infused virtue," is a concept which expresses the human autonomy and simultaneously the divine initiative.

The special character of the new creation is marked by the person of the Holy Ghost. Specifically this can be applied to the parts of man's rationality, his intellect and will, as well as to the ordering of the lower parts to his reason and to the Holy Ghost.

In the *intellect* the work of the Holy Spirit remains the same in kind as at the level of creation. He is the inspirer of truth; He "breathes in" all truth which the intellect apprehends. But there is a difference. Even though it is true that the Holy Spirit is the prompter of truth universally, He is so in a special way to the new creature. Thomas brings this out when he poses the question whether man can know the true apart from having received grace (II.i.109.1). After making the by now familiar distinction that the intellect can by nature know the natural truths but needs the additional light of grace to know the things of faith, he proceeds to point out, in reference to I Corinthians 12:3 ("No one can say that Jesus is the Lord but by the Holy Ghost"), that wherever truth is spoken and known it is so because of the natural light of knowledge which the Holy Spirit implants. But when it comes to truth that exceeds the natural capacity the Holy Spirit grants it not while standing on the outside, as it were, pouring it in but by Himself entering and working from the inside. The new-created intellect has not only its full power to know by its natural light but in addition the indwelling Holy Spirit, who inhabits it by saving grace. The light of God which shines on creation is like a light from without; the illumination of the intellect given with the new creation is like an inner light. "Many know God either

9. Bouillard, *Conversion et grâce,* pp. 197 f.

through natural knowledge or through unformed faith in whom nevertheless the Spirit of God does not dwell."[10]

Moreover, there are four "gifts" of the Holy Spirit, by which He inhabits the new creature without annulling freedom, which reside in the intellect.[11] By these the creature is enabled to act not only according to the guidance of his reason in attaining natural ends, but also according to the direction of the Holy Spirit in attaining the ends which exceed the natural ones. Faith does not suffice to do this directing, for it is an assent to divine truth without an apprehension of its inner meaning. Faith proposes things "not as seen but as heard," things to be taken on the basis of the reliability of their source. If they are to take hold in the hearer, the intellect must "penetrate" or "apprehend" them and must have a right judgment concerning them (II.ii.8.6). The gift of insight (or understanding: *donum intellectus*) makes this intellectual penetration possible. The other three gifts—of wisdom (*sapientia*), knowledge (*scientia*), and counsel (*consilium*)— make possible a right judgment concerning the things of faith. To wisdom it belongs to judge rightly the things of God; to knowledge, the things of the created world; to counsel, the application of principles of truth to single acts.

With these additions to the natural light of the mind, the human creature does not cease to be a rational creature. The gifts of the Holy Spirit, His indwelling in the reason, do not nullify reason's capacity. On the contrary, they extend it beyond nature. It is rational capacity-plus, not anti-rational or irrational capacity. As a natural creature is guided by its implanted reason, so the new creature is guided by the same reason and also the infused reason which is the Holy Ghost working in and through the intellectual *dona*. The gifts of understanding, wisdom, knowledge, and counsel are the habits in which the freedom of the rational

---

10. *Super ep. S. Pauli (I Cor.)*, I.173.
11. The gifts referred to here are seven in all, taken from Isaiah 11:2 f.: understanding, counsel, wisdom, knowledge; piety, courage, fear.

creature is preserved in the very moment in which he is joined
to the direct guiding of the Holy Spirit. They are reason and more
than reason; they are reason's fulfillment and extension. Thus the
renovation and completion of the intellect is describable in the
words, "faith" and "intellectual gifts." Faith provides the transition from natural reason to the Spiritually amplified reason. Faith
opens man to a reception of the divine truth, the illumination of
the intellect. The *dona* make it possible for the intellect to grasp
those truths rationally: to penetrate to their core by insight and
to discriminate concerning their implications and application to
particulars.

It is, nonetheless, in the *will* that the new creation has its
special residence and reaches its culmination. For the bond of
unity forged by love is more intimate than that forged by
knowledge. Between the knower and the known a certain distance always remains, for the known object is, in Thomas' epistemology, in the mind by representation—by the intellectual
form, the intelligible species. Between the lover and the loved
one, on the other hand, union is complete, for the lover is attracted not to a likeness of the thing loved but to the thing itself.[12]
Thus, in respect to the things of God, the union in love is "more
excellent" than union in knowledge and the virtue of *caritas* is by
the same token more excellent than that of faith (II.ii.23.6). This
fact should be kept visible when one is dealing with the question
of the primacy of the intellect over the will, as it is referred to in
the maxim that there is no love without knowledge (*nihil volitum
nisi praecognitum*). For Thomas' theology is not intellectualistic
in the sense that he maintains that the chief and indispensable
thing, the beginning and end, of the Christian life is correct
knowledge of the divine things. True, a certain knowledge is
demanded, but the decisive factor is not the intellect's knowledge
but the will's love, and the new creation is founded on the Trinitarian love which is the Holy Spirit. For the Christian life the

12. *III Sent.* d. 27.1.4.

crucial question is not whether a man believes the matters of faith to be true but whether he has love for the God who reveals them. Perhaps one can say that the intellect has primacy in creation—with regard to union with lower things that of knowledge is more excellent than of love—but the will has primacy in new creation in the sense that love of the things of God is superior to a knowledge of them. Primacy is not, however, superiority.

Again, it is true that the intellect always retains a primacy in the sense that it sets before the will the object of its love—there can be no love for the totally unknown. But it is *not* true that the intellect dominates the will, and that if the truth is once known it is necessarily loved. The intellect may set an object before the will but for that object to become the *finis,* that is, something to be striven for, the will must move itself toward it (cf. II.i.9.3 *ad* 3, and 17.6). Hence it is clear why in Thomas' conceptual framework "faith alone" cannot justify the sinner. Faith alone would have to mean faith apart from *caritas*—the simple acknowledgement that the things which God reveals must be true, since they come from so eminent an origin, but without a love for them. Thomas could, therefore, have agreed to the "grace alone" banner of the Reformers much more readily than to their "faith alone." To him *sola fides* meant something else than to the Reformers, and he might have objected to their conception as obscuring the essential *Trinitarian* character of all created reality, which reflects not only the Son (in intelligence and faith) but also the Holy Spirit (in love and *caritas*).

In the new creation the illumination of the intellect is complemented by the "inflammation of the affection" (1.43.5 *ad* 3). The virtue of faith in the intellect opens man to receive the illumination of the gifts. The virtue of *caritas* in the will enables man to love God as the final end, the "object of beatitude," and to love man as the creature of God. *Caritas* is complete in a way that faith is not, for it joins the new creature immediately to God Himself, and is indeed the presupposition of all virtues and gifts as well as that which binds them together. Faith disposes man to receive love (*caritas*), but *caritas* is its end and fulfillment: when it is received, everything is received. There are, to be sure, the three gifts of piety, courage, and fear which supplement the four named above (understanding, wisdom, knowledge, and counsel) and which properly belong to man's appetitive life, its intellective as well as its sensitive level; in the intellective appetite they would belong to the will rather than the intellect proper, and would therefore be rooted in *caritas*. But they are of the genus of *caritas*, specifications in its whole work, and not something extra. Piety puts man into an ordered relationship to God and to his fellow men by implanting a respect for them which is their due; fortitude strengthens the will against the terror of dangers which the Christian life may bring; fear holds concupiscence in check by its regard of consequences (cf. ii.i.68.4 f.).

With the endowment of *caritas* the vagrant will is united to its ultimate end and the rest of the parts of man fall into order and harmony. Acts directed toward natural ends are guided by reason through the moral virtues; acts directed toward ultimate beatitude are guided by the Holy Spirit through the *dona*. What is known is what is loved, what is true is what is good, and conversely. The insouciant creature becomes the inflamed new creature. The goodness of creation is transformed into the holiness of the new creation.

ITS DYNAMICS

The creature is universally "in order" to the good which is its fulfillment. In nature the striving toward fulfillment is by means of the innate forms directing toward their respective ends. In corrupt nature the striving has lost its purity and is partly replaced by external restraint, by imposed authority and discipline. In new creation the creature has been healed of corruption and endowed with a new set of forms, the virtues and gifts, which direct him to not only his natural ends but to his supernatural beatitude in God. Under the conditions of time the new creation is only partially actual; grace is implanted and works toward its end but does not accomplish it until after death, when the new creation is completed in the state of glory. The movement in new creation itself is thus from grace to glory, through an ever fuller working out of the new principles of life which have been endowed. This is not to say that progress is automatic and irreversible. Grace can be lost; yet, barring that, the general development goes on.

Here it is not only the natural forms which direct the creature but likewise the supernatural forms, the *dona* of the Holy Spirit, in which He Himself is actively present. The natural forms through which the Creator works and the virtues of grace through which the New Creator works more intimately are the total equipment of the new creature. He lacks nothing now to attain to his supernatural beatitude. What in creation was openness to God becomes in new creation cooperation with God.

Specifically the new creature's impulse comes from the three theological virtues as the soil in which the gifts are sown. Faith, hope, and love direct the creature to his ultimate goal. Whereas faith and hope are a part of new creation in the state of grace, *caritas* alone belongs both to grace and to glory. Faith and hope are still *indirect* junctures with the divine life. They make man cling to God not in Himself but as the source from which expected things proceed (II.ii.17.6). Faith looks to Him as the source of truth—but it is interested in formal truth not in His person. Hope looks to Him as the source of the power to overcome the hindrances in the pilgrimage to glory. *Caritas* alone is an immediate union with God as He is in Himself and not as the source of some good. Thus, it is through the gift of *caritas* that the Holy Spirit orders the human will to its supernatural good in God. He is the internally impelling power. True, authority remains partially external, as does also the discipline of the will, because the state of grace is only the beginning and not yet the fulfillment of the new creature. To the extent, however, that grace and not corrupted nature drives man, the externality of authority and discipline is replaced by interior motives. Instead of acceptance on the word of accredited witnesses, the intellect has insight into the truth of faith itself. Instead of external restraint on the passions and on its own rebelliousness, the will has an inner order. The gift of *caritas* enables the new man to strive willingly for ends that are his ultimate good.

Thus while Thomas has no single conception which covers precisely the same ground as the term "faith" in the theology of the Protestants of the sixteenth and seventeenth centuries, in *caritas* he approaches two characteristics which mark the Protestant conception: namely, that faith is a personal relationship of confidence or trust ("friendship" in Thomas), and that it is dependent solely upon the grace of God.

The overlapping and supplementation as well as the vivid contrast between the dynamics of creation and those of new creation can be seen in those sections of the *Summa Theologiae* where Thomas deals with the old and new law.[13] All law purports to direct actions to an end—and in that sense to make men good by directing them to good ends. In the old law given to the people of Israel is incorporated the natural law which is implanted in the human mind. The new law given with Jesus Christ surpasses the natural and old law in the same way that grace goes beyond nature. Both the old and the new are expressions of the one divine law, just as both creation and new creation are workings of the same God. The relationship between the two laws is like that between the imperfect and perfect, or between a boy and a man (II.i.91.5). Now, this seems to imply that the old law grows of itself into the new law in the course of time. But Thomas immediately amplifies and qualifies that comparison, so that the difference between the two appears not only as that between the immature and mature but as that between earth and heaven, be-

13. II.i.91 ff. Cf. 91.5; 98.1; 106.1 ff.; 107.1.

tween external force and internal motive, between fear and love —and these contrasts make it quite clear that there is more to the analogy than simply the relation of a child to an adult.

Thomas elaborates the functions of law as threefold. First, it serves to order things toward the general good, which can be either the sensible and terrestrial or the intelligible and celestial. The old law orders directly to the former: its aims are the peace and harmony of the social community. The new law orders directly to the latter and only indirectly to the former: its aims are eternal beatitude and ultimate good. Secondly, law serves to direct human acts according to the "order of justice," to make acts just and upright. In this function, the new law can achieve what the old cannot. The old can direct external acts to some extent but it cannot give internal motivation. Thirdly, law serves to lead men to observance of the mandates, the special commands of God. Here too the difference between the old and new is crucial. The old law can lead men to such observances only by fear and punishment; the new does so by love and the interior working of the Holy Spirit. The old law, being good but incomplete and in that sense imperfect, could "help" but not "cure" the creature. It could set goals before him and assist his external acts. Doing so, it was sufficient for the accomplishment of human ends by fear and punishment; but it was not sufficient for attaining eternal ends which demand the interior motivation of love. Whereas the old law in its essentials is inscribed in nature in such a way that it can point to the goals and the actions by which to reach them, the new law is implanted in such a way that it not only indicates but also works (*indicans et adjuvans*) what it commands. The new law, since it is the grace of the Holy Spirit working within, can justify, whereas the old could not. The new law supplies what the old lacked: the grace of the Holy Spirit, which enables man to fulfill the law also with regard to its motivation; the new man has *caritas,* the "bond of perfection," in place of fear. In terms of its relationship to the Trinitarian Persons the whole law is from

God, but the old stands especially under the Father from whom it originates and the Son who is prefigured in it, whereas the new stands under the Son who is its author and the Holy Spirit who is its expression and effectiveness.

In one way the old and the new law are alike, since the function of both is to make men subject to God, to make them just. In another way, however, they are dissimilar, because the old works externally, like a tutor of children, a *paedagogus puerorum*, whereas the new works internally as the law of love. Therefore, when Thomas discusses the imbedding of the new in the old (II.i.107.3) and uses two different analogies, they may reflect the ambiguity in the meaning of the word "law," but not of the essential relation of the new to the old. The new is contained in the old, he says, just as the species is contained in the genus or the total tree in its seed. But clearly the species does not grow out of the genus as a tree grows out of a seed. On the contrary, the first metaphor can best be applied (though Thomas does not so restrict it) to the new law as meaning the *addition of the grace* of the Holy Spirit. For His *caritas* is a species of general love. As species it needs to be posited separately; it presupposes a genus but it cannot grow out of the genus nor be logically derived from the genus. On the other hand, if law is taken to mean the *depth of understanding* that men have of the precepts, then the picture of the tree and the seed is appropriate, inasmuch as the new law as stated in the Matthean beatitudes is a more profound understanding of the old law as stated in the Mosaic decalogue. The latter was concerned with the external aspects of behavior; the former extends also to the internal aspects, the motives and intentions of the doer. The interior aspect might then be expected to grow out of the exterior in the course of time and thought, as a tree grows out of its seed; but the comparison still seems a bit forced. Thomas obviously did not reflect on the difference in relationship between, on the one hand, the seed and the tree (or the child and the adult) and, on the other hand, the general and the special.

THE RESTORED IMAGE

In the holy creature the image of God is restored and completed. Indeed, although Aquinas does not explicitly so describe or amplify it, the new creature implies a threefold image of the Trinity. The image appears in the creature's *esse* and *operationes* first at the natural level; then it is reduplicated at the level of grace and glory; and finally it is seen in the progression through the three stages.

First there is the natural image. In its *ESSE* this means universally the *modus-species-ordo* as the co-essential reflection of the Father, Son, and Holy Spirit. In the rational creature it means specifically the mental functions of *memory,* from which knowledge arises, *intellect,* in which knowledge is formed, and *will,* in which knowledge is related to its origin and end. Knowledge arises from memory and is reunited to memory by love, just as the Son proceeds from the Father and is united to Him in the Love which is the Holy Spirit. The image appears again in the creature's *operations,* as is indicated in the ternary of potentiality, habit, and act. The operations arise out of potentiality, are formed in the habit, and reach their fulfillment in the ordered act. Or again, with regard to the acquired habits, out of the abundance of possible, isolated, individual acts arise the habits which give them form, and out of the habits proceed ordered acts. The ordered act (like the Holy Spirit) presupposes the habit (the Son, the Word) as well as the plenitude of potential acts (the Father, the *Principium principiorum*).

Secondly, there is the image of grace. It includes not only the natural image, healed of its distortion, but the addition of the *dona* to each of the image's parts. The knowledge of the intellect embraces more, the will can attain more, and the memory has not only its own storehouse from which to form knowledge but also the fullness of divine wisdom. Upon natural memory, intellect, and will is built, as it were, a second story of grace. Moreover, the *modus-species-ordo* ternary is repeated on a higher level as the preparation for grace, the reception of grace, and the working out of grace. The *ESSE* of the image of grace thus reduplicates the natural image at a higher level. Furthermore, the operations of the new creature similarly exhibit the expanded image of the Triune Creator. In the working of acts meritorious of eternal life, there are the theological *virtues* as sources of power for those acts, there are the *gifts* as the forms of the virtues, and there are the meritorious *operations* themselves. The virtues are the principles of the acts, as the Father is the principle of the processions of the Son and Holy Spirit; the gifts are the formations of the acts as the Son is the form of God's gracious nature; the operations themselves are the expression of the gifts, as the Holy Spirit is the expression of the Son.

Thirdly, there is a Trinitarian reflection even in the interrelations of the stages from nature to grace. The Father is the cause of creation and the Son is its sufficient representation; the Son is the author of new creation and the Holy Spirit is its sufficient index. Thus the stages of temporal development themselves reflect the Trinitarian divine life. Not only creation viewed as a fixed cosmos, or new creation seen in itself against the background of God's grace, but the progression from creation to new creation is itself a Trinitarian progression. The age of the Old Testament was under the especial aegis of the *Father and the Son,* whereas that of the New Testament is under that of the *Son and the Holy Spirit.* The special working of the Father is placed at the beginning of creation; the special working of the Son is placed at the beginning of new creation; and the special working of the Holy Spirit is in the new creation which culminates in the state of glory. The world comes from God and returns to God under the guidance of the Trinitarian Persons. Thus, both in his nature and in his new nature as well as in his history, man reflects the Trinitarian life.

These levels of the image and their interrelations can be clearly seen in the following diagram:

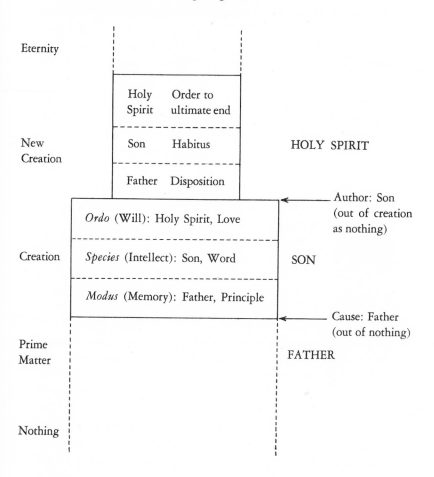

Two creations complete the image, just as two laws are the temporal expression of the one eternal law. The first comes from the Father, the second from the Son. But the question arises why *two* laws suffice to express the Trinity. Should there not be a third, given by the Holy Spirit? Should there not be a third and last creation? Why does the movement cease after two? The answer to these questions is contained in the nature of the inner-Trinitarian relations, of the "generation" of the Son and the "spiration" of the Holy Spirit. These are best developed in an article of the *Summa Theologiae* which has—for whatever reason—been largely neglected in the literature on Thomas.[14] He here makes a distinction between the "essential" and the "notional" relations expressed in the processions of the intellect and the will. The meaning of that distinction can best be clarified, I believe, by substituting two grammatical terms and using two pairs of brief sentences for illustration. Consider the relation between the verb and the object in the following:

> X knows something—X speaks a word;
> X loves something—X loves (a love).

In the first half of each of these pairs, the accusative is an objective one, whereas in the second half it is an internal one. That is to say, the word, "speaking," already implies that that which is produced is a word. And (this is the point Thomas seeks to make) there must be a parallel internal accusative in the procession of love, in addition to the objective accusative, so that the act of loving already implies that that which is produced is love. Just as the word (whether used of an unspoken intellectual conception or of a spoken or written word is of no import here) incorporates the object in a kind of intelligible similitude (the internal accusative), so "love" as an internal accusative is the bearer of the object in a kind of impressed inclination or affection, a *complacentia impressa*. The relation expressed by the internal accusative is the "notional" one; that which is expressed in the objective accusative is the "essential" one. The notional draws out something already immanent in the verb; the essential adds something which is not otherwise there.

14. I.37.1; cf. also *CG* IV.19.

Now, applying this distinction to the processions within the Trinity, we find that the following relations appear between the Son as Word and the Holy Spirit as Love over against the Father as the Principle of both:

	The word:	so used:	denotes:
PROCESSION OF THE INTELLECT	*intelligere* (to know)	essentially	the relation of the understander to the understood;*
	verbum (word)	personally	that which proceeds (in the Trinity, the Son as Word);
	dicere (to speak: produce the word)	notionally	the relation of the principle to the word itself;**
PROCESSION OF THE WILL	*diligere, amare* (to love)	essentially	the relation of the lover to the loved;*
	amor (love)	personally	that which proceeds (the Holy Spirit as Love);
	diligere, amare (to love, i.e., to "spirate" love)	notionally	the relation of the principle of love to love itself.**

*Grammatically, objective accusative in relation to the subject of the verb.
**Grammatically, internal accusative in relation to the subject of the verb.

Thus, the inner life of God as His knowing and loving of Himself implies the threefold movement and the three Persons—the knower (lover), the word, and love. The restriction, moreover, of God's immanent relations to those of knowing and loving depends on the fact that these are the only acts which do not "pass over into an external effect" but remain in themselves.

In his analysis of the two processions as shown above, Thomas does the same kind of reduplicating as in his rationale of creation and new creation. The procession of the Holy Spirit has the same structure as that of the Son as Word (1.37.1). He admits that, because the intellectual procession is "more known" to us, more proper words have been found to distinguish its elements than is the case with the procession of the will. Why the former is more known than the latter he does not say. But whatever the reason, we have two separate words to designate the essential and notional relations in the intellectual procession. In the volitional we have only one word serving both purposes, which makes it necessary to paraphrase.

In the two processions of the Trinity one sees the same structure and superstructure as in the two creations. But that is just one side of the picture. The Holy Spirit is indeed "according to origin" a *third* person. That would make it seem as if He ought to create something also—a third creation. Yet He is the bond of unity, the Love with which the Father and the Son love each other, and as that bond He is not a *tertium* but a *medius nexus* related to both the Father and the Son. He does not have His own creation because His proper function is to terminate and unite the work of the Father and Son, creation and new creation.

Indeed, it is in the nature of love as well as of spirit, both being a "motive and unitive force," to have this twofold character in Thomas' thought: on the one hand a kind of superstructure to the Word and on the other hand the invisible bond which unites the Word to its Principle. And because the new creation advances under the special banner of the Holy Spirit as Love, it too has

that twofold character: on the one hand appearing as a reduplication of nature but on the other hand being the reuniting of the
creature with the Creator as its *ultimus finis*. Sometimes these two
aspects function complementarily, as in the conception of free
will. Sometimes they pull apart and tend toward isolation, as
when in the Trinitarian doctrine Thomas treats the Persons as
three equally powerful people and comments that the Holy Spirit
or the Father might have assumed human form just as well as the
Son (III.3.5). The same tension is found in the doctrine of grace,
when Thomas finds in the ecclesiastical structure the undiluted
presence of the new creation superimposed upon the political and
social structure. Still the two poles never actually become separated, neither in the Trinitarian part nor in the whole of his nature-
and-grace doctrine. It remained for subsequent theologians and
philosophers to sense an irreconcilability and to bring about a
divorce.

When Thomas speaks of the ultimate meaning of new creation
and of the Holy Spirit's procession, he tends to employ the concept
of the *medius nexus,* the uniting of the creature with its ultimate
end and principle. He emphasizes then the intimacy in the union
of love which is lacking in the union of cognition (for example,
II.ii.23.6 *ad* 1). However, when he analyzes the rationale of new
creation or of the Holy Spirit's procession, he has recourse to the
superstructure which is a reduplication of the created structure.
Yet he does not far pursue that fugitive *complacentia impressa,*
which is to be a parallel in the will to the intelligible species in
the intellect, nor does he make any systematic use of it. It appears
on the scene in the Trinitarian discussion indirectly, demanded
by a specific question, but it departs abruptly and remains in the
shadowy background.

So the "image of God" sustains a reciprocal movement: because
he is made in the image of God, man can rise from a knowledge
of creation to a knowledge of the Creator—at the level of nature
and natural knowledge as well as of grace and new knowledge.

But having arrived at that dim knowledge of the Creator, he can turn back and look upon himself illuminated *sub specie aeternitatis*. His psychic faculties of knowing and willing are a clue to the inner life of God; the Trinitarian processions illuminate in turn man's psychic functions. Thus, man is by his very constitution partially equipped to translate his knowledge into the original of divine knowledge and to let that in turn illuminate the natural knowledge once more. He understands God by understanding himself; and he understands himself fully only by understanding God.

CHAPTER V

The Dialectic of the Court:
Gerhard's Rationale of the New Creation

In Chapters II and III we have sought to display the extensive similarity between Thomas' and Gerhard's views of man's nature. We should expect to find the same similarity regarding the new creation. Yet the expectation is not fulfilled. Gerhard does state, "Scripture testifies that two chief and greatest works (to which all others can be referred in a definite order and manner) were performed by God in time; namely, the creation of the whole universe and the restoration of the human race" (v.5). But he never develops a superstructure of grace like that of Thomas.

It is not the case here, as it was with regard to the conception of man's nature, that in spite of a widespread agreement there are points of disagreement attributable to the difference between a formal-objective and a dialectical-personal mode of conceptualization. On the contrary, the superstructure of grace does not fit anywhere.

Gerhard did not explicitly reject the validity of such a superstructure. At any number of places he makes statements and uses phraseology that would have enabled him, had he so wished, to proceed without much difficulty or inconsistency to an exposition of the nature and capacities of the new man. Had he done so, it is difficult to imagine how he could have concluded with anything greatly different from that of the Angelic Doctor. He speaks, for example, of the *novae qualitates,* of the *novus homo,* the *nova* and *altera creatio,* of *supernaturalia dona,* of the *novae donatae vires,* the "new powers by which man can assent to the call of the Holy Spirit," of *novi motus,* and of the cooperation with God made possible by those new qualities.[1] In conversion, he says in summary form, the Holy Spirit "makes the unwilling willing, that is, to those who by nature refuse, and cannot but refuse, he gives the capacity (*facultas*) so that by grace they can and truly do will it . . ."; the human will cannot "act . . . by its natural powers, though it can and does act by these new powers bestowed by God" (XI.81).

His viewpoint does not deny, he maintains (XI.69), that the "will freed from the yoke of sin cooperates by the new power given by the Holy Spirit" "because the Holy Spirit lights a new light in the mind and bestows new powers on the will so that the will in this state is no longer helpless but, through the new powers, cooperates with the Holy Spirit" (XI.141).

If there is a new faculty of willing, a new set of donated powers, and new knowledge; if, furthermore, these new qualities are the principles of actions[2]—then we certainly have the essential elements of the Thomistic superstructure of grace. Yet however many time he approaches it, Gerhard never completes the development. How are we to account for this?

Surely part of the answer lies in the fact that in Gerhard the dialectical rationale is most prominent precisely in those questions which relate to man's ultimate destiny. One can speak of the new powers, but not undertake to examine their structure.

---

1. See e.g. VIII.23; 36; 79. XI.36; 42; 57; 69; 72. XVI.247; 197.
2. XI.72: "Haec renovatio, quia non statim perfecta est, sed quotidie crescit, donec in aeterna vita perficiatur . . ."; XVI.232: "Renovatio . . . est principium actionum."

Indeed, even to undertake an exposition of them would seem to deflect attention from the proper object.

In other words (and this is the second part of the answer), Gerhard's attention is wholly concentrated on the transitional point between the fallen creation and the new creation. This point is called the "article of justification," which he expounds with a moving insistence—but only in a dialectical-personal rationale. For the article of justification refers to the criterion of theology *in use* as it brings hearers into real contact with the condemning and absolving God. This confrontation is the means by which God creates the new man. It is, therefore, not only central, but the condition *sine qua non* of the new creation.

Not the question: "What is the new creation?" but the question: "How does one articulate the transition so as to bring the hearer into direct confrontation with the voice of God?" is the question which preoccupies Gerhard. He does not deny the new powers nor the new character of the regenerated man. But he does insist that they be kept carefully distinguished from the article of justification. To distinguish faith and works and to assign to each its own is not the same as separating the two, and "to remove works from the act of justification is not the same as eliminating them from the justified man or exterminating them completely in the domain of the church" (XVII.1).

Again: "Although we are justified through faith without works and hence works are to be kept out of the area of justification, still the true and living faith through which we are justified is not without works since the benefits of justification and sanctification, regeneration and renovation, are always joined by a permanent and indissoluble bond" (XVII.1). It is, in other words, the act of justification, not sanctification, regeneration, not renovation, which claims his interest in the controversy with the earlier scholastics. But the justification of which he speaks, as the contrasting pairs above indicate, is not the "justification" of Thomas or, for that matter, of Bellarmine. In Thomistic thought, justification includes what Gerhard distinguishes as justification and sanctification. Thomas' *justificare* comprises not only the act through which God bestows his redeeming grace and *in principle* creates a new man, but also the process in which this new principle is actually realized in the concrete life of the redeemed. Sometimes, of course, especially in his commentaries on the New Testament books, Aquinas does use the word in the restricted sense; but its connotation is usually more inclusive. If we wish to compare the two theologians specifically regarding their rationale of the *transitional point* between creation and new creation, then we must do so by means of Gerhard's "article of justification" and Thomas' conception of the participation of the free will in the act of conversion, in which God moves the self-moving will. Gerhard, to be sure, retains a positive understanding of the participation of the human will in conversion (just as Thomas retains a more restricted use of "justification"), but such a formulation as that *the will moves itself as God moves it* is anathema to him. There is nothing in his utterances which would prevent his saying just that. Indeed, he does bring himself to say that, by confidence in God's mercy, "the human heart raises itself (*sese erigit*)" (xv.40). But for the most part he abides by phrases such as that God confers a new faculty of willing, and makes of the unwilling a willing heart. He thereby glides over the conceptual difficulty inherent in this voluntary act; and he has, as it were, repressed the paradoxical nature the act had in Thomas.

The Thomistic notion of the conversion of the free will is no less paradoxical than the Gerhardian conception of justification; but it is so in relation to the formal ascription of agency to an act. Gerhard does not find the formal rationale significant enough to be used in relation to man's critical position before God. It does not have the creative power that the dialectical-personal language of justification has. Thus, the article of justification embedded in the dialectic of a courtroom imagery is the center of his account of the transition. In this article, Gerhard, with his

vast biblical erudition, carries forth in all its religious vitality
the theological principle distinctively expressed by the Protestant
Reformers. Thomas' view of man provides a conspectus of the
whole field from nature to supernature; along the way it includes
the paradoxical point of transition, the conversion of the free will.
Thomas seeks to illuminate all points equally. Gerhard's view
continually reverts to the transitional point, and other points are
completely subordinate to it in importance.

In comparing Gerhard with Thomas concerning the conception of the new creation, I shall focus on three problems which
will disclose the extent and nature of the convergence and divergence of the two views. Those three areas are, in turn: the free
will (where Thomas had located the paradox of his formal rationale), forensic justification (where Gerhard locates the paradox
of his dialectical rationale), and the relationship of law and gospel
as replacing that of the old and new law (where the contrast
between Thomas and Gerhard is illustrated in a single problem).

FREE WILL

Gerhard's treatise on the free will (*Locus* XI) shows more clearly
than anything else how great was the agreement between his
position and that of his Roman opponents, as well as, by implication, that of Thomas. The treatise will serve, therefore, as an
excellent introduction to the other issues involved in the conception of the new creation.

Not only does this *locus* show the degree of substantive agreement, it also shows progress in the formal articulation of the
meaning of free will, the *libertas arbitrii* or the *liberum arbitrium*.
Virtually all of the ambiguities still present in Thomas' remarks
have been eliminated, as one would expect from the theological
discussion of the intervening centuries. The progress was not an
unqualified gain. It meant that one had to decide in favor of a
part of Thomas and against another part (and there was no clear

criterion in Thomas himself by which to make the decision) and that along with the removal of ambiguity went the removal of the genuinely paradoxical. We find, thus, that Gerhard sought to eliminate not just the ambiguities but also the paradoxical use of this concept. In so doing he crippled its functioning as the point at which God's movement and man's volition are paradoxically coterminous. What was for Thomas the interpenetration of the divine and human has become by Gerhard's time the *alternative* between the divine and the human. The result is that the transition to the new creation can be conceived as a justification through faith but not as a conversion of the free will. For a doctrine of the free will, even when correctly formulated, is still ambiguous and insufficient according to the criterion which Gerhard employs, namely, that the central doctrine must have the power of negating the self-evaluation of the despairing or the complacent man. To the details of this divergence from Thomas we shall turn in the following paragraphs.

Gerhard himself observes that there seems to be basic unanimity between his view and that of Bellarmine (and Thomas), especially since he can read in Bellarmine the explanation that in a good work (such as conversion) "God does all and man does all (*totum facit Deus et totum facit homo*)"[3]—an explanation which conveys the way in which Thomistic theology broke through the view of the divine and human agency as exclusive alternatives. What he opposes is not the fundamental intention of this Thomistic view, but the dangerously misleading way of formulating that intention. It is misleading because it—"in the sense in which Bellarmine asserts it" (XVII.102)—does not clearly repudiate every trace of Pelagianism. Thus, a number of times (e.g., XI.39 f.), after stating his position, Gerhard concludes, "Bellarmine himself seems to recognize this." Moreover, he can cite Thomas in support of his non-Pelagian view of the natural

---

3. *De just.* v.4; quoted by Gerhard XVII.102.

capacity of the free will.[4] But he labels "insidious" some of Bellarmine's formulations, not necessarily because they are false, but because they are so readily misleading. "It is insidious to say that a man before his rebirth can, through his free will, with God's assistance, be freed from sin; for if that is understood to mean that the assistance of God arouses the dormant powers of the free will—so that the grace of God and the will of man become equal causes (*causae sociae*) of conversion—it is false; but if it is explained to mean that man is different from a brute in this that even after the fall he is endowed with a will in which the grace of conversion resides (*cadere*) as in a subject—something which cannot happen in beasts—then it is a correct assertion" (XI.38). If the insistence upon the participation of the free will in conversion means that man is converted specifically in his manhood, Gerhard has no objection to the doctrine; but the "if" seems ineradicable.

Exactly the same objection applies to the talk about man's natural "remote and imperfect power to do works of piety." Not that this doctrine is wrong but, because of the ambiguity of its meaning, it can be insidiously misleading:

> That talk about the remote power [of the natural will] labors under an ambiguity that necessarily needs explanation. For if one understands by "remote power" that passive capacity and aptitude by which man, whose will is endowed with natural power of willing and not willing, can be converted and is capable of justification (a power or capacity of a kind that is not found in a dumb log or in demons confirmed in evil), we concede that such a remote power for conversion remains in man. (XI.54)

Only if one takes *potentia* in an active sense (however imperfect that activity be regarded), as Bellarmine may do, is this a doctrine which must be regarded as Pelagian. Similarly Gerhard finds

4. *De ver.* 24; *S. Th.* II.i.189.3.

remnants of Pelagianism in the scholastic notion of *meritum de congruo* (XI.51) and in formulations which make the activity of grace an "exciting" of the free will or a "rousing" of its powers or an external aid (*adjutorium*). From this last expression, though it too could be understood rightly (XI.68), he surmises that Bellarmine conceives the aid of grace as an external and supplementary impulse. "It appears that Bellarmine understands by the *adjutorium gratiae* not, so to speak, an interior change of the will but only an external assistance of grace which is necessary for laying bare its natural powers" (XI.72). He finds grounds for this judgment in the fact that Bellarmine compares the aid of grace to the light which is necessary for seeing, "that is, to disclose the hidden power of sight which was in the first act" (ibid.). However, because of the way in which it was used in Augustinian and Thomistic theology, this simile would in itself hardly provide grounds sufficient to support Gerhard's accusation; Bellarmine too knew his church Fathers. The image of turning to the sun does not have as its scope the externality of the sun's light, but rather its status as the presupposition of all sight. God is the presupposition of man's activity as much as the sunlight is of his seeing.[5] Sunlight is the presupposition but not the object of vision, just as God's assistance is that which qualifies human activity rather than a separate initial act. Gerhard may, therefore, be misinterpreting Bellarmine, but the misinterpretation itself discloses that the reason for his hesitation concerning such formulations is his suspicion that Roman theology had not actually eliminated the possibility of interpreting the capacity of the will in a Pelagian fashion.

His chief contention, therefore, against the *pontificii* and the Council of Trent is that they have misrepresented the Reformation doctrine of the free will. Consequently they have not issued a forthright repudiation of every possible semi-Pelagian view.

5. Cf. Thomas II.ii.4.4 *ad* 3.

Concerning the Council of Trent (session VI, canons Two to Five), he declares:

> The Council of Trent insidiously obscures (*involvit*) the true status of the controversy since the question has to do not with the will itself, nor with the freedom of the will from coercion, nor with any of its liberty with regard to externals, nor with the freedom of the restored will, but with its power to perform spiritual actions: whether it has that power of itself so that it can before its renovation cooperate with prevenient grace. And this the Council of Trent does not reject. . . . (XI.52)

Therefore "away with those dark accusations leveled by Bellarmine against our churches" (XI.8).

Thus the "true status of the question"[6] must be delimited in somewhat the following way, in negative and positive fashion. The controversy does *not* have to do with understanding the capacity of man's free will in the state of integrity, nor in the state of new obedience, nor in the state of glory. On these points the opponents were agreed. Man in his integrity was able to fully know and spontaneously will what was good, and to render perfect obedience, but he was also able not to do so; man in the state of new obedience, as reborn or renewed, has the capacity to perform the spiritual good in part, as he can perform it fully in the state of glory. The controversy *does* have to do with an understanding of man's capacity before and in the conversion from the state of fallenness to the state of renewal. It has to do not with the general picture of creation and new creation but specifically with the nature of the transition between the two.

Furthermore, it does *not* have to do with the essence of the will (whether it still *freely* wills its object) or with the participation of the will and intellect in the conversion itself, but with the nature of the object of fallen man's will. In spite of the fall,

6. Cf. XI.32, where he defines the *status controversiae* in nine points.

Gerhard agrees, man is still man, a rational creature whose endowment of free will distinguishes him specially from the animal world. The free will, as involving both intellect and will, participates in conversion precisely as free will. An act of cognition and an act of voluntary assent, together constituting the free will, are included in conversion: "nor does divine providence either annul or exclude this freedom of the human will; for it administers things in such a way that allows them their proper motions" (XI.9). The controversy, however, *does* have to do with the source and nature of that participation of the free will in conversion. Is the will capable of such movement "by nature" or must it await the new endowment which God gives as He converts? Are the movements of cognition and assent effects of the human will or of divine grace? Gerhard affirms the latter, and chides his opponent for not clearly repudiating the former. In the work of conversion "there is a concurrence of God in converting and man in being converted" (XI.33). There is no dispute about that. But what does God do and what does man do in this concurrence? What do the intellect and the will with their fallen powers contribute to the conversion? The controversy has to do with the answer to this question.

Finally, the controversy has to do with the question not of whether the will is capable of any good at all, but whether it is capable of "spiritual" good by its natural powers. "The whole question concerns freedom in respect to the object with which the will is occupied, that is, the freedom of righteousness (*rectitudo*), whether man after the fall is still furnished with power to perform good or evil equally" (XI.32). There is no dispute about man's capacity for doing "moral, political, or domestic" good. Through self-discipline or through discipline from the established powers, man can avoid acts of gross misbehavior and learn to lead an exemplary life; indeed, he can even read and listen to the word of God. But can he freely will the "spiritual" good which comes from acting with pure interior motives? Can

158

he hear and read the word of God "spiritually"? Is he indifferently disposed to the objectively evil as well as the objectively good, equally capable of choosing the one or the other? The negative answer to these questions is the theme which Gerhard expands in his treatise on the free will.

The preceding summary of the status of the controversy suggests that the concept of free will has, in Gerhard's thinking, lost virtually all of the dialectical and paradoxical functions which it had in the Thomistic use. The spiritual good and the rational ("philosophical") good, or—to use his other terms, taken from Luther—the hemisphere above and the hemisphere below, have been placed into separate classes. In the movement of the will it is not a question of interpenetration of the divine and human but of separate alternatives: the movement is either of God or of man.

Furthermore, the question of the relation of the civil good to the spiritual good is nowhere in the present *locus* decisively set forth. In what sense can they both be called good? If the civil good is a good which cannot survive God's final judgment, it must in some ultimate sense be not-good. But then what is the relation between the ultimate judgment and the proximate judgment upon the act of good? These problems do not trouble Gerhard at this point. He tacitly, on the one hand, accepts the ultimate good as having the characteristics of the civil good *and also* some others (the external propriety *and also* the interior motive, the hearing *and also* the inner assent), and, on the other hand, treats the civil good in conversion as *simpliciter* not-good, which indicates how formalized his sketch of the "good" has become. The profundity of the Reformation understanding of good and evil is to be found not here but in the exposition of the meaning of justification. There one finds the depth of the relation between the proximate and ultimate good.

Thus, with regard to the initiative in the act of the free will, Gerhard conceives the alternatives as, on the one hand, the grace of God and the will of man as coordinate causes (*causae sociae*) of conversion and, on the other hand, the human will as that empty subject into which the grace of conversion can come. (Logically there is, of course, the third possibility that the will is completely the originator, the *causa sola,* of its own acts; but such a possibility did not play into the controversy at all.) Similarly, with regard to the object of the will's movement, the alternatives are, on the one hand, the civil good which is external and this-worldly and, on the other hand, the spiritual good which is internal and other-worldly. In each case the distinction is made by separating the spheres in which a term is applicable—that is to say, by treating them as different genera.

Every such classification, however, falls into the Pelagian error, except the classification according to which the "philosophical" good and human agency are completely excluded from the spiritual good and divine agency. If you speak of the joint activity of man's will and God's grace, you must mean a sharing in it, either equally or in some other proportion. But whatever proportion you assign, you fall into the Pelagian error. Similarly, if you classify the philosophic and the spiritual as really and in the same generic sense good, you have not excluded Pelagianism as clearly as Gerhard wants it done.

The formalized nature of the rationale of this *locus* on the free will shows itself not only in the passing references which indicate how Gerhard conceived the alternatives. It appears also in the positive content of his doctrine on the free will. If the participation of the will in conversion is not its joint activity with God's grace; but if, at the same time, it is the will which somehow participates—the only possibility left is to conceive the will as similar to an empty frame into which God places (one is tempted to say, infuses) a new faculty of will. It is then still formally the will, but materially its powers are different.[7] The human will is

7. Cf. XI.40: "Vitalem illam vim, qua homo in conversione salutariter utitur, non excitat Spiritus s. quasi jam ante in homine delitescentem, sed plane de novo confert."

thus a *subjectum pathētikon* but not a *vis activa* or *energētikē*, a passive capacity but not an active one. "Of himself, man [after the fall] cannot soften and receive the tenderness of grace but requires that divine grace remove the inborn hardness and grant new powers for embracing the good, and that a new heart and new spirit be thus created" (XI.39).

The natural powers of the will would thus seem to be simply replaced by the new powers; grace is substituted for nature. The "natural" and the "new" *seem* to be effectively separated, without overlapping or fusion. Yet had he pressed on, Gerhard would have been led to raise the question concerning the characteristic of spontaneity which does carry over from the natural to the new. There must be a generic continuity unless the spontaneity of the new volition is the opposite of the spontaneity of the natural volition. In such a case, however, the whole rationale would be destroyed. So Gerhard's formalized description hides deeper problems beneath its smooth surface; it is not adequate for a doctrine of "justification," where such problems do emerge.

What, then, is the free will? Gerhard explicates his understanding neatly and in detail. At the same time his conception of a *subjectum pathētikon* avoids a great problem which Thomas' conception attempts to solve; namely, since it is a characteristic of the will to be self-originating and self-imperative, something of its voluntariness is lost if one conceives of the will as an empty receptacle for new volitional powers. The *liberum arbitrium,* or the *libertas arbitrii* (Gerhard uses the expressions interchangeably), is a faculty which is distinctively human. It involves both the intellectual and the volitional part of man's reason. The *arbitrium* pertains specifically to the intellect, the *liberum* to the will. Any act of the free will is, therefore, a mixture of the two. The relation of the two in the mixture is that of the antecedent (*praevium*) and the *complementum* (*formale*): "the judgment of the mind is as the antecedent, the choice adds the complement and formal element to this freedom" (XI.3). The judgment that something is good precedes the willing of that good, logically if not temporally; it is the ultimate disposition to the form. But it is participation of the will that makes the act a free one. Thus, Gerhard quotes with approval the definition of Thomas (1.83.3) that the free will is "a faculty of mind and will" but that "it inclines to the (rational) appetite." The proper definition of the freedom of the will is, Gerhard agrees, the way to resolve a major difficulty. For, as Augustine put it, when one defends free will, one seems to deny God's grace; when one defends God's grace, one seems to deny free will. Gerhard undertakes that definition.

There are two respects according to which the term can be defined: first by the manner of acting (*modus agendi*) and secondly by the object to which the will can direct itself. As to the former, the will is free; as to the latter it is free only to choose evil—and in that sense no longer really free.

There are two essential characteristics of freedom in the *modus agendi*. A free act is one which does not originate in external coercion or violence and one which is not the result of natural instinct alone. Positively, it is an action in which the will "spontaneously, or moved by internal principle, either embraces or rejects something" (XI.4). In this sense, to say that an act is voluntary is synonymous with saying that it is free; and to speak of something which is voluntary but not free is as self-contradictory as to speak of something which is hot but has no heat (*si quis dicere velit calidum absque calore*). In one phrase, the essence of the free will lies in this freedom from compulsion (*libertas a coactione*), whether the compulsion be external physical force or the force of animal instinct. An action in which the good is done consciously and because it is known to be good would be a free act in Gerhard's understanding.

Freedom from compulsion is not, however, equivalent to license (*libertas a jure, ab obligatione*). "True liberty . . . is to serve goodness (*justitia*)," for to disregard the norms of good or to act "without a guiding knowledge and binding order" is not freedom but brutal license.

The question, then, is whether, in its manner of acting, the will is always free, even in its fallen state. Gerhard holds that it is. When we come to the *object* rather than the *mode* of acting, the question is whether the will freely (i.e. without coercion) chooses things which are objectively good or objectively evil. What it does choose is, of course, in some sense good (since the object of the will is by definition the good); but the question is whether that which the mind has judged to be good and which the will has freely chosen is *in fact really* good. The answer here varies with man's state.

For the state of integrity, Gerhard and Thomas are agreed on the extent of the subjective (*modus agendi*) as well as the objective freedom of the will. Man could know and will what was good, and what he knew to be good was in fact good. In the fallen state, how much of that freedom has been lost? Gerhard's answer does not coincide with Thomas'. It is more detailed and has removed the paradoxical element. If freedom from compulsion is essential to the voluntariness of an act and if the capacity for voluntary action is an essential characteristic of man, then man must have this freedom of action even in his fallen state. "This liberty, since it is a natural and essential property endowed by God, has not been lost through the fall. *Substantia hominis non periit*" (XI.6). The subjective aspect of freedom remains.

With the objective side the case is different (XI.16–31). Whereas original man was poised between good and evil, able to sin or not to sin (*posse peccare et non peccare*), fallen man cannot but sin (*non potest non peccare*). That is to say, he cannot will what is objectively good, and he cannot but will what is objectively evil. The difference between that original freedom and this present freedom is the difference between "freedom from bondage and misery" and "freedom from rectitude (*justitia*)." Man is now not free from the bondage to sin. Before the fall "man had not yet given himself up to the tyrant of sin" (XI.20). The present state is one of freedom from righteousness "by which it is brought about that the spoiled human will freely and spontaneously is drawn only to the evil" (XI.24). The present freedom is linked with bondage to sin. "The freedom of will stands side by side with (*consistit cum*) the bondage of sin, for man sins and cannot but sin; yet he sins freely and sinning delights him. Although he is drawn only to evil, he chooses it freely—that is, of himself and spontaneously, not unwillingly or by force. . . . Besides that he employs a certain freedom even in the selection of evils" (XI.29). The mind errs in its judgment concerning the good, the will errs in its love. Even if the mind should judge rightly, "still the will divorces itself from the intellect and unites with the immoral feelings and follows their leadership" (XI.30).[8] The freedom which man now has is a freedom which enslaves. It is still freedom, a "lesser freedom" in contrast to the "greater freedom," which is "freedom from misery or servitude." The supreme freedom is that of God, who cannot will evil. The freedom next in rank and greater than in prelapsarian man is that of the angels because they have been confirmed in the good and "cannot will what is not good (*non possunt non bonum velle*)." "The highest liberty is not to be able to be miserable, the highest happiness not to be able to be unhappy" (XI.28).

Everything which man in the fallen state does is sin, that is, a transgression of the law of God. However, the law of God is to

8. Cf. XI.118: "Infirmitas intellectus et voluntatis, quia ipsae illae naturales vires adhuc reliquae in mente et voluntate hominis misere sunt infirmatae, ac languor ille et stupor virium animae peccato originali maxime debilitatarum, vario ac multa humanae voluntati impedimenta objicit. Hinc in consiliis saepe erramus, etiamsi omnes ingenii nervos intendamus et bonum finem propositum habeamus." "Vehementia atque impetus affectuum saepe tantus est, ut instar torrentis voluntatem secum abripiant, et judicium rationis intervertant, et tunc 'fertur equis auriga, nec audit currus habenas.' Hinc illud Medeae: 'Aliudque cupido, / mens aliud suadet, video meliora proboque, / deteriora sequor.' Hinc etiam philosophus disputat 7. Eth. 3, quod 'homines saepe faciant ea quae sciunt esse vitiosa.'"

Gerhard not essentially a code for guiding behavior (though it is partly that) but the articulation of God's will, which provides man with his *opportunity of expressing trust* in his Creator. Thus what man does is evil, not in the sense that every aspect of it is absolutely vicious, but in that it always falls short of being a *perfect* expression of confidence in God. It is, therefore, man's self-assertion against the law of his Creator. This evil is also objectively evil because its ultimate result is the opposite of its intention, the destruction of the man who asserts himself.

The conception which emerges from Gerhard's discussion of the freedom and bondage of the will in fallen creation appears at first to be not paradoxical but self-contradictory. The contradiction then appears to be removed by a formal classification or, as it were, stratification of its terms. Thus, we are met with the following contradictions: (1) on the one hand fallen man can do only evil. Even where he may know what is good, his will follows the path of evil lust against his better judgment. On the other hand, however, he can do some things which are good: he can keep his *externa membra* subject to the rule of reason and can do many acts of civic justice.[9] (2) On the one hand, fallen man is able to do good things, acts which judged objectively are morally good rather than evil (XI.113). On the other hand these morally good acts are not "truly pleasing" to God. Every good pleases God, but man's moral good does not.

How are we to bring the two sides together? Does everyone (in Gerhard's thinking), when confronted with a choice between murder or friendship, always choose murder if he is not restrained by civil law? Certainly not. Is not the action of the man who refrains from murder more pleasing to God than the action of the murderer? Certainly, yes. The problem hinges on the relation between what is "pleasing" and what is "truly pleasing (*vere placens*)" to God, between "knowing" and "truly knowing," between "living" and "living according to the Spirit." But no clear

9. Cf. XI.32 (6) and 109 ff.

solution is offered in the *locus* on the free will. The relation which is here implied is quantitative, of more and less. What is truly pleasing to God is what is good morally *and also* spiritually. Knowing God truly is knowing that He is just, almighty, etc., *and also* that He is merciful.

In the light of the meaning of justification, however, we can say, negatively, that bondage to sin means not that every act is absolutely corrupt (if such a conception were even possible) but that no act is free of the taint of sin; it means not that every act is totally evil according to all standards of good and evil, but that every act *falls short of being totally good*. Man can do only evil, because everything he does is short of perfection. Man can do some good things, if "good" is restricted so as not to imply perfection. In the latter case, then, some acts can be said to be good because they are not absolutely evil; in the former case, all acts are said to be evil because they are not perfectly good.

Why it is, however, that the moral good, which in relation to the spiritual good is evil, can still be called good; or what the conditions are under which the rational good changes to evil; or why and in what sense it is that the additions of the "spiritual" amount to a negation of the moral and rational—these considerations we shall defer until we discuss the network of *loci* concerning justification.

In summary, the question which pertains to the act of conversion and man's participation in it is connected indissolubly with the taint of imperfection in all man's activities. Does he have by nature the power freely to overcome that taint? Or must the power be given him from elsewhere? In other words, does he of his own resources have the power to turn away and avoid the ultimate destruction which sin's bondage brings? Gerhard's answer is No. But so is that of Thomas and Bellarmine.

In the act of conversion man's will does nothing but receive. His will and his intellect have only a passive capacity and no active *energeia*. Gerhard, therefore, objects to conceiving the process of conversion as a waking or exciting of dormant powers. Man is *dead* in sin, not asleep. "Thus, just as a dead man can provide no help in the resuscitation of his body, so a man spiritually dead in sins cannot help in his spiritual resuscitation, that is, in conversion, illumination, regeneration, and renovation"; "the natural life itself is death in the sight of God" (XI.40).

If the analogy of rousing from sleep is used, as Gerhard himself does use it (XI.82), then it must be clearly noted that it is the power of the Holy Spirit, and no natural power, which wakes man *ex somno peccatorum,* from the sleep of sins. When the Holy Spirit issues commands, such as "Be converted!" "Awake, you who sleep!" these indicate "not what man can do but what God, by those efficacious admonitions, is able and willing to work in man" (XI.82). Thus, the words of Jesus to Lazarus to rise did not indicate what Lazarus was able to do of himself, nor that Lazarus was co-operator in the resuscitation, but rather that the *words of the command were themselves the power by which the command was fulfilled:* "to Christ and his life-giving word the whole work is attributed."

The power to resuscitate himself does not lie in natural man's capacities, for the removal of the taint of sin would mean the complete obedience to God with perfect knowledge and a perfect will. It is true that he still has a partial knowledge, but it is "weak and imperfect; reason knows a little part of the divine law, it can learn from the universal innate principles (*koinai ennoiai*) and the book of nature that God is, that He is just, wise, etc." (XI.65). But that partial knowledge, as well as the partially ordered will, is enmity against God because it is imperfect. "Therefore even though the mind of man forms for itself thoughts which in its opinion are sufficiently excellent, still in God's judgment they are vain" (XI.34; cf. 35–37). The will cannot incline itself to God before conversion; it can only flee from God (XI.37).

How, then, is it that an imperfect knowledge can *coram Deo* be no knowledge, and an imperfect will be no good? How is it that what Gerhard himself calls the privation of the soundness, rather than the annihilation, of the powers of man (XI.32) can do nothing but lead him "to eternal death"? In a formal rationale it cannot, without destruction of the rationale itself. But in a dialectical rationale it can.

Gerhard objects to the Roman doctrine of free will because it seems to him to posit something in man's natural powers which enables him to turn himself to God. To his more formalized conception of the will, the dialectic of God-and-man in conversion can appear only as a joint activity of two powers, and Gerhard is intent upon excluding every active contribution of man. The whole work is to be attributed to God alone; man does nothing except be the receptacle for the new powers which God bestows; whatever cooperation there is comes after the conversion (XV.79). One can still speak of man as having free will, because what he does he does spontaneously and without external coercion; this is true of him in all states. The difference, however, between the regenerate and the natural is in the object; the former can will both the spiritual *and* the moral good; he can know the true mind of God and not only some characteristics of Him.

Here we are, therefore, on the threshold of Gerhard's doctrine of the justification of the sinner, the dialectical account of man's conversion and the paradoxical account of the relation of the righteousness of faith to the natural goodness of morality.

JUSTIFICATON: AS FORENSIC

In the treatise on the free will, the spiritual good appears to be something additional to the rational (moral, "philosophical") good. Yet there are indications that this *additum* has another character. It seems not only to supplement but to reverse. What shall we say is added when a person changes from mere "living" to "living according to the Spirit," or from "hearing" to "truly hearing" the voice of God in the gospel? Are new parts added to one's attitude? Are more powers added to the mind and will? If the natural mind knows that God is just and the spiritual mind knows that He is just and merciful, is the additional knowledge the same as, for example, knowing that B is an American and also that he is red-haired? The answers to these questions are given, at least implicitly, in the conception of justification as consisting "not in the infusion of a habit but in the free remission of sins and the imputation of the righteousness of Christ" (XI.42).

In Thomas, the "article of justification" does not cover the same ground as does the term, "justification." For Aquinas there is no radical distinction between the justification and the sanctification of the Christian. Bellarmine is, therefore, following a Thomistic lead when he insists that justification consists not only in the forgiveness of sins but also in the interior renovation.[10] Gerhard, to the contrary, makes it clear that "not everything that belongs to being a Christian belongs to justification" (XVI.157). To a genuine and unfeigned Christianity do indeed belong regeneration *and* renovation, faith *and* works, justification through faith *and* the fruit of justifying faith. Yet in the article of justification, the second half of each of these pairs is to be carefully excluded, for it is a consequence and not a part of justification. The act of justification itself is only that point of transition between the old and the new man. It consists (says Gerhard) "in a relation" rather than a quality of the man;[11] in the remission of sins rather than in the infusion of grace (XVI.2).

This restriction of the use of justification does not derive simply from Gerhard's desire to make the meaning of the term coincide with the meaning of biblical terms like *dikaioun* or *zadak* and their derivatives. He concedes that there is a variation in the

---

10. Quoted by Gerhard, XVI.232.
11. XVI.168. According to XVI.232 the "relatio seu *logismos* Dei" is the "justitia imputata," while the "justitia inchoata" is a "qualitas vel actio seu *energeia* in nobis."

usage of the terms (XVI.2; 3; 246). If we say, for example, that we are justified *by or before* the Lord, the word is "in the third conjugation and signifies that we are absolved or pronounced just." If we speak of our being justified *in* the Lord, the word is "in the first conjugation and signifies that we are in a positive sense just" (XVI.3). The restriction of the term's meaning is due rather to the *pre-eminent status of the forensic doctrine of justification as containing the theological criterion which is indispensable* for the church's proclamation, the "golden key" which opens or closes heaven (XVI.2). It is not a doctrine to be believed as a dogma; it is rather the criterion according to which the use of all dogmas is judged.[12]

That is the reason why he maintains untiringly and often repetitiously the distinction between justification and renovation. They differ, he says (XVI.232), in the following ways: *formally* (or essentially, *tō einai*), in that justification is the remission of sins and imputation of righteousness, whereas renovation is the "reduction of impure qualities to pure ones"; as to *subject,* in that the justice by which we are justified is rooted in Christ whereas the subject of renovation is the mind, will, affections, and all external members; as to *object,* in that justification looks toward Christ, renovation toward the law; as to *cause,* in that justification does not have a cause inherent in man, whereas renovation does have the will as its cause or principle of actions; as to *effects,* in that justification absolves man in the judgment of God, whereas renovation would do the opposite; as to *extent,* in that justification is an indivisible act (*actus adiairetos*), whereas renovation is divisible "for it is carried out in the course of time (*successive*) according to God's good pleasure."

Man can, of course, be considered from other viewpoints besides his continual falling short of perfection and disrupting his relation to God. He can be considered in his animal nature, or in

12. Cf. XVI.129, where Gerhard names the doctrine of justification among neither the principal nor the less principal dogmas of the church.

his rationality, or from other scientific viewpoints. But when he is considered in the most intimate presence of God, then the single relevant characteristic is not his rationality but his imperfection. The fact that he is not what he should be, a fact which is universal and beyond his capacity to correct, is the determinative factor of his ultimate standing.

In connection with justification, Gerhard, like Luther, "invariably viewed good works in the light of their imperfection and therefore in their incongruity with the grace of God."[13] In terms of the originally intended relationship to God, man has not rendered perfect obedience to the divine will as expressed in the divine law. In terms of everyday reality, this means that nothing he does or is reaches up to what it could and should have been. In relation to man's ultimate standing, Gerhard can thus assert that "good works are always perfectly good, evil works are perfectly evil" (XVII.116).

But where, in this world, does man find himself in that intimate presence of God? Gerhard would answer in the Reformation tradition: when the word of God is so proclaimed in a concrete situation that the hearer hears himself addressed in the depths of his being by the voice of God. Gerhard's conviction, as we shall see presently, is that the doctrine of forensic justification provides the basic "image" through which God thus speaks. For that reason it also provides the criterion for the use of other biblical material in the actual proclamation.

Thus, Gerhard's discussion of justification is motivated by the question of how to preserve the efficaciousness of the biblical message. How does one speak to man so that God Himself confronts him with judgment and mercy? Does a description of the free will do it? Does speaking of the infusion of grace as a new *habitus* do it? Gerhard answers these latter questions negatively. Such descriptions may not be false in a formal sense, but they do not concretely come to the hearer as the voice of God.

13. A. Ritschl, *Justification and Reconciliation*, pp. 137 f.

To tell the man who is condemned by his own guilt that he can act freely does not give him the power to overcome the stain of imperfection. He already knows he can act freely. He also knows that none of his free acts is pure. To speak to him of the infusion of grace misleads him into thinking his imperfection cannot be overcome until that infused grace has completely taken control of his life. This is, in effect, to address only God's condemnation to him.

Against this background Gerhard delimits justification as meaning, in principle and effect, the complete forgiveness of sins. First he establishes that justification is a *forensic* term. By this he means (as his proofs will presently show) that the doctrine of justification is tied to a courtroom scene. "Forensic justification" does not assert that in conversion something happens, as it were, exclusively in the distant mind of God, which has no transforming effects within the justified person. This misconception, which motivated the Council of Trent's condemnation of the doctrine and was called by various derogatory names by the polemicists— "the craziest insanity," by Andradius; "the ghost that haunts the Lutheran brain," by Stapleton; and, untranslatably, the *"mathematicum solifidianum commentum,"* by Rainold—is still to be found. Aubert, for example, calls it a doctrine which "reduces to nothing the personal part of man in the justificative process"[14] and makes of justification a matter of *foi-confiance* "independently of the practice of good works."[15] And Hans Küng[16] believes that Roman Catholic theology has underestimated the value of the biblical material on forensic justification because of its fear of being forced into accepting "the (allegedly) Lutheran concept of a *purely* forensic exoneration (*Rechtsprechung*)."

If such were indeed the meaning of Gerhard's forensic justification, then the accusation that the doctrine leads to ethical

14. *Le problème de l'acte de foi*, p. 76.
15. Ibid., p. 74. Cf. also Bouillard, *Conversion et grâce*, p. 222.
16. *Rechtfertigung*, p. 208.

anarchy or cynicism would be well grounded; then righteousness would indeed be, as Gerhard's opponents maintained, only "putative and imaginary." Its actual intention is, however, quite the reverse. It combats moral complacency as well as frees a person to act ethically by overcoming his guilt. Misunderstanding of the emphasis upon the forensic character permeates Bellarmine's objection to the doctrine. He maintains that even if justification *is* attributed to God as a judge, yet when He justifies the sinner, He (unlike judges) "by His declaring just makes just (*declarando facit*) because His judgment is truthful (*secundum veritatem*)."[17] If He did not *make* the accused just at the same time as He declared him so, His judgment would be simply untrue. It would ignore the real state of affairs. Thomas had already formulated a similar view. In his commentary on Romans he interpreted *justificare* as meaning, among other things, "that someone is said to be justified when he is considered (*reputatur*) just." But in *De veritate* he wrote, "God does not accept the just but the acceptation makes us acceptable."[18]

Gerhard agrees that God's judgment is *secundum veritatem*. But he does not agree that Bellarmine has properly specified the reason.

> To be sure, the judgment of God is just when He justifies man on account of the righteousness of Christ imputed through faith, even as His judgment was also just when on account of our sins He struck down His Son; but one ought not and cannot infer from that fact that He justifies us either through or on account of our inherent righteousness; otherwise it would be not the sinner but the righteous who is being justified—which is contrary to what the apostle declares in Romans 4:5. (XVI.5)

17. *De just.* II.3. Quoted XVI.5.
18. Quoted by Küng, *Rechtfertigung*, p. 216, from *Ad Rom.* 2.13 and *De ver.* 27.1.

In the Thomistic rationale of Bellarmine, a *purely* forensic justification would mean that God declares a sinner just even though he is and remains in truth unjust. This would be sheer illusion or self-deception on the part of God, if He would not, by the declaration, also change the situation and make the sinner just, in principle if not yet in full actuality. In the Lutheran rationale of Gerhard, forensic justification means that God accepts the sinner as just even before he is just. This is not an ignoring of a real state of affairs. It is a judgment made on the strength of the work of Christ. Only thus can the uncertainty be removed from the grace of God. Gerhard would have, I should think, no objection to the phrase, *declarando facit justum,* if the ground of the change is found in the work of Christ rather than in a man's infused quality or qualities. That a change does take place in the sinner, both are agreed. "We do not deny," writes Gerhard, "that the grace of God not only remits sins but also renews our nature in conversion. But that that renovation is to be called the infusion of the *gratia gratum faciens*—this indeed is what we deny and contest with all our powers" (XVI.220).

"In the article of justification this word [*justificari*] has a forensic or judicial signification" (XVI.4). Gerhard supports this assertion with four types of proof. First, the term is forensic because it denotes a judicial act. The biblical support for this can be omitted here, but, in summary, Gerhard says that

> the word for justifying is properly and in kind to pronounce someone just, whether he be really just or unjust. With reference to God it is used either actively for His absolving from sins and pronouncing just or passively for the recognition and predication of His righteousness by others. (XVI.4)

But to pronounce a man just is an act performed by a judge in his capacity as judge; his pronouncement is his verdict of not-guilty. The term does, therefore, have a forensic connotation.

A second proof is the fact that it is set in opposition to another judicial term, "condemnation," which is—to use Bellarmine's definition—the "act of the judge when he commits (*deputans*) to punishment the one who was found guilty in the trial (*judicium*)." Bellarmine insists, however, that the word also has a non-judicial sense "if we say, as we do, that both Adam and God have condemned us." It means then the effects of the wrongdoing. But Gerhard is satisfied as long as his opponent concedes that the term when applied to the act of God has a forensic signification. "For we can add that in all those passages condemnation is ascribed to God as to a just judge and in opposition thereto we are said to be justified by faith in Christ. Therefore justification has a forensic meaning in those statements" (XVI.5).

The third proof resides in the fact that the whole act of justification is described in judicial or forensic terms, such as trial, judge, court, accused, accuser, witness, bond (*chirographum*), debt, advocate, absolution. And man's situation before God is described as the accusation of the law *coram Dei judicio* and of the gospel's showing Christ as the Mediator. Man's justification is his being set free; "the sentence is suspended and he is pronounced free (*justus*)" (XVI.6).

The fourth proof consists in the fact that the synonyms of *justificare* have judicial characteristics. "To be justified" is used interchangeably with "not to be called to trial (*judicium*)," "not to be condemned," "not to go to court (*venire in judicium*)," "not to be judged," and so on.

It seems clear that the object of Gerhard's argument for a forensic conception of justification is twofold. He wants to establish, first, that the term is a courtroom term and, secondly, that fallen man's relationship to God must be articulated in these courtroom terms if the power of God's grace is to be kept undiminished. To take justification as the infusion of righteousness invalidates the distinction between justification and sanctification; it obscures the working of God's grace. "Through sanctification the righteousness of new obedience is acquired, but justification consists in the forgiveness of sins and the imputation of the righteousness of Christ" (XVI.10). He does not contend that the sinner's relation to God is determined by a change of mind on the part of God with no real effects in the state of the sinner. Nor does he contend that the term, "justification," has always been used only in the forensic sense in distinction from sanctification. He freely admits that some Fathers and Doctors have followed the "grammar" of the word and used it to mean the whole of justification and sanctification (XVI.8). Others have underplayed the forensic notion, because they wanted to emphasize (and rightly so) the indissoluble connection between the forgiveness of sins and the interior renovation of the forgiven sinner: *nexu arctissimo invicem sint conjuncta* (XVI.246). But without a doctrine of justification as distinct from sanctification, theology has no means of dialectically countering the despairing or the self-satisfied man. Thus, the Fathers also, however they may otherwise have understood justification, *in situations of extreme temptation and anxiety* have held to the forensic meaning, that "to be justified in Christ's name is nothing else than to accept the forgiveness of sins by faith in Christ, to be absolved of the accusation of the law, and to become a participant in salvation" (XVI.10).

Methodologically this insistence upon the forensic character of justification suggests, if indeed it does not actually imply, the claim that a formal rationale is not adequate for articulating the ultimate dimension of man's nature, his standing *coram Deo*. The man who has never himself been in extreme situations of dread and anxiety of conscience (*in seriis pavoribus et angustiis conscientiae*) does not understand his status before God. But the man who is in such situations can be helped only by being brought before the voice of God. This is what happens when he hears himself spoken to in terms of the courtroom scene with God-in-Moses as the Judge and God-in-Christ as the Advocate and Mediator.

To be in *angustiae conscientiae* is to be in the situation where one's own awareness of imperfection becomes the voice of the Other, the very *vox Dei,* which utters condemnation of the self. The agony of the situation lies precisely in the fact that it is constituted not by a conflict of one part of the mind (the intellect) with another part (the will) but by the dialogue of the whole self with what is concretely the voice of God. Therefore, in Gerhard's view, the only ultimately adequate doctrine is the one which is so articulated that it has the power to be concretely the voice of God which condemns and yet affirms the troubled self.

The image of the courtroom, a forensic doctrine of justification, has that power. The doctrine of the infusion of grace does not have it. As soon as one speaks of the infusion of grace, the hearer is led to measure objectively the value of the newly infused quality and to ask whether it is worthy of new life. Instead of that, he needs to be led to listen for the Yes or No of God. Such an evaluation of one's qualities, be they natural or infused, only deafens one to the *vox Dei,* either by withdrawing the hearer from the dialogue or by converting God's final word into a No.

Both of these points, that the knowledge of the ultimate standing of man before God comes only in the dialectic of the concrete situation and that the dialectic of a judicial process is an adequate rationale of that situation, Gerhard makes fairly explicit. After his description of the judicial dialectic he concludes, with a reference to I Corinthians 4:4 (*Nihil mihi conscius sum, sed in hoc non sum justificatus, qui enim me judicat, Dominus est*): "All this cannot really be understood except in the situations of trembling and anxiety of conscience (*in seriis pavoribus et angoribus conscientiae*)" (XVI.6).

Forensic justification is, in other words, not a purely formal and objective understanding of the nature of the transition from the old man to the new. It is the language through which, when it is spoken to man, God speaks *in concreto* as Judge and Redeemer. It is the courtroom "image" which translates man ever and again into the situation of crisis in the presence of God.

The dialectical criterion of a doctrine, then, relates to its effectiveness in addressing man in his concrete situation rather than to its completeness and consistency in stating the formal conditions of salvation. Gerhard must, therefore, take issue with Bellarmine concerning the possibility of being certain of one's salvation (XVI.83). The Protestant doctrine of justification seems to say that God forgives and imputes righteousness to any man who is truly penitent. Bellarmine naturally concludes that the doctrine implies that if a man is truly penitent he can be certain of his salvation. "If the question is proposed conditionally whether a man can ascertain for certain that his sins are forgiven if it be established (*si constet*) that he has truly repented or is truly repentant (*egisse vel agere poenitentiam*), there is no Catholic who will not reply that he can and ought [to be certain of his salvation]."[19] Yet Gerhard (even apart from his objection to the ambiguity of the word "penitence") insists that "those words, 'in earnest penitence,' do not propose any meritorious condition but *contain a description of the subject*." They are words which describe the concretely given situation; they do not set a condition to be met. Thus, while Gerhard can state that the article of the forgiveness of sins shows "no one's sins are forgiven *unless* he is earnestly repentant and embraces Christ in true faith" (XVI.107), he does not turn the formulation around to say that "*if* anyone does penitence, *then* he is forgiven" when this latter sounds as if a condition were set up which must be met before salvation is possible.[20] Nor does he make a direct address thus: "*If* you are penitent, then God *will* forgive you."

Now, in a formal rationale it is, indeed, true to say that the statement, "If a man is truly penitent, God forgives him," is logically equivalent to the statement, "God forgives all who are

19. XVI.83, quoted from *De just.* III.2.
20. The single apparent exception I have encountered is in II.158: "Peccatorum nostrorum [Deus] obliviscitur, si poenitentiam seriam agamus, sed gratiae suae non potest oblivisci." But this is in a different context and precedes the article discussing justification.

truly penitent." But Gerhard's preference for the latter and rejection of the former phrasing shows that formal criteria are not the ones which determine his position.[21]

Thus, one can say in general, God will forgive any man who is truly penitent. One can say dialectically only one of two things, either "God forgives you," or "God does not forgive you." To attach a condition, "if you are truly penitent," will only geld the forgiving or judging word so as to leave the despairing man deep in his despair and the complacent man confirmed in his complacency.

Moreover, the "image of the judicial process" is an adequate account of the situation of man before God. It is able to provide the effective No to the two types of false understanding of that situation. The one type is that of the "pharisees" or "Epicureans" who underestimate the gravity of sin. "Epicureans are of the opinion that justification is a very easy matter, and so they are not sufficiently concerned about sin; pharisees clothe themselves with the conviction of their own righteousness by which they stand before God. But *when the doctrine of justification is presented under the image of a judicial process* before the court of God, those Epicurean and pharisaic ideas quickly vanish" (XVI.6, emphasis mine).

The second type of false understanding is that of the man in

---

21. A particularly clear illustration of this is given in the rationale of Gerhard's rejection of Zanchius' doctrine of an eternal predestination to damnation, VII.181–84. There he states the general rule: "The legitimate interpretation of Scripture must be so directed that it has regard for the instruction and consolation of men." So his reasons for rejecting the double predestination are such as the following: "si introducitur absolutum aliquod reprobationis decretum, adimitur hominibus consolatio" (181); "quomodo tunc erigendus est talis homo?" (ibid.); "quid . . . restat misero isti tentato, quo se sustentet ac erigat, si dicat se non sentire fidem . . . ?" (182); "nos vero tentatum hominem deducimus ad divinas promissiones, et jubemus in tentatione de perseverantia eum niti his tribus columnis: Dei omnipotentia . . . , fidelitate . . . , bona voluntate" (184); "si obmurret tentatio, multos vere renatos vicissim gratia Dei excidisse, respondeat fides . . . non ex absoluto quodam odio a Deo sunt rejecti . . . non delinquet me in aeternum, nitor enim istis Dei promissionibus Rom. 11:29 . . ." (207).

despair, who takes his sin with absolute seriousness and who, therefore, imagines that he must be excluded from God's presence. "To the man who is a sinner, in extreme troubles of conscience, the gospel's promise of Christ's benefits should be presented. Having accepted it in true faith, he is justified; and having been lifted from the depths of despair, he is brought to the harbor of eternal life" (XVI.1). In the doctrine of forensic justification Gerhard finds the divine No to complacent man, who is either untroubled by the fact of his imperfection or ignorant of it, as well as the divine No to the despairing man, who takes his imperfection with absolute seriousness. An account of justification as the infusion of grace muffles that No.

> Those who convert the gospel into law and contend that a man is justified by the merit of his dispositions and works cannot accomplish anything by their doctrine except perpetual doubts since the goodness of our works is imperfect and impure and cannot pass the severe test of divine righteousness. (XVI.82)[22]

Even the "righteousness of the new obedience," though it is a genuine righteousness "with respect to philosophical righteousness," cannot withstand the judgment of God, because it is "imperfect and impure" (XVI.8).

Thus, although Gerhard does not reject every use of such terms as "inherent justice," "habitual grace," and "the infusion of grace," he does deny them a place in the article of justification and does reject the account of justification as an infusion of *gratia gratum faciens* (XVI.197; 220).[23]

22. Cf. XVI.157: "Si illa promissio penderet ab impletione per nostram caritatem, nunquam foret firma, quia caritas nostra est multis modis imperfecta."

23. Cf. also XVI.233: Bellarmine is said not to understand the remission of sins as "absolutionem a peccatis, sive non-imputationem eorum propter Christum, sed totalem eorum deletionem et expunctionem per infusam gratiam. . . . Longe ergo alio sensu Bellarminus accipit remissionem peccatorum, quam in nostris ecclesiis accipitur, nimirum confundit eam cum renovatione et carnis mortificatione."

JUSTIFICATION: AS FORENSIC

In the forensic metaphor, the mediation of Christ provides the possibility of God's negating the No of His own verdict of condemnation. "Free justification through Christ shows God to be merciful, just, and true" (XVI.249). Justification is not a matter of arbitrary changes in the distant mind of an inconstant deity; it is a matter of truth (*secundum veritatem*). If the accused is guilty in the judgment of the judge as well as of himself, there is only one way in which he may legitimately escape his *deputatio* to punishment—and that is through the *imputation* of the righteousness of the One who can really represent him. "In Christ, therefore, not in us, is to be sought that worthiness because of which eternal life is given" (XVI.24).

In the notion of the imputation of the righteousness of Christ one finds the "image" which is, in the concrete situation, the effective No to the No of God's judgment. It is the No which is heard as coming from the same God who is the judge. "Justification is the action of God the Father, Son, and Holy Spirit, by which . . . He remits sins, imputes the righteousness of Christ . . ." (XVI.251).

If it is true, as the preceding paragraphs have sought to show, that Gerhard has moved the articulation of the ultimate relation of man to God out of the formal into the dialectical mode, it is likewise true that his dialectic preserves the limiting paradox, the Yes-in-No and No-in-Yes, just as in Thomas' conception of the free will's conversion there was a totally divine and yet totally human agency. When does the paradox appear? The doctrine of forensic justification functions with respect to the concrete situation. It places the hearer into a final and critical relation to God. There placed, he responds to God and God to him. Man's Yes to himself, in which he points to his own qualities of goodness, however limited, is countered by the No of a God who is pleased with nothing less than absolute perfection. Man's self-defense before the judging God is his attempt to find something in himself on the basis of which he can effectively refuse God's No. But everything he finds is inadequate. If he points to his moral goodness or to his standing as a good creature of a good God, he does no more than increase the power of the returning No. For whether he points to the qualities of his goodness or to his *ur*-relation as creature, he still hears his own imperfection as the bearer of God's No: his goodness is not perfect and his creaturely relationship has long since been disrupted by a failure of trust. This part of the dialectic, which leads man nowhere except further into his own guilt, continues indefinitely until the turning point, when the paradox appears.

When the man who hears his own condemnation is finally driven to silence, with no further response to God's condemning No, he has reached his limit. But upon mutely accepting God's unqualified No he is surprised by the discovery, the revelation, that in this No there is a Yes, the Yes of Christ's merit. Beyond this point of No-in-Yes and Yes-in-No, the dialectic is not that of man's self-defense against God's judgment but of God's judgment and God's mercy in Christ.

In Thomas' formal conceptualization the paradoxical appears in that movement of the will which is both God's and man's, not *partim-partim* but *totaliter-totaliter*. In Gerhard's dialectical rationale it appears as that point in which the final Yes-No (and No-Yes) is reached, the *adiaireton* in a dialectical *successivum*. In the concrete situation this implies that the awareness of imperfection crowds out all else and becomes God's total No to man's person, and that in the mute acceptance of that No, God's Yes becomes audible. Has the universal stain of imperfection turned out after all not to have been significant? Indeed not. Precisely because of its critical and final importance, the only answer to it is to point to the Mediator as the One who, as representative Man, was able to receive the full force of God's judgment and by accepting it to overcome it. Thus, the doctrine of Christ's *satisfactio* turns out to be not simply the requirement of the metaphysics of legal relationships, but the requirement of a doctrine of justification which can be effective in the concrete situation of the believer or non-believer, and which can enable man to face his imperfection in its radical significance.

PER FIDEM

The first mark of Gerhard's conception of justification was his insistence that it is a forensic conception. The second mark, closely associated with it, is that the righteousness which man receives by imputation comes not through works but through faith.

The doctrine of *sola fides* or *fides sola*—faith alone or only faith—which was the partisan characteristic of the Protestant theologians against their Roman opponents, even though the phrase was older,[24] was subject to grave misunderstanding, as Gerhard's extended explanations of various issues will testify. What was it that these *fidesolarii* maintained? The answer can be given negatively, by showing that "through faith" meant "not through works," and positively, by analyzing the elements constituting the act of faith.

Negatively, to be justified by faith[25] means to be justified not by one's own works or merit.

> Since justification and renovation, grace and the gift given through grace, are always joined, therefore, lest anyone think we are justified on account of those new movements as pleasing to God, the particle *gratia* is added [by the author of Romans] so that the sense is: we are justified before God without any merit of ours, indeed contrary to our deserts; and the cause of the free acceptance is not in us but alone in God. (XVI.18)[26]

24. It is found, for example, in Thomas' commentary to I Timothy 1:18. See Küng, *Rechtfertigung*, pp. 243 ff., where other occurrences are cited.

25. When speaking precisely, Gerhard writes "through faith" (per fidem) and "by grace" (gratiā, ex gratia, or per gratiam) and "on account of Christ" (propter Christum). "By faith" (fide, or sola fide) is an abbreviated expression for the same: by grace through faith on account of Christ.

26. The reference is to Romans 3:24.

In the act of justification God looks not "at the worthiness, merit or anything else inherent in us" for we are justified freely, "that is, doing nothing and returning nothing" (ibid.). Gerhard sees but two alternatives: that which is of faith and looks solely to God, and that which is not of faith and looks at least partly to man. Justification comes only when man looks entirely away from himself. Therefore, only faith, and not works, can serve as the "organ and medium" for apprehending salvation. "In justification we say faith reigns alone" (XVI.120). The only act by which man is able to apprehend Christ is one by which he turns completely away from himself. For the problem of his justification is precisely to find something which he can set against God's and his own judgment upon his imperfection. The name of that act in which he, accepting the total No to himself, casts himself upon the mercy of the Judge because of the mediation of Christ is the act of faith. It is as the apostle shows:

> No one can live in the extreme spiritual straits and the jaws of eternal death, which man, terrified by the threats of the law, sees himself deserving by his sins unless he is righteous (*justus*); and no one can be righteous before God except by faith in Christ which is kindled by the promises of the gospel. (XVI.122)[27]

Not to accept Christ and His merits means simply to try to oppose to the judgment of God any trace of goodness that can be found in the condemned man. On the other hand, to cease to oppose anything in man against the judgment of God is, in the concrete situation, the act of faith in which Christ is apprehended and the accusing law is fulfilled. "Faith or the trusting heart (*cor fidele*) fulfills the law by believing, that is, by apprehending Christ who by His most holy obedience and satisfaction fulfilled the law, an obedience which is imputed to us through faith" (XVI.157).

27. The reference is to Romans 3:22 f.

Man cannot fulfill the law by anything he does, only by the acceptance of its having been done for him in Christ. If this sounds like an easy way out, a way of escaping due deserts without suffering punishment, then this doctrine, Gerhard would say, has not been understood. For it is not offered in the abstract or in general, but as the message or image which can effectively address man in a situation of despair. One who has experienced the *terrores conscientiae,* the jaws of death, and has been saved through the mediation of Christ, is transformed in his whole person because he is able to face his imperfection knowing that it will not ultimately condemn him; and he can conquer it *graduatim* in the power of the new life lived in Christ.

When the merits of Christ become the merits of the stricken man, he has accepted God's promise in faith.

> Through a genuine and justifying faith we not only believe that we are diseased (a fact which even a "historical faith" can accept) but we also receive the precious medicine set before us in Christ for our health; for faith is described in John 3:14–15 as a spiritual and effective intuition of Christ hanging on the cross, by whom we are freed of the wounds of our soul and are made well. So faith in Christ is far different from an invalid kind of faith, which is neither a cause nor a part of health (*sanitas*). (XVI.168)

A caution should be repeated: it is not the case that man reflectively decides to accept God's No and then also His Yes on the basis of a demonstration that God must have spoken them. For the doctrine of justification is the articulation of man's condition which has the power *to be* God's word in the concrete situation. The hearer does not ask, "Is this God's word?" He only listens and responds. That is to say, the man confronted with the divine law does not ask, "Is it true?" On the contrary, according to Gerhard's Lutheran understanding, to be confronted with the law of God, the *vox legis,* is to hear the voice of one's conscience (or the voice of another person) as God's No, His non-acceptance of the person so confronted. In such a situation man can only respond or reply; he cannot reflectively and objectively evaluate. If he utters the question, "Is it true?", this is not the question of reflective, critical reason, but the attempt of the man addressed to reply to the God he hears. In Gerhard's view, therefore, the response is shaped not by the question, "Is it true?", but by the question, "What shall I do? Shall I defend myself or shall I accept the judgment?"

Similarly, the faith which accepts the Yes of God in Christ is not the acknowledgment that God has demonstrably said something which must, because He has said it, be true. It is rather the hearing of a promise as the promise of God and the acceptance of that promise. The one who hears the *vox evangelii* is engaged by it. In Gerhard's terms, faith is the effect of that *vox evangelii* through which the Holy Spirit kindles the hearts of men, and it is at the same time the organ of apprehension.

> The good things offered in the gospel we apprehend through faith and apply to ourselves, so that there is a perpetual relation between the offering and the receiving medium, between the gift and its acceptance, between the promise of grace and its apprehension in trust. (XIV.33)

Any good works which man does must be totally excluded from this apprehension of justification. They grow out of faith and faith is not genuine without them, but they are not its cause. This is the famous *sola* in the doctrine of justification *sola fide*, by faith alone. Salvation is to be attributed alone to faith and not to faith-and-works. Not that the works are absent; indeed, they are the signs of the living faith and are indispensable. But they cannot bring about justification.

> It must be carefully noted, because of the calumnies of the adversaries, that the particle, *"sola,"* does not refer to the

subject, as if justifying faith exists by itself and separate from
caritas and the other virtues—if, as is the case, a genuine
faith is living, not dead, active through *caritas,* not impotent
and idle. . . . Hence it may seem to someone that this proposition, *Fides sola justificat,* expresses more clearly that the
exclusive particle belongs to the predicate; it is less subject
to the false charges of the adversaries than if it is formulated
thus: *Sola fides justificat.* (XVI.150)

The *sola* does not remove the works, but it denies their causality
in the act of justification. If it be asked whether salvation is
attributable to faith or to faith-and-works or to works, the answer
is, to faith alone. Although faith is never alone, it justifies alone.

Not only the start but also the completion of salvation is to
be attributed to faith. Still we do not divorce *caritas* and
the other virtues from faith but we attribute a double power
(*energeia*) to faith: one formal (as it is called), by which it
apprehends Christ, whose righteousness is imputed to us
through faith; the other effective, which grows through love
and the other good works in which the righteousness of the
new obedience consists, whose foundation, mother, and origin
is faith. (XVI.168; cf. 154)

The rationale of Gerhard's "through faith alone" as meaning
"not through merits or works" and that of Thomas' "through
merit on the presupposition of grace" may be compared in the
following way. If man in his freedom attains to any end, he does
so, in Thomas' rationale, because he has merited it. This is a
matter of definition. It distinguishes man as a freely acting creature from the non-human creatures who attain their ends without
reflection or conscious choice. To speak of man as freely attaining
something which he did not merit would amount to a self-
contradiction; it would be saying that he attains to something
which he does not attain. Given this reflexive relation between

end and merit, when Thomas poses the question concerning man's attainment of eternal life, his logic must proceed along the following lines. The fact that man can attain to eternal life is a datum of the Christian conviction. This implies that in some sense man earns—merits—eternal life. But what is there which is *aequale* to eternal life? Nothing in man's pure nature, because eternal life exceeds the bounds of nature itself. If man attains eternal life (and he does), there must be a *donum supernaturale* which is a principle adequate to reach it.

The two questions which are answered in this rationale, if it is presupposed that man *can* reach eternal life, would be the following. First, what is an adequate principle for bringing man to his end, that is to say, what is meritorious of eternal life? Answer: something which is capable of leading to a supernatural end. Second, since nothing in nature, and still less in fallen nature, can by definition lead to a supernatural end, what is there that can reside in man as a principle of actions to overcome the limits and defects of his natural principle? Answer: the grace which is the Holy Spirit. Here we have a particularly clear illustration of how the rationale gives shape to the conviction concerning man's ultimate destiny. Thomas' is a formal rationale. Hence, the questions and answers arise from an assessment of the nature, the definition, of such terms as "man," "end," "merit," and "principle of action."

Gerhard's rationale of the same problem moves dialectically in the Yes and No of the concrete situation. The axiom of the Christian conviction which he shares with Thomas is that man can and does attain to eternal life. From that point, however, he proceeds not to the formal implications of the datum, but to a consideration of what can be announced to an individual in order to create the encounter and response through which he is brought to that life. "The Gospel announces grace not to the secure and hypocritical but to the penitent" (XIV.107; cf. XVI.I). *To the complacent man*—be he Epicurean or pharisee—

who does not acknowledge the gravity of his sin, is spoken that *vox legis* through which he hears God demanding nothing less than perfection. This word of the law is genuine and true, not because it accords with the definition of man's nature, but because it has power to claim man's attention unconditionally and to engage his self-interpretation. *To the despairing man,* whose interpretation of his sin is such that he discounts all possibility of salvation from "eternal death," is spoken that *vox evangelii* through which he hears God accepting him for Christ's sake. This word also is true because it is an effective No to the self-interpretation of the despairing man.

Where Thomas asks, "What is *adequate* to a supernatural end?" Gerhard asks, "What can *please* God?" To Thomas' question there is a uniform (even if complex) answer, given in terms of supernatural principles and merits. To Gerhard's question there are two answers which, viewed formally, would contradict each other. The first answer (spoken to complacent man) is: "Nothing can please God." The second answer (spoken to a despairing man) is: "Everything can please God." Both of these assertions are implicit in the courtroom image and are to be made without qualification. Neither of them is true or false in the abstract; both of them are true or false *in concreto*.

Secondly, Thomas' typical question would be: "What principle is there which can reside in man and lead him to a supernatural end without destroying his humanity?" Gerhard's would be: "How must God speak to man in order to overcome the complacency or despair which shuts him in and which prevents his doing anything pleasing to God?" Again the answer is twofold, the voice of the law and the voice of the gospel, heard respectively by the complacent and the despairing man. To a complacent man it cannot be truthfully said, "God is pleased with you for Christ's sake"; and to the despairing man it cannot be truthfully said, "God is displeased with you because of your imperfection." Both of these statements would be untrue because they would lack the power to be a No to the concrete situation. It is this dialectical power to which Gerhard refers when he (1.36) calls Christians those who "sense [*sentiunt:* that is, without reflection or theoretical deduction] the power and efficacy of the word in their heart and through it recognize themselves as reborn to eternal life." He also calls it the inner testimony of the Holy Spirit:

> God entered a covenant with us . . . and in lieu of a downpayment gives the Holy Spirit, who makes us certain of the fulfillment of the promise . . . [by a testimony which is] internal, when He inwardly assures us that we are in the grace of God, out of which peace and tranquillity of conscience arise . . . (XVI.87)

The effectiveness of a doctrine is, thus, a criterion of its soundness. Theology is "practical" in Gerhard's conception (*Prœm.* 28), not as the application *in concreto* of general theories to special cases, but as "spiritual medicine," that is, as the *habitus* of speaking the words which have the power to effect justification. "Efficacy of doctrine," meaning the power of a doctrine to convert, rather than the popularity of a doctrine (XXII.256), is a mark of the true church because it distinguishes a sound from an unsound theology.

Although it is true that there are formal strains in Gerhard's rationale of justification (for example, that God can be pleased only with the perfect is true by definition) and that there are dialectical overtones in Thomas' (for example, man's beatitude consists in his enjoyment of God *Himself*), the predominant emphasis of *per fidem* is dialectical while that of *per meritum* is formal.

We come then to the second part of the doctrine of *per fidem solam.* If negatively faith is the dialectical negation of works or merit, what is it positively? What (in Gerhard's words) are the *materiale* (the constitutive elements) and the *formale* (the essential nature) of justifying faith?

The material acts which concur in justifying faith can be distinguished but not separated. They are to be understood as "diverse acts following on each other (*invicem consequentes*) and coming together in justifying faith" (XVI.67). From the standpoint of the *formale,* faith "is only trust or the trusting apprehension of Christ's merit and in this sense it does not have (*non agnoscit*) diverse parts" (ibid.). The three constituent material elements are knowledge, assent, and trust—*notitia, assensus,* and *fiducia.* As knowledge, faith's proper object is "the word of God set forth in the prophetic and apostolic Scriptures" (XVI.70). Faith is, however, not only the knowledge that these things are true; it is also the intellect's assent to them. "Faith is furthermore not only knowledge but also assent, for it is not sufficient for faith just to know the divine doctrine; it must also give assent to it" (XVI.71).[28] Assent is, in Thomas' definition, the disposition of the intellect to follow the command of the will (II.ii.4.2 *ad* 2). Gerhard implicitly accepts that meaning without troubling to provide a definition, because there was no interconfessional dispute concerning it.

There was dispute, however, as to whether *fiducia* were an element in the act of faith. Gerhard insists that it is not only an element but the essence of justifying faith. *Fiducia* necessarily implies knowledge and assent, whereas the converse is not true. His opponents preferred to exclude trust from the act of faith, on the grounds that faith is an act of the intellect whereas trust belongs to the faculty of the will (XVI.74 ff.). But to Gerhard, saving faith must include more than the bare knowledge or even knowledge-with-assent of what God has said. Indeed, the *notitia* of faith leads inevitably to *fiducia,* unless it is short-circuited.

Since the object of faith, namely, the revealed word, contains the gospel's promise concerning the free mercy of God and

28. Ibid.: "Ad *phôtismon* igitur sive *epignôsin* accedere debet *sygkatathesis,* consensus et judicium approbans ea, quae in verbo credenda proponuntur; hic assensus pulcherrime Hebr. 4:2 vocatur *krasis tês pisteôs kai tou logou.*"

the forgiveness of sins on account of Christ the Mediator; and since true faith assents to every word of God, how could faith not be a fiducial apprehension of Christ—or, what is the same thing, a trust in the divine mercy offered on account of Christ in the word of the gospel? (XVI.71)

As a form of knowledge faith has for its object whatever is in the *verbum Dei,* which includes promises about Christ's merits. Christ's merits, or the mercy of God, cannot, however, be apprehended except by an act of the whole heart, a complete reliance upon God with the confidence that He will fulfill his promises. Any faith which lacks *fiducia* is incomplete. Abraham's acceptance of God's promise of a son is an illustration of this fact (XVI.73). "Abraham not only believed *that he could hope for* a son from Sarah but *did in fact hope* and, relying with full confidence on the divine promise, was sure that a son would be given to him." The fullness of faith which the apostle Paul attributes to Abraham "signifies not only the kind of conviction with which the mind assents to the divine promise as to a reality most true but also the conviction with which the heart relies completely on the divine promise." *Fiducia* is that confidence "by which we apply the divine promises to ourselves and rely on them completely." A "historical faith," by which we believe in general in God's omnipotence, truth, and mercy "is not sufficient to make us pray according to God's will"; what is also needed is "that we are certain (*statuamus*) the evangelical promises apply *in specie* also to us and that we hold to them with a firm and unshaken trust." It is not enough just to know that God has made promises of mercy for Christ's sake and to assent to them because He has made them; it is not enough to believe *that* His promises are reliable. What is needed yet to make such faith a saving faith is *the very relying upon the promises.*

Whereas, therefore, the object of faith as *notitia* may be the word of God in general, the object of saving faith is Christ Himself as the Mediator. *Notitia* leads to *fiducia* because the heart of the word of God is His promise of mercy. If faith does not include *fiducia,* it is not a saving faith.

> The proper and adequate object of saving faith is Christ in His office as Mediator; for it is He whom faith beholds and His benefits that faith applies to itself (XIV.15). . . . The proper and adequate object of justifying faith is, I say, that by which, when we have apprehended it, we are justified before God and absolved of our sins; that and nothing else. But the grace of God in Christ or, what is the same thing, Christ in His office as Mediator, or the obedience and satisfaction of Christ, is that by which we are justified before God when we have apprehended it; and nothing else. Therefore, the grace of God in Christ or, what is the same thing, Christ in His office of Mediator, or the obedience and satisfaction of Christ, is the proper and adequate object of justifying faith. (XVI.131)

The "form and, as it were, soul of justifying faith" is "the fiducial apprehension of Christ with all His benefits offered in the word of the gospel" (XVI.72). In accordance with this conception of saving faith Gerhard must, of course, reject the notion of a faith that is formed by *caritas.* That there is a distinction between an incomplete and a complete faith, an "historical" and a "saving" faith, he grants. What gives faith its *plerophoria* or its essential form, however, is not *caritas* but the fiducial apprehension of Christ. His basic objection to the *caritate formata* is recorded in a quotation from Luther's commentary on Galatians:

> If *caritas* is the form of faith, I am immediately forced to think (*sentire*) that *caritas* is itself the greatest part of the Christian religion and thus I lose Christ, His blood, His wounds, and all His benefits, and I hold on to *caritas* and fall into moralism. But the Holy Spirit, who gives to everyone mouth and tongue, knows also how to speak. He could

well have said, "The just lives by a formed faith," but he intentionally omitted this and said simply, "The just lives by faith."[29]

From this last statement an acute opponent would, of course, draw an argument to invalidate Luther's own *sola fide;* he would suggest that similarly, if the Holy Spirit had wanted to say man is justified by faith *alone* He could have done so, but in fact He did not.

Gerhard does not object to the use of *caritas* as a summary designation of the fruits of faith and of the Christian life. "We do not object to saying that *caritas* is in a way the sum of Christianity if the question is about the life of the Christian man, who indeed ought to do everything out of *caritas* . . ." (XVI.120). What he does resist is the introduction of works into the notion of justifying faith, for it is not *caritas* but rather the grasping of Christ which makes faith able to justify.

> *Caritas* does not perfect that spiritual life but affords external testimony of its presence and arises from it (XVI.122). . . . Justifying faith is what it is through its form, namely, the apprehension of Christ in the gospel, and is distinguished from all other things. . . . *Caritas* is a form only external, like a garment; therefore, it would be better to say that faith is the form of *caritas* than to say that *caritas* is the form of faith. Among the heathen writers one finds examples of those who were so devoted to each other with *caritas* only that the one would not have hesitated to lay down his life for the other. And yet, because this *caritas* was without faith, was it in God's sight anything more than a dead body? (XVI.121)

From this last quotation it is clear that Gerhard, in speaking of *caritas,* is speaking of something other than was Thomas. That

29. Quoted by Gerhard, XVI.118.

there could be *caritas without faith* is a conception impossible in Thomas' frame of thought, where *caritas* is not the name of a certain kind of act (namely, an unselfish one) but the name of that which perfects the act of faith as an adequate principle and form of action. It is an adequate principle because it is a new power given by grace; it is a form because, being located in the will "whose object and form is the *finis*" (II.ii.23.8), it directs and guides. It is as impossible in Thomas' conception to have *caritas* without faith as it is to have faith without *caritas* in Gerhard's.

Both theologians accept a distinction between a faith which does not save and a faith which does. The non-saving faith Gerhard calls *fides historica,* the knowledge that God has said or promised something and the assent to that knowledge; Thomas calls it *fides informis,* the faith which has not yet received its final form. Saving faith, according to Gerhard, is distinguished from historical faith by the element of trust; in Thomas it is distinguished by the element of *caritas* which makes it meritorious of (that is to say, able to attain) its ultimate end.

Furthermore, besides making a similar distinction between an incomplete and a complete faith, both theologians agree also with regard to how man's faculties participate in each kind of faith. Non-saving faith (historical faith, unformed faith) is that faith which resides alone in the intellect as bare knowledge-with-assent of the truth of revelation (the assent being the disposition of the intellect to heed the will). Saving faith resides in the intellect and the will in their joint function. The act of saving faith in its integrality is an act of the "heart," the will and intellect together. Gerhard asserts

> there are, as it were, two parts to this faith, knowledge-with-assent and trust; with respect to the knowledge-with-assent we say it is in the intellect; with respect to trust, in the will; with respect to both, in the intellect and will simultaneously,

that is, in the heart or soul (*animus*) of man. . . . As the will presupposes the intellect, so trust in Christ must presuppose knowledge of Him. (XVI.75)

To support his contention that saving faith proceeds from both intellect and will, and to oppose the argument that if faith is in the intellect (as it is) it cannot also be in the will, Gerhard adduces Thomas, even though he rejects what he believes to be the Thomistic "formed faith." Adopting the Thomistic terminology to make his point, he goes so far as to suggest

> What if we were to say [as we might] in the same way that justifying faith is in the intellect by disposition (*per modum dispositionis*)? For such historical knowledge is not the whole of justifying faith (*nondum absolvit*). There must also be a fiducial apprehension and special application of the promises of the gospel. For that reason some give only one genus in the definition of justifying faith by defining it as the fiducial apprehension of the divine grace or mercy through Christ the Redeemer in the gospel promise, which arises from the truth of the divine word known through the Holy Spirit and which leads to eternal life. (XVI.75)

This is less opposed to Thomas than Gerhard thinks. For in the Thomistic view, *fides informis* is not the *materia*—contrary to what Gerhard, following Luther, says against the notion of *fides informis* (XVI.12)—but the "disposition preceding the ultimate form" (II.ii.2.9 *ad* 1). It is, as in Gerhard, the bare knowledge-with-assent that something of God is true. What makes it faith is that it is an acceptance as true of something which God has said to be true, but which is not seen to be true with the intellect; its "formal nature" is objectively, truth itself, and subjectively, the not-seen (cf. II.ii.1.1 and 1.6 *ad* 2). Faith is as certain as knowledge; it is not just opinion. But its foundation is the conviction that God has spoken, coupled with an assent to whatever

God discloses about Himself and about other things in relation to Himself.

In contrast, *fides caritate formata* is an assenting knowledge *joined to the will* which is committed to God, for that commitment to God is what makes the faith "formed or living" (II.ii.4.4 *ad* 2). True, the presence or absence of *caritas* does not alter the essence of faith, because what makes faith faith is its manner of knowing, or believing; but it does alter the believing person. "Faith itself is not changed; but the subject of faith, which is the soul (*anima*), is changed" (II.ii.4.4 *ad* 4). Thus, the form of saving faith (that is, what makes faith *saving* but not what makes faith faith) is *fiducia* for Gerhard; to Thomas it is *caritas*. Gerhard's *fiducialis apprehensio* is Thomas' *fides caritate formata*. An unformed faith-as-trust is as impossible a conception as is an unformed *fides-caritate-formata*—in both cases one would have an unformed formed faith.

When the question is posed as to whether *caritas* is the form of salvific faith, Gerhard's negative answer proceeds as follows. *Caritas* cannot make faith into saving faith because *caritas* is the name of a type of action theoretically capable of being performed by anyone. An act of *caritas* is one which, judged externally and objectively, is unselfish, even if the subjective motive may be selfish. The external cannot be the form of a reality any more than clothes can be the form of the man wearing them. We should say rather that faith forms *caritas,* because faith is the internal principle of actions which are pleasing to God. Thomas' affirmative answer, by contrast, proceeds thus: *caritas* is the form of faith because the bare knowledge of the *prima veritas* is not sufficient to be a principle of actions which attain the ultimate end. It is the will, not the intellect, which rules actions. A formed action—that is, one which is directed toward its end—must therefore proceed from both the will and the intellect. Since *caritas* is unity of the will with God and presupposes knowledge of Him in faith, it is that which forms faith and makes it salvific.

Trust makes an act of *caritas* (that is, "works") *pleasing* to God (Gerhard); *caritas* makes an act (that is, "works") *meritorious* of its supernatural end (Thomas). The distinction between a dead and a saving faith is common to the two theologians; the rationale of that distinction follows the different patterns of each. The integral act of saving faith is, to Gerhard, that which pleases God; it is, to Thomas, that which merits its end. Ask the question of Gerhard, "What is it that pleases God?", and his answer is, "Christ's merits imputed to man." Ask of Thomas, "What is it that merits a supernatural end?" and he replies that it is the *donum* of grace, earned by Christ and implanted in man as a new principle of action. Ask Gerhard whether the believer is just before God and he replies, "Yes, because trust is the utter reliance on God which restores the broken relationship." Ask Thomas and he replies, "Yes, because God has placed within man a principle adequate to attain a supernatural end."

Trust is the grasping of God's general promises in the individual situation (XVI.73), made possible by the inner *testimony* of the Holy Spirit who assures us that we are in grace and the children of God (XVI.87); *caritas* is the gift given to the individual as a *habit* to direct him to a supernatural end, a movement which is possible because this created grace is also the *uncreated grace,* namely, the Holy Spirit. The indwelling of the Holy Spirit, both for Gerhard and for Thomas, distinguished between the redeemed and the unredeemed man; but the emphasis in Gerhard is naturally upon the "testimony" of that Holy Spirit, and in Thomas upon His new direction of the will with new enabling powers. The background question in Gerhard's conception is: "What can overcome the despair of a concrete situation, the despair caused by an awareness of the bondage to sin?" And his answer is: "Only that which will turn man completely away from himself, to rely not at all upon what he finds in himself but solely upon what he finds in Christ." The difference between the unsaved and the saved is determined by the difference in what they *rely on.* The background question in Thomas' conception is: "What is capable of directing man to a supernatural end by overcoming the imperfection of sin and supplementing the power of nature?" And the answer is: "Only that which is a perfect and adequate principle of action—the grace of the Holy Spirit working in man, a principle of action which, in power, is perfect because it is the eternal Spirit but which, in action, is still imperfectly realized." The difference between the saved and the unsaved is determined by the kind of *habitus* he has, whether simply natural and sinful, or supernatural.

Gerhard's conception is shaped by the dialectic of the courtroom, where the accused has the alternative of relying upon himself (unsuccessfully) or of relying upon the Mediator; Thomas', by the "natures" of things. Since *caritas* would imply a reliance on the self, Gerhard must reject it in the article of justification.

"LAW AND GOSPEL" OR "OLD AND NEW LAW"?

To complete the picture of the new creation it is necessary to say something more about the conception of law which is operative in each of the systems. Gerhard denies that the gospel is a new law, except in a severely qualified way, whereas Thomas cheerfully affirms it. This is to be expected since Gerhard is interested in the article of justification (that is, effecting the transition from the old to the new man). His contrast is between law and gospel, between demands and promises, between attention to man's situation and attention to God's acts. But Thomas traverses the whole area from nature to grace, and so his contrast is between the old law as containing the rules to attain natural and terrestrial ends and the new law as containing the directives to the supernatural. The new law adds *caritas* to the old law. It is the interior motive of love and the indwelling Holy Spirit. Gerhard has this conception of law also in his "first" and "third" use" (XII.203). The role of the first, or "political," use is to restrain men from overt actions of wrongdoing. The role of the third, or "theological-didactic," use is to instruct the converted in what is really good in the sight of God.

But it is in the second, the "theological-practical (*elenktikos*)," use that the divergence becomes clear. Here the distinction of law and gospel is the summary of the dialectic of forensic justification.

> The chief announcements (*conciones*) of God in the whole Scripture are two; one is the accusation of the law, the other is the promise of the gospel. The former is the announcement of wrath, the latter the announcement of grace, and each of them is universal (XVI.250). . . . With good reason . . . the doctrine of the gospel follows in order after the explication of the divine law. For those whom the hammer of the law has pounded down . . . the preaching of the gospel heals . . . and makes joyful; the gospel announces that the obedience which the rigor of the law exacts is rendered by Christ in our stead. (XIV.2)

For Gerhard as for Thomas the law *is* an expression of the eternal will of God. But for the Protestant theologian its function, instead of being that of directing actions to an end, is to announce to man what his relation to God is—but to announce it effectively as God's concrete No. The law does not direct, it accuses. The gospel does not give new directives; it heals by its announcement of God's grace as His Yes subsuming His No. Law and gospel, therefore, perform complementary functions; the one is "subordinate" to the other (XIV.53). They are both *sermo Dei.* Yet they are to be distinguished on a number of points (XIV.54). As to the manner of their disclosure:

> the law is in a way naturally known since it was implanted in the minds of men in creation and was not completely erased by the fall. . . . But the gospel is a mystery entirely

hidden from human reason, brought forth through the Son from the bosom of the eternal Father and revealed to us.

As to their matter or content:

> law is the teaching of works, for it prescribes and commands what we are, what to do, what not to do. . . . The gospel is the teaching of faith, for it sets forth Christ as Mediator and through Him announces the forgiveness of sins, righteousness and salvation. . . .

As to form:

> the promises of the law are conditional, for they require perfect obedience, they demand as cause the condition of perfect fulfilment. . . . But the promises of the gospel are free and are, so to speak, donative; for that reason they are called the word of the grace of God (*verbum gratiae Dei*) . . .

As to effect:

> the law convinces of sin and terrifies man. . . . But the gospel announces forgiveness of sins and lifts man up by its life-giving consolation.

As to object:

> the law is to be presented to the wicked, the secure and hardened sinners, for it pertains to the old man. . . . But the gospel is to be announced to contrite hearts and consciences terrified by the sense of sin.

In short, whatever turns man's attention to himself and his capacities is law in the article of justification, because it strengthens the accusation, the awareness of the distance between the sinner and God. Whatever turns man away from himself and his capacities *when he is in anxiety because of his imperfection* is gospel. The priority of the law is thus a dialectical, not a formal one; it provides the No (man's terror) to which the gospel is the No (and Yes in the No). If the law is effectively announced, man hears himself rejected by God; if the gospel is effectively announced, man hears himself accepted by God. The "genuine and proper" doctrine of the gospel is the

> free promise of forgiveness of sins, of righteousness, and eternal life on account of the Christ promised in the Old Testament, testified to in the New Testament, who for our sins made satisfaction on the cross and earned for us a perfect righteousness, which He gives and applies to us through faith. What belongs to the gospel, therefore, are all those pronouncements of the Holy Spirit, whether in the Old or New Testament: 1) which speak of the grace and mercy of God, for from the law and works there is no hope of salvation since the fall, but only in Christ . . . ; 2) which speak of the person and saving office and benefits of Christ as Redeemer and Mediator, for the law demands our solution and obedience but ignores Christ and His benefits . . . ; 3) which deal with faith through which we are made participants in the benefits of Christ, for "the law is not of faith . . ."; 4) which speak of the purpose and use of the sacraments, for they are the seal of the gospel's promises, means of arousing, increasing, and confirming faith . . . (XIV.13)

As Gerhard interprets them, the scholastics maintained that

> the old law contained precepts only concerning external works, to be performed out of fear, and promises only temporal or corporal, whereas the new law brings more perfect, more excellent, and more severe precepts which bring to the doers an abundant righteousness which exceeds that

of the pharisees and scribes and which has the promise of salvation and eternal life . . . (XIV.58)

He rejects in this very context a statement of Thomas (II.i.91.5): "the old law leads to observances of mandates through fear of punishments; the new law accomplishes this through love, which is infused in hearts through the grace of Christ."[30] But, according to Thomas, the new law contains not new *promises* but new *principles* or *powers* of action. To the conception of the new man as having new powers Gerhard, as we noted at the outset, has no objection. He does, however, insist that the law, even in the Old Testament, made demands about the interior aspect of moral actions.

Not only external sins but also sins in the heart—and thereby the whole inner (*intima*) corruption of nature—are accused by the law; for, among other reasons, the *vox legis* was given and repeated after the fall that it might make known those precepts whose cognition in the law of nature was erased through sin. (XII.53)

Thus the distinction between Gerhard's law and gospel is not equivalent to the distinction between the Old and New Testament; whereas Thomas' distinction between the old and the new is, when viewed from the divine standpoint, the same whether applied to Testament or to law. For Gerhard law is the expression of God's absolute *demand;* for Thomas it is the expression of His *ordering.* That God demands absolute obedience and that man's failure to render it is sin, Thomas does not deny; but the function of the *lex* is not to point to that failure.

Are the precepts of the law then capable of fulfillment? Gerhard answers No (as far as fallen man is concerned). God demands the impossible. But the reason for holding to this doctrine

30. Gerhard does not quote the clause which follows: "which in the new law is conferred but in the old law was prefigured."

of the impossibility of the demand (XII.202) lies in the doctrine of justification:

> The first . . . use of this doctrine is in the article of justification, lest, namely, we should set against the judgment of God that imperfect and in many ways contaminated obedience which we render to the law; but we teach that we are justified by faith in Christ. The second use of this doctrine is in the article on good works, as we teach that we cannot by the natural powers of the free will begin to render the sincere and true obedience which is due the law but that it is necessary that the "law of God be written in our hearts" by the Holy Spirit.

Take the law, however, not as an expression of God's demand, but as the order by which God leads man, and the answer to the question whether it is impossible of fulfillment becomes a modified No, as it does in Thomas. Here the function is not to make man aware of his miserable state, but to direct him to his ends. To direct him to external ends, a certain type of law is adequate; to internal and supernatural ends another type is adequate. The education through the divine law in this latter conception is not one of driving man to despair before his healing, but of starting him in those actions which are easier and leading him to those which are more difficult. As a child is capable of less than an adult, so the Old Testament was less perfect than, and preliminary to, the New Testament.

Never does Thomas deny that the power to do works is a gift of God. Yet God does not *simpliciter* command the impossible, because He Himself makes the impossible possible. Indeed, the distinction between law and gospel in Gerhard comes closest to that between the *lex humana* and *lex divina* in Thomas (rather than to the *vetera* and *nova lex*), in that both are present in both Testaments and the divine is in each case the grace of God in contrast to man's natural powers and knowledge.

Gerhard's ultimate defense of his doctrine of the law rests, as does his whole doctrine of forensic justification, on his conviction that it alone is able to engage a man in his given situation, to be the very address of God, to provide that upon which man can rely. It meets the dialectical-personal criterion.

Thomas' defense of his doctrine would, in turn, rest upon the claim that it gives a complete and consistent picture of the whole of the relation of man and God as objectively knowable. It meets the formal-objective criterion.

It is possible for both of them to be right.

CHAPTER VI

Caritas

Caritas contains a microcosmic view of the rationale of nature and grace. It is the reality *sine qua non* of the new creation; he who has it has all, he who lacks it lacks all. It gives ultimate meaning to man's being and action. Who is the man that attains ultimate beatitude? He on whom God has bestowed grace, of which *caritas* is the center. It is the bond which ties him to God as his first principle and his ultimate end.

Caritas is, in a word, the whole order of creation and new creation. As a kind of *amor,* it exhibits the continuity of the two creations; as a gift or *infused* virtue, it points up the discontinuity, the newness of the new creation; as a *form* or principle of being and action, it unites the freedom of the new creature and the sovereign direction of God; as *ordered love* it recognizes that all things have their divinely appointed place; as *friendship* it is the elevation of the new creature not only to higher ends but to a personal relation with the Creator.

Caritas as a special case of general love (*amor*) exhibits the continuity, the lack of contradiction, between the new and old creations. *Caritas* presupposes *amor,* which is founded upon the "communication of natural good" and by which every creature in its proper manner loves God above all and more than itself

(II.ii.26.3) since He is the universal good in all particular goods. In fallen nature this love is distorted; it prefers particular to the universal good or mistakes the good which it seeks. As bestowed grace, *caritas* thus restores that natural love by healing it before adding the special characteristics of grace. *Caritas* is indeed an addition to natural love, but no contradiction of it. It is a *multo magis* rather than a *sed contra*.

Furthermore, the continuity appears in the area of love of the self and of others. By nature every creature loves itself because it is at one with itself—it is an identity. Self-love in this sense is not evil but natural. For a creature not to love itself is a self-contradiction, destructive, irrational, a consequence of an inner split. Thus love of others naturally implies an *amor sui,* a love as of oneself. Self-love is in a way both the measure and the origin of love for others, because without it the creature cannot act in a centered way. If this is the case, then it follows that *caritas* too must contain an element of self-love. And it does, but there is a difference. Whereas natural love is directed toward the self because of the self's proximity to the lover, *caritas* is directed toward the self because it is one of the creatures which pertain to God. *Amor* loves the self because of its identity with the lover; *caritas* loves the self in God. *Amor* says to the self (to speak metaphorically), "I love you because I am you." *Caritas* says to the self, "I love you because I love God and you are God's."

With respect to the love of others, the same continuity and qualification appear. Natural love says of the fellow man, "I love you because you are an upright person (or appear useful, or likable, etc., to me)."[1] In that way it is based upon the *amor sui.* *Caritas* says of the fellow man, "I love you because I love God and everything which pertains to Him, and you like my self are a creature who belongs to Him."

Thus, the difference between natural love and "gracious" love

1. *De car.* 4.

is not the difference between self-love and love of others. One cannot say that man by nature loves himself and by grace loves God and others. True, Aquinas assents to the Augustinian description of man as enclosed in himself (*incurvatus*), but applies it to sinful man and not to man as natural. It denotes the inordinate type of self-love. Proper self-love and other-love appear both in the state of nature and in the state of grace. But the perspective of the two differs according to the difference between, on the one hand, knowing oneself and others to be the creatures of a Creator and, on the other hand, knowing oneself and others to have the ultimate end and beatitude in that very same God who is the Creator. Natural love recognizes and evaluates all things according to their status as originating from God. *Caritas* recognizes and evaluates them according to their participation in beatitude.

Again, the continuity of the two loves appears in the identity of their basic character. Both of them are a directedness toward the good. The difference is not in the affirmation or negation of this directedness but rather in the object to which the mind and heart are directed. Natural *amor* flies arrow-like to the common good, the universal good: that element which appears in everything as the cause of its goodness but is not identical with any one thing. The good toward which *caritas* flies is the supernatural, the specific good of the ultimate end, in relation to which all other good is preliminary or peripheral. *Amor* loves God as the source of being; *caritas* loves God as the "object of beatitude," that is, as Himself being man's beatitude. All creatures, rational and non-rational, want to live, and so they love the source of their life; rational creatures want to live and in addition to be happy, and so they love the source of their life and seek it as their happiness; graced creatures want to live and be happy eternally, and so they love God as the first principle and ultimate end. This is the movement from the general to the special love of God.

Finally, *amor* and *caritas* are continuous because the latter's act is still (actively) "to love" (*amare*). Thomas pointedly asks (II.ii.27.1) whether it might not be true that *caritas* is more a "to be loved" than a "to love." After all, it is a gift from God, and the more a person has of it the more lovable he must be. Those who have most *caritas* are by definition the best people—and what is best is by definition the most to be loved. But this, Thomas answers, hinges on a confusion. Certainly, the one who has more *caritas* is more lovable and may accordingly evoke acts of love from others toward himself. But his *own* act is still to love. Unlike *amor*, *caritas* is thus both the source and the object of love. He who has *caritas* is good because of it and he can love others because of it. *Amor's* act is to love—if it finds one worthy. *Caritas'* act is also to love—but it need not find a good outside itself since it is its own source. "Caritas est illud bonum quod optamus omnibus quos ex caritate diligimus" (II.ii.25.2). *Caritas* is the good by which one loves and it is the good which one wills to another in love. In short: love loves love. This is formal perfection.

Caritas, as being a special case of the genus of love, completes without contradicting *amor*, just as does every species its genus. But there is also a *dis*continuity between the genus and species and therefore also between *amor* and *caritas*. As the species can never be derived from the genus so *caritas* can never be derived from *amor*. As a genus never evolves into a species, so *amor* never evolves into *caritas*. The species, like *caritas*, needs to be posited anew even though it is always posited in relation to the genus. Thus, when understood as a "gift of God," *caritas* shows the break between nature and new nature. It is "infused" as a virtue or *donum:* that means, it does not originate in and derive from nature. "*Caritas* and nature do not belong to the same genus," Thomas reminds us in an attempt to emphasize their discontinuity (II.ii.24.3 *ad* 2). On the contrary, the new nature springs newborn out of nothing. The natural virtues which empower acts cannot lead to eternal ends. It is only through the power of additional virtues that the human act pierces through to the good which is infinite. *"Caritas* attains to God Himself as He is in Himself, and not just according to the things that have their source in Him *(non ut ex eo aliquid proveniat)"* (II.ii.23.6). Eternal ends are beyond all human natural faculties. They are not natural nor attainable by natural faculties, but come as the ends of new, infused virtues, the indwelling of the Holy Spirit as *caritas creata* (II.ii.24.2).

This element of discontinuity is consistently carried through in Thomas' thinking. The *caritas* which is infused has its residence in the human will, as does *amor*. Nevertheless, whereas *amor* remains subject to reason as its guiding principle, *caritas* remains directly subject to God. The guidance of God is not irrational but it adds the power and insight which is lacking—permanently lacking, naturally lacking—in reason.

Again, discontinuity is emphasized in the contrast between the externality of good in creation and the internality of good in the new creation. In created humanity the ultimate good is outside man; God is known as the cause of all that is, but remains unknown. The good which man loves is outside him. But the external does not spontaneously and necessarily become internal. Insight into God's Trinitarian life and the love of Him as being Himself man's beatitude, come only from a new act of God. When it comes, it illuminates and orders all good and all knowledge from within; but if it is not given it cannot be derived from the external and unknown. Nature rests on one communication of God, grace rests on another. Both of them have their own circle. Nature's circle is also its prison. It allows development from potentiality to actuality, but the latter never includes the supernatural. A natural habit, as a principle of action either innate or acquired, cannot issue in an act which results from the internal freedom of grace. Only the new habit of *caritas* can open the gates of the prison.

The quality of *caritas* as gift, proceeding from and uniting most intimately with God, makes it unnecessary to posit imperfection in the gift itself. Because of the element of discontinuity, of newness, of givenness, *caritas* is *as a habit* perfect, even though it is imperfect *as an act* or series of acts. Here in the distinction between habitual *caritas* and actual *caritas* we meet a Thomistic parallel to the distinction between justification and sanctification (or regeneration and renovation) which Gerhard considered absolutely essential to theology. *Caritas* is given as a habit, complete, perfect, total; it leads into acts, partially, incompletely. In the sight of God man is just, in empirical actuality he is not. This is fundamentally the same distinction which Gerhard preserves in his insistence that justification takes place by grace through faith without works, but that it is always followed by the works of sanctification if it is not a dead faith.

As a virtue which is infused, *caritas* points to the discontinuity of the creations, but as a virtue it is the habit which points to the freedom and responsibility of the new. For as the formal principle of action it expresses the freedom of the new creature to act voluntarily. *Caritas* is located in the will; it is a new principle of voluntary action which can issue in acts worthy of eternal beatitude (cf. II.ii.23.3; 24.1). Whatever good is attained is due to a virtue. When supernatural good is attained, the good which is God Himself, it is due to the virtue which joins the creature to God directly. Thus both God and *caritas* can be said to be principles of life (II.ii.23.2 *ad* 2). God is man's life "effectively," *caritas,* "formally." These are not two separate principles of life but the former is in and with the latter. *Caritas* as a form is the means through which God effects eternal life; it is the finite analogy of the richness of God's life in Himself.

That *caritas* as a new form does imply the freedom of the new creature appears most clearly if one looks at a question which was the subject of much discussion in the Middle Ages; the question whether *caritas* is the Holy Spirit or whether it is something created in the soul. It is a striking fact of the theological discussion on this question that Peter the Lombard, who identified *caritas* and the Holy Spirit, found almost no followers of significance, even though his books of *Sentences* served throughout the period of late scholasticism as the basic dogmatics textbook upon which beginning university instructors held their first lectures.

The question has to do with the interpretation of the fifth verse of the fifth chapter of the book of Romans ("God's love has been poured into our hearts through the Holy Spirit which has been given to us"), of which Augustine had written, "This God, the Holy Spirit who proceeds from God, inflames the man to whom He is sent to a love of God and the neighbor; and He Himself is the love."[2] Shortly before the time of the Lombard, perhaps prompted by Abelard, the question had aroused renewed interest. It was Peter Lombard who, apparently on the basis of an oral controversy, raised the question to one of first importance in the famous Seventeenth Distinction of his *First Book of Sentences*. He is aware of the pre-eminence of love in the Christian life. The conclusion which he draws from that pre-eminence is that *caritas* must be a unique virtue in which the Holy Spirit works acts of love directly, without any mediating created virtue. Faith and hope both have mediating virtues which issue in their acts. But the Holy Spirit Himself must work the acts of love. To assert the opposite would, Peter seemed to believe, disenfranchise theological love, strip it of its rights of eminence.

But the identification met with opposition. Before the time of Bonaventure and Thomas, the chief argument against it came from Simon of Tournai and Philip the Counselor. The latter's seven arguments seem to have been convincing to his contemporaries, although the axioms he uses are not nearly so self-evident as we might like.[3] He asserts axiomatically, for example, that

2. *De Trin.* XV.31. See Landgraf, *Dogmengeschichte der Frühscholastik,* I/1, 220–37, and Johann Schupp, *Die Gnadenlehre des Petrus Lombardus,* p. 235.
3. *Summa de bono.* Quoted in Landgraf, *Dogmengeschichte,* I/1, 235 ff.

caritas must be a created virtue because working with, instead of without, means is a more perfect way for the Creator (though a less perfect way for the creature). Hidden in this kind of axiom is the view of creation (or at least the matter of creation) as a negative force to God's power. It would be a simple undertaking for Him to do things without tools; it is a more difficult thing for Him to use created tools, which resist His working. In other words, Philip implies, if one wants to preserve the eminence of *caritas,* one ought not to do so by eliminating the created virtue as a medium of its power.

Thomas, while accepting this basic criticism of the Lombard, gradually shifts the emphasis of his own answer. In his commentary on the *Sentences* (written in the years 1253–57) he argues in the fashion of Simon and Philip, pointing out that Peter does not accomplish his goal by his means. By the time of the *Questiones disputatae,* in which the treatise on love appears, and the *Summa Theologiae* (1269–72 and 1266–71, respectively), the argument has indeed not changed fundamentally but it revolves more cleanly around Thomas' concern to protect and preserve the freedom and voluntariness of the acts of *caritas,* to prevent understanding the creature as only an instrument, an inert tool, in which God works. Thus Aquinas maintains that a movement from the outside on the creature is not natural and not even God can make it so. As a stone cannot naturally fall upwards, a man cannot naturally act under compulsion. Therefore, a movement on the will from without can never be voluntary, for that would contradict the nature of the will. So if man as man, as a willing creature, is to attain an end which exceeds the capacity of his natural will, he must be endowed with a new *intrinsic* principle to perfect the will. That new principle is *caritas creata.* Without that inner habit, therefore, an act either would not be voluntary or it would not reach beyond purely natural ends.[4]

4. *De car.* 1 and *S. Th.* II.ii.23.2.

Caritas as a virtue, as "a created something in the soul (*anima*)," enables man to act voluntarily to attain ends beyond nature. Yet at the same time Thomas insists that it is indeed the Holy Spirit Himself acting in and through that *caritas*. He is the uncreated love, the *caritas increata*, operating through the created love in the same way that the Creator works through the natural forms. The forms, together with the gifts or virtues, enable the creature to attain the ends natural and supernatural "not as under compulsion but as free."[5] The concepts of virtue and form comprehend the divine and human activity in an inseparable union.[6]

Creaturely freedom has, moreover, the aspect of responsibility, betokened in the conception of the theological virtues as *accidental* habits. They do not belong to essential humanity. Man is still theoretically man even without grace. When he has grace it is not a permanent possession, but needs to be actively retained. It can be lost by one act of mortal sin—where mortal sin is by definition that act which expels *caritas*. An "accidental gift": thus does *caritas* mirror man's freedom and responsibility, conceived in Thomas' formal terms.

Furthermore, *caritas* is love in right order; where it is realized everything is in its own divinely appointed place. This order implicates everything without exception. Love of God, love of men (even enemies), love of the world of nature and the heavens —it is all in *caritas*, which is a love of God (and from God) for His own sake and a love of creatures because they belong to God. Thus, with regard to enemies, Thomas makes it a matter of "necessity" to love them out of *caritas*. *Caritas* loves them not in the degree to which they are enemies but because they are still essentially something of God's in spite of their enmity. "The more one loves God, the more one shows love to his neighbor, any

5. *De car.* 1: "non coacte sed quasi sponte."
6. Harnack, *Dogmengeschichte, 3,* 620 f., saw in the rejection of the Lombardian solution a missed opportunity for a "more evangelical posture" on the part of medieval scholasticism. But this is surely too great an oversimplification of the issue.

enmity notwithstanding" (II.ii.25.8). Sometimes, indeed, it becomes necessary to exclude from one's fellowship, or even from the fellowship of all the living, those enemies who are incorrigible in their perverseness. Thomas insists that such an exclusion is also an act of *caritas:* the act of love "by which the public good is preferred to the life of the single person" (II.ii.25.6 *ad* 2). Yet this is a work foreign to love, the reverse side of its proper activity. For, as Thomas goes on to say, traffic with sinners is to be avoided, indeed, by those who are weak and susceptible, those who may be led astray, but not by those who are strong. In other words, dealing with the perverse negatively, by exclusion and avoidance, is an admission of the weakness of *caritas* in the person who must so deal. Where *caritas* is at full strength its way of conquering is by inclusion and fellowship. It is greater, and proper to *caritas,* to overcome evil with good rather than forcibly to exclude the evil. Thomas seems to implicitly acknowledge that exclusion, or the execution of heretics and criminals, is not a final conquest of their wickedness but the self-defense of a weak *caritas.* The power of evil is conquered only when *caritas* is strong enough to overcome it with good, to embrace the neighbor in love and restore him to his place in the order of things.

But can *caritas* imply also self-sacrifice? This question is one that caused great difficulty to Thomas and other medieval theologians. Rousselot distinguishes two main lines of thought, the so-called "physical" or Greco-Thomist view of love, which sees no ultimate contradiction between self-love and the love of others, and the "ecstatic" view which emphasizes the aspects of self-surrender and self-sacrifice that are prerequisite for the full blooming of genuine love.[7] The former view retains a minimal amount

---

7. Perhaps no single writer, as Rousselot grants, represented either view exclusively. Bernard of Clairvaux, for example, is found in both lines. For this reason the division seems to have met with little agreement. The most extensive attempt to re-analyze the problem according to a different typology is that of Z. Alszeghy, *Grundformen der Liebe.* Instead of the dichotomy of "physical" and "ecstatic" he uses four types: the objective-ecstatic (*sachbetont-*

of self-preservation at all times; the latter emphasizes love's demand of absolute self-negation where it is needed.

The special occasion for the discussion of this problem was Romans 9:3, the passage in which the author declares his desire to forfeit himself if by such means his people could be brought to salvation. It was a knotty problem; if taken literally, Paul was, in the view of the scholastics, suggesting that he sacrifice not his temporal life and goods but his eternal blessedness itself, in exchange for the beatitude for his people. "Optabam anathema esse a Christo pro fratribus meis." Such a desire went *against the order* of *caritas,* according to which one should not love one's fellow man more than one's own eternal beatitude. And since that order was divinely established and not arbitrarily determined, to attempt to violate it was blasphemy. The notion that the willingness to make absolutely no claims for oneself at all might itself be the essence of love was not one to which Thomas could have eagerly assented.[8] Not only was such a notion absurd because of its

---

ekstatisch), the objective-physical (*sachbetont-physisch*), the personal-ecstatic (*personbetont-ekstatisch*) and the personal-physical (*personbetont-physisch*). He sees the difference between the love of a thing (*Sache*) and the love of a person as a principle of division which has a validity equal to that of "physical" and "ecstatic." His analysis is not so much a contradiction as it is a further refinement of Rousselot's pioneer work. The interpreters of Thomas are not unanimous concerning the rationale of his solution to the question. Rousselot finds it in the part-whole relation, E. Gilson in the image-relationship, M. Coconnier, L. Geiger, and H. D. Simonin in the nature of the "spiritual" good which transcends the opposition between self-love and other-love—how it does so remaining always a bit of a puzzle. M. D'Arcy's fascinating *The Mind and Heart of Love,* presenting a solution which goes beyond Thomas, finds it necessary to preserve a polar tension between the egocentric and ecstatic drives within man, neither of which can be eliminated without self-destruction. Also among non-Thomistic solutions one should notice a strikingly original, but apparently not well-known, attempt to resolve the problem, that of L. Grünhut, *Eros und Agape,* who develops his view on the basis of the proposition that nature (*Wesen*) is evil.

8. Although he does recognize it: in III.49.6 Thomas states, as the rationale of the exaltation of Christ, the principle, "If anyone out of a just will deprives himself of that which he was entitled to possess, he then deserves that something should be superadded to him as the reward of his just will."

practical impossibility (self-sacrifice too often meant self-defeat) but also because of the blasphemy to which it was hospitable: that of wanting to dispose of something which was not at man's disposal, of rejecting the divinely established order of all things. To bargain with one's eternal beatitude was to forget one's creaturehood. Eternal life was and remained at the disposal of God alone. To wish to be accursed for one's friends or compatriots was tantamount to playing god, in opposition to God. It contravened the order of *caritas*. For even the love displayed in the Crucifixion and Resurrection was not conceived exclusively (perhaps not even primarily) as self-sacrifice united with power—where self-denial meant not defeat but final conquest—but as the re-establishment of an order disturbed.

All of these reasons combined to make Thomas seek another explanation of the Romans passage. In his commentary on the *Sentences*[9] he adds the qualification that this passage is to be understood to mean Paul's exclusion only for a certain length of time or under the condition that it be acceptable to God Himself. The interpretation which he gives later in his *Commentary on Romans*,[10] his *De caritate*,[11] and his *Summa Theologiae*,[12] is consistent with that initial position. There are two ways of understanding the apostle's meaning, he declares. Either the past tense in *optabam* ("I wished") means that Paul is referring to a time before he was in the state of grace and, therefore, does not himself condone such a blasphemy; or the sense of the verb is optative ("would that") and means not that Paul loved his compatriots more than God but rather that he wished to be temporarily deprived of the fruition of blessedness (which is a matter of self-love) in order that the honor of God be manifested in others first (which belongs to a love of God). In this latter case the order of

9. *III Sent.* d. 29.1.3 *ad* 6.
10. *Ad Rom.* 9.1 (v. 3).
11. 11 *ad* 6.
12. II.ii.27.8 *ad* 1.

caritas is preserved because it places God's honor above one's own immediate delights.

Now, the order of the objects of love was not an idle question devised for entertainment in leisure hours. On the contrary, it was a microcosm of the whole order of nature and grace. For even though it was true that *caritas* was indiscriminate and promiscuous in the sense that it willed the same good (namely, eternal beatitude) to all, yet when it came to the degree of "affect" or "exterior effect" decisions of preference had to be made. Thomas, accordingly, devotes thirteen articles to a discussion of the question of the order of love's objects (ii.ii.26.1–26.13). In this discussion arise considerations which have to do with the relation of the creatures to their *principium* (creation and the Creator), with the relation of the new creation to God, and finally with the relation of the creation to the new creation. The proper order of the objects of love is the following:

1) One loves *God* above all, because He is the first principle and the universal good.
2) One loves the *community* above oneself, because the common good is "more lovable" than the private.
3) One loves the *spiritual part of the self* next, because it is participant in the eternal good.
4) One loves one's *neighbor* next to oneself, because one's neighbor is an associate in eternal good (*societas, consociatio*).
5) Finally, one loves the *corporeal part* of oneself, because it is partaker of beatitude not directly by participation or association but indirectly *per redundantiam.*

But under "neighbors" there are problematic situations. Does one love one's father more than one's son? Or father more than mother? Or parents more than spouse? Or benefactor more than beneficiary? In deciding these questions Thomas points out the two major principles upon which the answers are based. Both principles are formal. From the standpoint of the *loving subject,* that creature receives greater love which is more closely related to the subject; whereas from the standpoint of the *loved object,* that receives greater love which is more closely related to God, whether by its creative power or its degree of goodness.

Thus, there are two answers to each of these questions, corresponding to the two viewpoints. From the side of the *object,* the father is loved more than the son, because the father is more similar to God. As God is the principle of the world, the father is the principle of his family. From the side of the *subject,* a person loves his son more than his father because the son is more closely related—*magis conjunctus magis amatur* (II.ii.26.7 *ad* 3). First, the son is a product of the father; secondly, a father always knows his son even when the son may not know his father; thirdly, the son is a vital part (*pars existens*) of the parent whereas the parent is not of the son; fourthly, parents love their children longer than children their parents because children do not begin to love immediately at birth. The answers to the other questions are given in similar fashion: one loves father more than mother because the agent of procreation is more similar to the Creator than is the *patiens,* whereas under such other aspects as the amount of care bestowed upon the child, the mother may be loved more as the greater good.

Again, *objectively* one loves parents more than spouse, but *subjectively* spouse more than parents, because the one-flesh relationship of marriage is more intimate than that of children to parents. So also under one standpoint the benefactor is more loved; under the other, the beneficiary. Moreover, if there are two relationships equally close (say that of brothers among themselves and of soldiers in an army or of citizens in a community), then normally preference is given to the more *stable* relation. Since the natural ties of the family are indestructible, they provide the basis for other relationships, rather than conversely.

A third explicit (but somewhat incidental) criterion which Thomas employs is the *number of reasons* one has for loving (cf.

II.ii.26.7 and 26.11.3 and *ad* 3). Thus, one has greater love for a Christian who is a member of one's family than one has for other Christians. For *caritas* has but a single reason for loving others, but many reasons for loving members of the family.

In addition to these explicit criteria, however, the implicit one should not be lost from view. The order of love's objects is based on their metaphysical status and not on psychological considerations. In other words, love of God claims absolute priority because where it is lacking all else is lacking too. The love of one's spiritual nature has precedence over love for one's neighbor in the sense that it is in the nature of *caritas* to work first in the mind. If it is absent there it is everywhere absent. And so on through the other grades. A *caritas*-love for one's own body presupposes a love for one's neighbor, which in turn presupposes a love for one's spiritual good, etc.

In the same sense one should interpret the idea (which Thomas took from Aristotle) that self-love is the measure of all love. Where there is no self-love, there is no love whatever. Grammatically speaking, one might say that the coloring of the genitive in "love of self" is as much subjective ("the self's love") as it is objective ("the love for oneself"). Self-love, in other words, only occasionally takes on the meaning of *selfish* love, a seeking or working for one's own delight or comfort or advantage at the expense of someone else. Therefore, although Thomas is prevented from ever expressly stating self-sacrifice as the final expression of *caritas,* in the many and various qualifications upon self-love it is certainly approximated, for each object of love has its own place which is restricted and limited by all other objects.

The charge that the Aristotelian, or Greek, strain in medieval thinking about love emerged as selfishness is not, therefore, fully true. For it becomes clear that these considerations concerning the sequence of the objects of love are not immediately *ethical* principles if one attempts to apply them to a concrete situation. Suppose, for example, that one is confronted with a choice between meeting the claims of a father or those of a spouse. Let us say that the both of them are in such a condition where they need full attention, so that the (legitimate) claims of both cannot be met. Under such circumstances one obtains no answer from the consideration that the father is to be loved more in his objective character, whereas the spouse is to be loved more because of his closer relationship to the subject. The two principles in this case demand two contradictory actions, and lead to the circumstance, in the words of Jacques Barzun, that "principle never forgives and its logic is to kill." In order to resolve the ethical problem some further principle or some mediating agency would be needed. The point is that this whole scheme of *caritas'* objects expresses not an ethical solution, but a view of creation as an ordered and harmonious whole.

Thus, when Thomas repeats such axioms as that every creature naturally loves the good of the whole more than his own private good, one need not conclude that the Doctor was blind to the common fact that there are some who do exploit others for the sake of personal advantage or comfort. On the contrary, such statements as "Every creature naturally loves . . ." are not statistical generalizations of observed behavior. They are articulations of the vision of a fundamental harmony in creation and new creation, a fundamental harmony named *caritas*. Where people do in fact pursue their private good to the detriment of the public good, they are examples of fallen nature, and their actions are contrary to their own nature; they are, in that sense, irrational. Where *caritas* has healed and elevated, there the truly natural is restored and supplemented, germinally in the present life and consummately in the next.

In sum: as ordered love, *caritas* is the name of the vision of a creation that has all its parts in place.

Thomas does, moreover, make room for a conception of man's relation to God in a way which is more dialectical-personal. We have already noted that his conception of the knowledge of God as the "object of beatitude" is virtually the knowledge of God as the Thou with whom dialogue is possible. That fact is included in *caritas* too, for, as a kind of friendship with God, it marks the elevation of the creature to a status in which personal communion with Him is possible. In this sense the friendship-character of *caritas* is its grandest expression. R. Egenter[13] indeed points out that, apart from a single reference in the commentary on I Corinthians, Thomas reserves the word "friendship" for the relationship in love of the *new* creature to God. Natural love for God is not a friendship (*amicitia*) because at that level God is an unknown. He is known as Principle but not as Thou. Friendship presupposes familiarity and mutual responsibility, an intimate commerce which is possible only because the new creature knows God Himself, not as a stranger but as a companion.

Nygren, in his analysis of the Thomistic concept of love, sees in the incorporation of this Aristotelian friendship a violation of the integrity of Thomas' doctrine of love.[14]

> As Thomas has affirmatively answered the question, *utrum amor sit in concupiscibili,* and will not surrender his principle that all love is acquisitive love, it is undeniably strange that he can immediately afterwards give a new definition of love, based on Aristotle, as follows: *amare est velle alicui bonum.*

On this point Nygren makes both a technical and an interpretive error. Technically, this is not a "new" definition, since Thomas uses it throughout the *Summa*. It occurs, for example, very early in connection with the question whether God loves all things (I.20.2). The mistake in interpretation: it is at best misleading to state that Thomas maintains the principle that all love is acquisitive love. There are two types which appear consistently in his thought, the *amor concupiscentiae* (the appetite for the good) and the *amor amicitiae* (the willing of good to someone in

13. *Gottesfreundschaft*, p. 51.
14. *Agape and Eros*, pp. 644 ff., commenting on *S. Th.* II.i.26.1.

222

friendship).[15] The latter he even calls love "in the pure sense" (*simpliciter*); the former is love in a derived sense. If one were to give priority to one of these two types, it would seem more just to Thomas' view to give it to friendship.

It *is* true, however, that Thomas did not give a detailed account of the relationship between the two objects of love, the good which is willed and the someone to whom it is willed.[16] Sometimes he distinguishes the two thus: concupiscence is the desire of a thing's good for oneself, friendship is the desire of it for someone else (II.ii.23.1). But he seems to have assumed that they were mutually complementary and not contradictory. It seems preferable, therefore, to see in the element of friendship not a change in the definition of love but the use of a more openly dialectical conceptualization of God's relation to the creature of grace. Rather than violating the unity of meaning, it seems to enrich it by contributing another articulation of the same reality.

At any rate, Thomas unhesitatingly states that *caritas* is a friendship with God (II.ii.23.1). As such it is a privilege only of the creature of grace. For friendship implies that there is benevolence and also mutuality—*amicus est amico amicus*. The mutuality is possible only on the basis of a "communication" from God which goes beyond the communication of natural goods. How is it possible for the creature to return benevolence to God? Only as his free response to God's free gift. *Caritas* makes it possible for man to participate in God's eternal life, to become intimate with Him, to call Him friend—to address Him as "Thou." The special communication upon which *caritas* is founded is the communication of His beatitude itself and not of natural gifts. Yet it is a communication which confirms man in his creaturely freedom. So founded, the equality or mutuality is not absolute in respect to

15. Cf. e.g. II.i.26.4; *De car.* 8 *ad* 16; *In Jn.* 15.4, n. 2; *III Sent.* d. 29.1.4.
16. Egenter and Hatheyer have, therefore, tried to stress the significance of a concept of *complacentia* as a union of the benevolence in friendship with concupiscence.

man's friendship for God; it is based on man's relation to Him as "in His image." The pattern of that dialectic between friends, however, Thomas nowhere describes.

The whole structure of nature and grace is an articulation of *caritas,* and *caritas* is in summary that structure. *Caritas* explains the structure of nature and grace—why it is what it is (because it is God's ordering of things); that structure in turn explicates *caritas.* The order of *caritas* is the embodiment of the will of God; the will of God is the order of *caritas.* Thus grace does not contradict but rather fulfills nature; and *caritas* does not contradict *amor,* the natural striving for natural goods, but fulfills it by rectifying the distortions in the fallen state and by endowing it with more principles of action. Grace presupposes nature; *caritas* presupposes *amor.* Grace does not annihilate human freedom; *caritas* does not destroy man's responsibility, but rather lifts him to participation in the eternal life of God Himself, to friendship with Him. Finally, grace is not derived or deduced from nature, and *caritas* does not grow out of natural love but awaits a new creation.

CHAPTER VII

Fides

Thomas' ultimate answer to the question, "Who can stand before God?" is "The man of *caritas*." With Gerhard it is, "The man of *fides*." These answers reflect the difference in the more exact formulation of the question. In Thomas' rationale, the form of the question is: "How can man *attain* his supernatural end?" In Gerhard's it is: "On what can man *rely* in the face of the annihilating judgment of God against every imperfection?" Faith in Gerhard's sense will not answer Thomas' question just as *caritas* will not answer Gerhard's. *Fides,* therefore, summarizes the dialectical-personal rationale of Gerhard as *caritas* does Thomas' formal one. The latter's *caritas* cannot be neatly fitted into the former's rationale any more than the former's *fides* can function effectively in the latter's rationale.

This is true in spite of Gerhard's concurrence with the view that *caritas* is "in some sense the sum of Christianity" (XVI.120) and that the "practical definition" of God is found in *caritas* (II.94). For although he can make such an acknowledgment because every "good fruit" in the behavior of the Christian proceeds from *caritas* as from its root, he must always add the qualification: "nonetheless, in the article of justification, faith alone reigns,

225

whose fruit is *caritas,* and without which *caritas* itself does not please God" (ibid.).

It is true, further, in spite of Thomas' and Gerhard's common conviction that the cause of salvation lies in God alone and not in man. Gerhard articulates this *sola gratia* in relation to *sola fides,* implying pre-eminently that man *relies on* Christ's mediation rather than his own goodness. *Fides* is the *sine qua non* for Gerhard as *caritas* is for Thomas—and they both emphasize the absolute sovereignty of God as well as the freedom in man's participation.

It is true, finally, in spite of the fact that point for point Gerhard can speak of the relation of creation to new creation in almost the same terms as does Thomas. As Thomas uses the relation of genus to species to express both the continuity and discontinuity of the creations, so does Gerhard. As God's love of man in Christ and His love of man qua creature are distinguished in Thomas as the *dilectio specialis* and the *dilectio generalis,* so also they are in Gerhard. As Thomas speaks of the communication of nature and the communication of grace being the two positing and creative acts of God, so too may Gerhard. Does the new creation bear additive characteristics in that it bestows new powers above and beyond the old? It does so in Gerhard's view also. Thomas may speak of the new creation as being a new form or set of forms, lending both freedom and responsibility; so does Gerhard. If Thomas can describe the closeness of the relation of *homo justus* to God in terms of friendship, Gerhard can agree. "All these things," he says of the medieval distinctions in love, including friendship as the designation of a "reciprocal and mutual love (*amor*)" of the rational creature with God, "can in a sound sense be allowed, provided it is clear that love in the rational creatures is not considered a condition meriting the divine love" (II.223).

All of this agreement becomes disagreement in the article of justification as Gerhard senses an obscuring of *fides.* The object of Gerhard's scrutiny is not the whole picture of man as he is by nature and by grace, but the picture of man precisely at the point of transition between the two states. How man looks at *that* point —and how man *looks* at that point is not separable from how man *is brought* to that point—is his consuming interest. *Fides* thus reflects the following marks which are the paramount characteristics of Gerhard's whole view. It reflects, first, the fact that his concern is precisely for the *articulus justificationis.* There and only there one can speak of faith alone; there and only there faith crowds out every other consideration, because *caritas,* nature, and free will are intrusions and obfuscations.

> The question does not concern the absolute rank of *fides* and *caritas;* it concerns their ranking in the article of justification. In justification, we say, faith reigns alone without our love; indeed, it is the task of faith alone (*soli fidei competit*) to lay hold of Christ and, in Him, of God's grace, the forgiveness of sins, and eternal life (XVI.120). . . . Our position is not refuted by the fact that *caritas* is called in some sense the sum of Christianity if the question concerns the life of a Christian man . . . ; in the article of justification faith alone dominates—*caritas* is its fruit and without it not even *caritas* would be pleasing to God (ibid.). . . . If the promise [of the gospel] depended on a fulfillment through our *caritas,* it would never be sure because our *caritas* is imperfect in many ways (XVI.157). . . . It is very true to say that only unbelief condemns a man (XVII.116).

Secondly, it reflects the fact that his conceptualization of justification through faith is in dialectical terms. Justification is a forensic procedure, in which man has nothing to do but to listen to the voice of the Judge and the Mediator. This is the counterpart to the *discontinuity* in Thomas' *amor-caritas.* In the formal relation of the species to the genus, there is nothing in the general-natural which of itself leads to the special-gracious. In the dialectical relation of the accused to the judge, there is nothing the accused can say which will lead him out of the state of guilt. Nature cannot produce grace; and the guilty man cannot renew his innocence by self-congratulation. The first is an impossibility formally, the second dialectically. Nature is "nothing" formally in relation to grace—except recipient; man is "nothing" dialectically in relation to God—except hearer.

Thirdly, it reflects the dialectical counterpart of the *continuity* between nature and grace. In formal terms the species is always posited in relation to the genus; grace presupposes and perfects nature. Dialectically, there is not only the No of the accuser but also the Yes of the Mediator. What is the No of one moment becomes the Yes of the next moment in the forensic process. And at the turning point where the guilty becomes innocent, the total No of the Judge is also His total Yes. Formally, with Thomas, we speak of continuity and discontinuity, which at the precise point of transition are fused, with conversion exhibiting both the continuity and discontinuity of nature and grace. Dialectically, with Gerhard, we speak of the Yes *and* the No, which at the precise point of transition are the Yes *in* the No and the No *in* the Yes.

Finally, *fides* as trust (*fiducia*) is to the dialectical rationale what ordered love is to the formal. The *tranquillitas* of the new creature in the intimate presence of God is the state of utter reliance upon Him or the state of perfectly ordered love. "Ordered love" suggests that all parts are in their proper place; "trust" or "reliance" suggests that the continuous traffic between man and God will bring communion but no quarrel, a Yes and No containing surprises but no disappointments. Like *amicitia* in Thomas, *fiducia* expresses the personal character of the relation between man and God; but unlike *amicitia* it retains the connotations of *obedience-in-law* rather than of the encounter of equals and friends.

CHAPTER VIII

"Through a Glass Darkly"

In this concluding chapter I shall first summarize the results of the previous chapters by stating three conclusions and two rules. These will be followed by an evaluation of the whole. The chapter is concluded by a suggestion.

Thomas and Gerhard both employ formal, dialectical, and paradoxical concepts. The difference lies, however, in the emphasis given to each. In Thomas the formal predominates and has dialectical overtones or supplements; in Gerhard the dialectical predominates but there are formal additions. Furthermore, the paradoxical in each case appears in relation to those predominating modes: in Thomas in relation to the formal, in Gerhard in relation to the dialectical.

Thus, the pivotal concepts in *Thomas' formal-objective rationale* are nature and supernature, form and end, order and merit. They articulate what man is and does as a creature and as a new creature. The type of question which Thomas asks and answers is tied to the formal character rather than the dialectical effectiveness of these concepts. God's sovereignty and man's freedom are articulated in those terms. For example, the question of man's merit of his supernatural end would have the following rationale. The given conviction (a datum of revelation as far as Thomas is concerned) is that man *can* achieve a supernatural end. But if a free creature achieves an end, then by definition he has merited that end. The actual achievement of an unmerited end on the part of a creature of free will would be a self-contradictory notion. The form and end are the priorities in this case, not the merit. That is to say, the means by which the form attains its end, in the case of the rational creature, will by definition be his merit; merit is defined in relation to the form and end. "Merit" is not the name of a morally perfect act; it is not that which can in an absolute sense successfully claim a due reward of eternal life. Instead it is part of the rationale of that which can be named man's participation in beatitude as a creature of reason and will.

In the interpretation of some of the Thomistic maxims it is, accordingly, of capital importance to note how the concepts are used. If the concept of merit is a name applied to a concrete reality (for example, an inner disposition or a kind of moral act) from which one may infer eternal life as a necessary consequence, its function and implications are surely different than if it is part of the formal rationale of man's freedom and God's sovereignty. Moreover, it is also important to note that at decisive points the formal scheme is broken through. When the subject of discussion is the relation of man's doing to God's doing, Thomas is consistent in holding to the sovereign initiative, the absolute prevenience, of God as the *principium* and *finis ultimus,* as well as to the participant freedom of man, the "cooperation" of the creature. Thus, the "aid of God (*auxilium Dei*)" and the "conversion of the free will" are concepts in which the formal scheme is broken through as well as maintained. That is to say, they are paradoxical in the formal conceptualization. In every act the aid of God is presupposed in the same way that, metaphorically, the light of the sun is presupposed in every act of seeing. To interpret the *auxilium Dei* either in purely formal and straightforward terms or in dialectical terms would be to misunderstand it. If interpreted in a non-paradoxical way, the aid of God would have to be distinct from the initiative of man. The result would be to say that God is the agent of this *part* and man the agent of that *part* of an act; or that at certain times (the very beginning, for example) God is solely at work and at other times man is solely at work; or that in certain respects it is God's act and in other respects it is man's. But any of these three interpretations would involve theology in the Pelagianism or semi-Pelagianism which Thomas rejects. The only way to maintain the scheme as he preserved it is to use the concept of God's assistance as he used it; namely, as the paradoxical breakthrough of the formal rationale. In this way God's agency is not separate or absolutely distinct from man's agency; it is rather man's agency in an ultimate perspective.

The paradoxical becomes focused in the concept of the conversion of the free will, which is at once the purely voluntary act of man and the sovereign movement of God; it is the point at which creature and Creator touch. Under ordinary circumstances the notion of an act of the will which is impelled (rather than attracted) by something outside of the will is self-contradictory. The good is external to the will and moves it by attraction, but only the will itself can move itself to that good, for its principle is interior. Yet the movement of God on the will in conversion is neither the attraction of the exterior good alone nor the interior movement of the *voluntas*. It is both. Only God as the Creator as well as the final end is able to be the unqualified object of the will's desire *and also* the agent who can move the will interiorly precisely as free will. As the Creator He can give an impulse to the will which does not destroy the reality of its self-impulsion. The rationale of this interpenetration of the divine and human is not simply formal, for the movement of the free will when it turns to God is simultaneously the impelling action of God and the uncoerced action of man. Here again the interpreter, especially if he is a Protestant, must be at pains to discern the nature of the concept, to avoid interpreting it as purely formal (or even dialectical) instead of as the paradoxical in the formal. The usual oppositions between the agency of God and the agency of man are overcome in the notion of the movement of the free will toward God.

Moreover, the air of self-contradiction in such paradoxical concepts can be quite frankly recognized. That is to say, the fused elements can be distinguished in the abstract, and even separated at specific points of a discussion, but this separation can never be made absolute; for the presence of the paradoxical in the formal rationale is evidenced by the refusal to make formal distinctions absolute. Thus, even though for long stretches Thomas may speak of God and man as if they were either separately or jointly acting in concrete situations—as if, in other words, the formal oppositions were absolute—still at decisive points these oppositions are overthrown in order to bring to light the paradox which is in them. Thomas can speak of conversion as if it were due totally to man's (implying "and not to God's") agency; or as totally God's (implying "and not man's"); or as partly divine and partly human. Yet he can also reject all, from the crassly Pelagian through the Manichean to the semi-Pelagian, because he knows of the limitation, the latent paradox, in his rationale. His use of concepts to articulate, in spite of their limitations, something of man's ultimate status is the well-known Thomistic analogy, the use of terms in such a way that they are neither univocal nor equivocal but both.[1] Although one must grant that a greater degree of precision in delimiting the analogous use of concepts and words may be desirable and possible, there can be little doubt of the main direction of the notion of analogy, as it is presupposed in Thomas' actual employment of such concepts as the conversion of the free will.

In Gerhard's dialectical-personal rationale, on the other hand, the pivotal concepts are justification and related concepts. To be

1. I prefer to describe analogy as *both* univocal and equivocal rather than, as is usually done, as *neither* univocal nor equivocal but a mean between them.

sure, in those articles which are not drawn into the rays of the
central doctrine of justification, he operates with formal concepts
as much as Thomas does. But the terms around which his thought
characteristically revolves are those of forensic justification, of
judge and accused, of mediator and the just-by-faith. The ultimate
status of man is described in these terms rather than in those of
form and end. They are terms which have the power to engage
the hearer in his situation, to engage him with the concrete *vox
Dei.* Then Gerhard must reject the notion of merit, because he
transposes it into his dialectical rationale in which it can concretely be only an ambiguous or false *vox Dei.* The question
which guides him in this area of problems is not the formal one
of what is presupposed in the fact that man attains a supernatural
end as a free creature (though Gerhard does not deny that fact)
but the dialectical one of what can be set against the concretely
heard voice of the judging God. It cannot be man's merit, because
nothing of man has the power to be a No to God's No to sin.
If there is to be a No to God's No, it must come from God Himself. It is, therefore, not the concept of man's merit but the image
of Christ's mediation which provides the No to God's No.

The criteria applicable to Gerhard's theological assertions are
accordingly dialectical and not formal. If he says that man can be,
and is, completely rejected by God, completely under the wrath
of God, this is an assertion validated not by reference to the nature
of God and of man but by reference to the concrete situation.
The picture of God's wrath as His absolute judicial No to *homo
peccator* is true because it is able to drive the complacent man to
the recognition of the depth of his imperfection.

Similarly the doctrine of the mercy of God in Christ is not
formally validated, nor is it the result of a historical study of the
events in the New Testament; it is that doctrine or image which
has the power, in the concrete situation, to negate the despair of
the man who is overwhelmed by his sinfulness. Because the doctrine has the power to do this—that is, because it is efficacious—

it is the adequate theological account of man's relation to God. In relation to the man who is self-satisfied, the doctrine of Christ's mercy is not true—because it does not have the power to overcome his complacency. Relative to the man who is in despair at his sins, the doctrine of God's wrath is not true—because it does not have the power to overcome his despair. The doctrine of justification through faith, with all its implications, is thus the pre-eminent doctrine, the *articulus stantis et cadentis ecclesiae,* because it is an adequate interpretation of that radical encounter of the sinner, as sinner and nothing more, with God. That is the crushing and saving drama of salvation in the life of the individual.

Furthermore, as the paradoxical in Thomas' thought emerges in relation to his formal rationale, in Gerhard it emerges in relation to the dialectical. The paradox is the implicit criterion in justification through faith. In the radical encounter of the despairing *homo reus* with God the dialectical progression (*successivum*) is ended. Man receives the absolute No of God, and in and through that absolute No His Yes. When the dialectic between man and God reaches the point where the two are completely over against each other; when, that is to say, man becomes aware of himself as nothing more in the sight of God than a sinner who can, because he is a sinner, speak no word of self-defense; then the dialectic has in principle ended. Henceforth it is not God and man but God alone who speaks. In that *adiaireton* He speaks His No and through the No, His Yes-for-Christ's-sake. Here the dialectical rationale is broken through and transformed. Normally every dialectical No is followed by another Yes (which is a negation of the No) and there are no limits to this progression; there is never a final No or Yes. Yet the No-Yes in forensic justification is precisely the final one. For when man is nothing but a sinner, when the only quality that counts is his imperfection, he can hear only an unqualified rejection of himself by God. No rejection can be imagined beyond that one, for it is total and final. But the rejection is also a hidden acceptance which becomes audible to the ears of faith. No more complete acceptance can be imagined than this one, for it is an acceptance of the wholly unacceptable. For that reason Gerhard can regard the article of justification as the final criterion, the article with which the church stands or falls.

The paradox is presupposed in the dialectic between God and the new creature. The Yes and No which has passed beyond the final Yes-No is the dialectic, not of man the accused with God the Judge, but of God the Judge with Christ the Mediator and Advocate.

It is clear that some terms which are common to both Thomas and Gerhard appear in different modes in each of them. Gerhard's interpretation of merit illustrates a transposition from the formal to the dialectical. He must reject the idea of man's merit because he understands a recourse to merit as an attempt to find grounds upon which to defend oneself against God's concretely heard judgment against sin. He does not understand it as the term in which the positing freedom of God and the participating freedom of man are formally enclosed. Again, his interpretation of the freedom of the will is, like Thomas', primarily formal. But unlike Thomas' it lacks the ragged edges of the paradoxical. His extensive formal analysis of the notion is a refinement of Thomas' doctrine, a purification from all paradoxical coloring. That is to say, Gerhard sees the oppositions between God's agency and man's agency in a radically exclusive way. The conversion of the free will must be assigned entirely to God; to man can be assigned at most a passive receptivity. The difficulties which this solution overlooks do not trouble Gerhard because, as we noted, he has undertaken to resolve them in the article of justification.

The fundamental tenets of the two theologians are the same. In both cases the rationale explicates on the one hand the sovereign initiative of God and the purely receptive role of man, and on the other hand the real and active participation of man as a free creature in his salvation. What has obscured the underlying unanimity, as far as the rationale is concerned, has been the mis-interpretation of formal terms dialectically or of dialectical terms formally. Thus, if Gerhard's forensic justification is interpreted formally it leads to nonsense, to ethical chaos, and to a denial of man's real participation in salvation. The assertion that man is absolutely worthless before God is, viewed formally, self-contra-dictory; but dialectically and properly expounded, as Gerhard intended it, it is that doctrine which can be set against man's *complacency* in a concrete situation. Again, a non-dialectical interpretation of man's righteousness in the sight of God leads to ethical chaos. The dialectical interpretation of it implies, however, that the doctrine of free grace on the basis of the merits of Christ is that which can effectively be opposed to man's *despair* in a concrete situation.

Conversely, a dialectical interpretation of concepts like "faith formed by *caritas*" leads to an obscuring of the initiative of God in creation and especially in salvation. That is to say, if the doctrine that man is saved by his *fides-caritate-formata* is taken as a doctrine which can be set against a person in the situation of despair, then it is ineffective because it does not call the despairing man away from his self-condemnation to the voice of the mercy of God which is outside him and which is absolutely prevenient to anything he does. The despairing man is one who finds nothing in himself or in his understanding of the world which can bring him out of the ever more constrictive circle in which he is caught. To call him to his *caritas*, even his *fides caritate formata*, will cause him to listen all the more to his self-accusation; it will not help him out of his despair because it does not enable him to hear the sound of God's accepting voice.

On the basis of the foregoing conclusions we may now state some general rules for the analysis and understanding of the theological controversy between Roman Catholicism and Protestantism in the period represented by John Gerhard.

The first rule, it would seem, is that anyone examining this controversy should be aware of how its terms are used, and should judge them according to the criteria which are applicable; he should, in other words, not divorce doctrines from methods. One cannot fairly judge Thomas' *caritas* by dialectical criteria, nor can one fairly judge Gerhard's *fides* by formal criteria. The type of argument which G. C. Berkouwer presents in *Recent Developments in Roman Catholic Thought*[2] suffers, I believe, from precisely this failing. He writes, "It seems to me that it is precisely against *sola fide* that Trent turns, against the faith that directs itself exclusively upon the grace of Christ." If we assume for the moment that the canons of Trent are fairly Thomistic on this point (as Küng would maintain[3]), half of Berkouwer's criticism is correct—Trent does turn against justification "by faith alone." But the other half is not correct, for a Thomistic rejection of *sola fide* is not a rejection of the sovereignty of the grace of Christ nor, therefore, an actual rejection of the Reformation doctrine. Thomas' *fides* is not the total reliance upon Christ's merit, but the dispositional stage of the completely ordered being and action of *caritas*. The Thomistic question does not ask for that on which one can *rely;* it asks for the nature of *caritas* as the ultimate ordering principle of life. The Reformation's *fides,* through which justification comes, is more nearly equivalent in meaning and function to Thomas' (and, I think, Trent's) "faith formed by love." For *sola fides* in Thomistic thought would be faith without its final form; it would be the faith which is roughly parallel to "historical faith" (knowledge and assent without trust) in Gerhard; whereas in Reformation thought, as in Gerhard's, "faith alone" means faith without works, or more precisely, faith as the trust which negates the ultimacy of works.

Berkouwer's argument is marred, moreover, by an additional error. In opposition to the thesis of Küng (that there is no funda-

2. Pp. 61–63.
3. *Rechtfertigung,* pp. 215, 248, 259.

mental opposition between the Tridentine and the Barthian doctrine of justification), he holds that Trent *did* misunderstand the Reformation notion of faith alone *and* (but?) that it did reject the Reformation conception of *sola fides*. Küng contends that Rome rejected the "Reformation's external concept of justification." Now, if it is a mistake to interpret the Reformation's concept of justification as purely "external" (that is, without effect in the justified man), then Trent was mistaken in so understanding it. How then does Berkouwer's conclusion follow: "It is impossible to draw any other conclusion than that the declarations of the Council of Trent actually have reference to nothing but the Reformation *sola fide*"? If on the one hand one says that Trent misunderstood the meaning of faith alone, how, on the other hand, can one say that therefore what it anathematizes *is* really the Reformation doctrine of faith alone? It would seem only consistent to conclude that, if Trent rejected a doctrine which was not really the Reformers' doctrine (as Berkouwer himself proves), then Trent cannot have rejected what was really the Reformation doctrine of justification by faith alone.

A student of these controversies should, it would seem, be aware that the modes of conceptualizing have not only their legitimate and necessary functions but also their distinctive dangers. The overriding danger for the formal mode is that its concepts deaden rather than enliven the material being interpreted. When definitions of terms can be made only in relation to other terms, and when concepts can be understood only by a memorizing of those purely formal relations without reference at all to concrete reality, then formal thought is sterile. It no longer illuminates, it oppresses—or at best entertains and bewitches. Thus, the prevailing objection of the twentieth-century mind to the scholasticism of the thirteenth as well as the seventeenth century is not so much that scholastic thought is false but that it is irrelevant; that it consists of nothing more than a vast array of definitions to be learned, which when learned have no further function than to admit one to the society in which the rataplan of the terms is the identifying mark; that it does not do what it is intended to do, that is, to illuminate the reality we confront or to resolve actual problems. From our present conviction it does not, of course, follow that the concepts of those philosopher-theologians failed to interpret their actual experience satisfactorily at their time. Indeed, their zeal and passion show that the contrary was the case; Aristotelianism as they understood it had its power precisely because it did interpret experience and give shape to actual questions and answers, providing in a formal rationale the satisfying explanations that the mind sought.

For the dialectical mode the chief danger is that the doctrine which is effective in one situation is not effective in another. Much of Gerhard's defense of the doctrine of justification through faith is entwined with his conviction that the account of man before God in terms of a court trial has an unfailing dialectical effectiveness. To be sure, there can in retrospect be little doubt (at least for a Protestant) of the vitality and revolutionary power of this conception at the time of the Reformation; it did provide God's concretely heard No and paradoxically redeeming Yes-in-No. But there can also be little doubt that the doctrine did not have the same power for those who remained in the Roman Church and for some of the humanists. Theologians like Gerhard faced a grim alternative: either to assume that (however things might *seem*) the teaching of a forensic justification was *really* effective also among the opponents and that their rejection of it was simply a refusal to acknowledge what they knew to be true—this would be to call into question either their sincerity or their courage; or to assume that the situation in which forensic justification was a dialectically effective doctrine is the only situation which is redeemable. The former assumption excludes in advance any evidence which could controvert it. The latter assumption entails a contradiction of the principle of justification through faith alone, for it demands by implication the performance of a "work" as a condition of salvation; namely, the work of transplanting oneself into the situation of the Protestant-Lutherans of the sixteenth and seventeenth centuries.

Beyond this alternative there was a way out which Gerhard was on the verge of taking but did not actually take. It would have been first to abstract a formal statement of the criterion in his forensic justification and secondly to regard the extreme situations of which he speaks as universally possible but not necessarily universally actual. He came close to performing the first task when he acknowledged that *whatever* drives man to despair (summarily called *tentationes,* XVI.250) at his own resources is the *concio legis,* the accusing voice of the law before God the Judge, regardless of how it happens: whether through the "image of a trial before God" or through another image or through natural calamities or through intellectual pursuits. But Gerhard did not perform this task. Furthermore, he might have accounted for the experience embodied in forensic justification in terms of its universal possibility: that is to say, the situation of being *in extremis,* in despair over one's sin, can be presented as a universal possibility even though actually the number of people who are, or the number of times at which they are, in that situation is limited. This I think Gerhard partly recognized also, for he does seem to acknowledge that there are other ways of regarding man than from the standpoint of his sinfulness, but his most important question is whether a man can still be saved if the only thing that ultimately matters is his imperfection. When regarded from the standpoint from which man is seen in the worst possible way—as worthless, as nothing, as the object of God's undiminished wrath—he is still redeemable. It was this fact that the Reformation theology witnessed—the possibility of redemption out of the most radically evil situation possible, namely, the situation in which the one overwhelming fact is that man is not perfect. The extent to which this extreme situation is communicated, and its salvation made effective, is the extent to which a doctrine has met its dialectical and paradoxical criterion. Gerhard did not, however, explore this path to any length.

The fact that the same elements of form, dialectic, and paradox are to be found in both Thomas and Gerhard, though differently emphasized and differently related, does not mean that there is a final identity of their whole views. On the contrary, the wholes are not interchangeable. Why this is the case can be seen if we look at the different primary criteria which *caritas* and *fides* imply. To illustrate, let us suppose we are within the *caritas* perspective, and we begin by asking the moral question whether act *x* was a good act. We are told it was good. We proceed to ask why it was good. To that question initially many different answers might be given. Thomas might show, for example, how it exemplifies the principle that parents are to be loved more than a spouse "objectively."[4] But we can ask further (as we could with regard to any other answer that might have been given), "Why is it morally good to love parents more than a spouse objectively?" As the questions and answers continue, the final answer will always be (if the questioner and answerer are patient and acute enough), "Because this act, or this principle, exemplifies *caritas.*" If we then ask, "Why is it that an act of *caritas* or a principle exemplifying *caritas* is good?", the only answer is, that is how God has ordered things. That is to say, the order of things encapsuled in the concept of *caritas* is (to use Collingwood's phrase) an absolute presupposition of the rationale. To deny that order from within this rationale would be a self-contradiction. For anyone who is actually within the system of thought named by *caritas,* the reduction of answers to *caritas* is the grounding of them on an answer which is actually and most completely satisfying. To ask whether the order of *caritas* is really good is like asking whether the order which God has established is really the order He has established. It is a question which cannot be raised as a

4. Cf. above, Chapter VI.

matter of practical concern within the *caritas*-whole. If it is raised, it is done only methodologically and its answer can be only a reverse formulation of the question itself—this is God's ordering of things. When the question can be practically raised, when it is *actuel,* then the questioner is no longer within the *caritas*-whole. Such was, of course, the case with Gerhard.

Fides functions similarly in Gerhard's rationale, implicating not only the final answer but also the dialectic which is involved in the very asking of the questions. Thus, if we start with the same question, "Is act *x* a good act?" and receive an affirmative answer, we may go on to ask, "Why is it a good act?" "Because it proceeds from *fides*" is the final answer which could be reached through many possible intermediate answers. The only answer to the question, "Why is it good if it proceeds from *fides?*", is, that is how God is pleased. But *fides* does more than provide the final answer concerning the nature of a good act, for its significant rationale is not a formal one alongside of *caritas.* That is to say, the question, "Is act *x* a good act?", not only occasions an account of the nature of a good act; it is also a question actually raised by some person in a concrete situation and put to another person (even if that other person be the answering self). The raising of the question implies that the person senses that he cannot *rely* on his morality as a basis for being accepted; it implies that he has heard or sensed, in the ambiguity of his act, a condemnation of himself either by himself or by another person. The answer, given by himself or by another, is, therefore, one through which he hears himself either further condemned or accepted by the other. Furthermore, when the question, "Is it good?", is the form in which a person expresses his despair, that is, his awareness of God's total rejection of him, then the question has reached its highest dialectical pitch; and the answer, which is the final one, is that through which he hears himself accepted by the very God who totally rejects him. That is the answer of *fides.*

If, then, *fides* and *caritas* perform the same function in the rationale, we may perhaps be inclined to think that Thomas and

Gerhard are after all saying precisely the same thing in different words; that when we read Thomas through Gerhard's eyes we shall simply substitute *fides* for *caritas* and when we read Gerhard through Thomas' eyes we shall simply put *caritas* wherever Gerhard has *fides;* that it is like translating from one language into another when the cultural background is largely the same—you may miss a few shadings here and there but nothing of the essential content if you translate carefully; and that what we need is a dictionary to bring the two together.

Such a view overlooks too many difficulties. For although faith-as-trust and faith-formed-by-love are in many respects interchangeable in meaning and function, there still is a difference which emerges when one examines the relation they suggest *to other wholes.* This difference makes it impossible to translate the one into the other, but it does allow the hope that there is a perspective which can unite the two.

To make this difference clear, let me construct an extreme example. It is possible to suppose that there are two total perspectives set over against each other, with no points of contact between them. (Actually one may perhaps always find *some* points of contact, if only minor ones.) One may suppose, further, that there is no one who is not either within the one or within the other of those two total perspectives. In such circumstances two major problems are met if any attempt at relating or comparing or confronting the two wholes is made. The one problem is to determine from within the one whole what the other even means; that seems impossible as long as there are no points of contact whatsoever. The only procedure open would seem to be to interpret the one in terms of the other—and whether that would or would not do justice to it, one could never know. The second problem, not entirely distinct from the first, arises if, by the standards of the one, the other is basically false and if, moreover, there is no third and superior perspective from which to criticize both. How shall one account for the fact that there are people who believe it with an apparently unassailable genuineness of conviction?

In those extreme circumstances there seem to be only two options. The first one may be called the imperialistic. It is the simple reassertion of one's own perspective together with the suppression or recasting of the other. The second may be called the open option. It is the reassertion of a perspective "under the forgiveness of sins." That is to say, one can always find a point of contact with other views if that point is the imperfection in all of them. The one thing which can be said of every given perspective is that it is not incorrigible. Each one is, to be sure, ultimate for those who are embraced in it. There was, for example, no serious question for Thomas that the order of *caritas* was ultimate, that is, God's own ordering of things; and Gerhard had no serious question about the ultimacy of justification through faith. And one cannot, by an act of the will or intellect, escape from the truth by which one is caught. Yet even that which presents itself as incorrigibly and ultimately true may be held open to the possibility, which sometimes but not always becomes an actuality, that something else might also show itself to be true. This way of maintaining a perspective involves the paradox. For if there is no serious or practical doubt as to the truth of its founding principles, and if one takes the question of truth with an unconditional seriousness—then it seems to be self-defeating to allow that an opposing perspective may be equally true. This posture seems to negate the seriousness of truth as well as the commitment to a perspective which has shown its truth. That it is, however, a paradoxical and not a self-contradictory posture is shown by the fact that the consequences which ought to follow as a matter of fact do not. Neither the seriousness of the quest for truth nor the power of its claim on the mind and heart is actually destroyed by holding thus openly to truth.[5]

5. This is not to say, of course, that everyone is actually unconditionally concerned about the truth of his views or principles—he may be satisfied with dogmatically held opinions. But granted the passion for truth, the option of the open perspective is paradoxical; it is neither unconcernedly relativistic nor imperiously absolutistic.

Both Gerhard's *fides* and Thomas' *caritas* represent, I believe, the open alternative rather than the imperialistic one. This can be said in spite of the suspicion under which scholasticism in every form has been placed by psittacistic successors who tended to forget that, as Hans von Balthasar has said of Thomas, "Thomistic spirit and thought, as it is found in the historical person of Aquinas . . . , is . . . a posture of openness toward all the fronts of the world."[6] But Gerhard and Thomas represent this openness in different ways. This difference constitutes the impossibility of substituting the one for the other or of adding them together. It is a difference which not only marked the limits of the rapprochement of Leibniz and Bossuet in the seventeenth century, but is still the typical difference between the Roman and the Protestant confessions.

What is that difference? *Fides,* we must remember, was not only the utter reliance of the whole self upon Christ as the Other person, the Advocate and Mediator. It was also the dialectical and paradoxical negation of works. The assumption in Gerhard's notion of justification is that men are striving for good works and are burdened by their awareness of the impossibility of perfection in performing them. To such people *fides* offers the only consolation.

> People are to be encouraged, nay urged, to do good works according to the norm of the law; but they are not to be brought into the theater of our justification before God, for there the opposition between believing and doing, grace and works, law and gospel is permanent (*perpetua*) (XIV.55).
> . . . There is nothing which can lift and console one who is burdened by the weight of sin and terrified by the sense of the divine wrath except the free promise of the gospel concerning the remission of sins on account of Christ. (XVI.250)

6. *Thomas von Aquin im kirchlichen Denken,* p. 72. Quoted by Robert Markovics, *Grundsätzliche Vorfragen einer methodischen Thomasdeutung,* p. 19.

To be saved through faith is interpreted positively as being saved through reliance upon the merit of Christ; negatively it is interpreted as being saved through that which negates the claim of works. The full significance of this negative side becomes clear only when it is set against the background of that to which the Reformation sought to witness. The question which gripped the Reformers (on this point there was no disagreement among Luther, Calvin, and Zwingli) and aroused their passion and despair was how to be or to become good enough to endure the intimacy of God's presence. Their religious concern was, in other words, expressed in the quest for moral (rather than cognitive) perfection; their problem lay in the fact, not that no answer to this question was available, but rather that the available answer did not satisfy. That answer was the following: you could become good enough to stand before God by following the various procedures that the church had, according to its divine authority, laid down. Those procedures were in short one's "works."

Now, to make sense of the Reformation it is not necessary to assume that everyone except the Reformers was too naive to see that, judged by the standard of absolute moral perfection, even the person who did the works of the church was far from perfect. On the contrary, if you accepted the presupposition of *caritas,* that the existing church's system of works (which had, of course, become a rather distorted version of *caritas* by the sixteenth century) was the way of attaining a supernatural end in spite of the empirical actuality of moral imperfection; if you believed that these works did achieve their end because they were according to God's plan—then you had the answer to the moral question. The *aporia* of the Reformers arose precisely from the fact that they did not and could not in actual life accept that basic presupposition; they had no effective answer to their quest.

When the breakthrough came with the discovery or revelation that the sinner is justified through faith, this was not the discovery of another system of procedures or a new set of moral principles.

It was not the case that henceforth, instead of doing the works of the church, one did the work of believing in Christ's promises. On the contrary, *per fidem*, instead of providing a new moral principle, pointed to the paradoxical in the given moral principles. *Fides was the negation of the absoluteness of that which, in the given situation, presented itself as absolute;* namely, the demand for moral perfection, together with the means by which it was to be accomplished.[7]

Fides was the power which made it possible to transcend a system from within. Good works were still to be done, but out of faith. The worth of the works was still the same as before. The principles according to which one decided in specific cases on a course of action were no different from what they had been. Only they were *now* done *per fidem*, that is, redeemed by the recognition that they could not and need not be used as a base on which to stand against the annihilating judgment of that God who is satisfied with nothing less than the perfect. "Through faith" opened the moral realm *from within* by placing it under the criterion that there was no moral principle or act to which one had to hold absolutely. Unless, therefore, *fides* is understood not only as a reliance upon Christ, but also as the paradoxical element in a total moral perspective, the principle of "through faith" either is transformed into a new "work" or topples over into moral chaos or license.

It is this *fides*, then, which characterizes Gerhard's outlook and stalks, as an indefatigable huntsman, every part of his rationale. It provides the contrast in the whole between him and Thomas. For while *fides* is (as paradoxical) the self-negation of a whole ("works") or the transcending of a perspective from within, the

7. Similarly the *sola Scriptura* as a theological principle meant not only that one heard (positively) the voice of God in the Scriptures but that (negatively) one did not hear it in the church which claimed to be it. "Scripture alone" negated the absoluteness of the tradition of the empirical church which presented itself as absolute.

caritas of Thomas has another character. *Caritas* suffuses the whole rationale but does not bear in itself explicitly and totally a criterion for self-judgment. There are, to be sure, the paradoxical concept of the movement of the free will and related concepts, which are included in the whole order of *caritas;* but *caritas* itself is that order without at the same time transcending it. *Fides* provides the criterion which opens it in principle to all other perspectives. In principle, that is to say, the perspective of *fides* includes a total self-corrective element which is not explicit in *caritas*.

Certainly Thomas himself, in his actual work, was as open to any truth, regardless of its source, and as open to correction of his own conclusions, as Gerhard might have been. But Gerhard was heir to a power which was able to go beyond a whole even while staying within it. Thomas did not have to overthrow a cosmos of convictions in order to construct his system; he had only to face Aristotelianism and adjust it. In Gerhard's thought, on the other hand, there is still recorded the fact that in the Reformation a whole way of thinking was overthrown and transcended from within. It matters not that that way of thinking was, at least to some extent, a misinterpretation and distortion of the scholastic system of Thomas. The significant fact is that it was a whole perspective dearly held, the giving up of which seemed to mean at the outset the forsaking of God Himself.

In *caritas* and *fides* one has, therefore, two characteristically different ways of facing the new and changing. The *caritas*-outlook adapts to it gradually; it can change elements in its outlook, it can redefine old concepts and thereby grow into something actually new; but it can never say of itself *as a whole* that it is, like all things, imperfect and transient. In this sense it is always acquisitive.

The *fides*-outlook, since it denies in principle the perfection of any thing or totality of things, is less concerned about continuity with the old. It need not be concerned to show that new convictions are underneath the same as the old or at least implied in the old. On the contrary, it is concerned to show, first, that no given conviction, dogma, or presupposition, however ultimate it appears, can claim an absoluteness which exempts it from a possibly annihilating criticism; and, secondly, that *this* is the only continuity it need find in the history of things or in their present interrelations. It finds its maximum in the minimum; the abiding and ultimately significant characteristic of all things at all times in all places is their fallenness, their *im*perfection. *Fides* is, we may say, revolutionary; *caritas* is evolutionary. *Fides* is self-transcending; *caritas* is self-expanding.

Yet perhaps they require one another. *Fides* is concerned to show that even the worst possible is still redeemable. Where all positive continuity or relation has vanished, there still is *this* continuity that everything finite is also fallen.[8] But the *caritas*-outlook can provide the sober corrective which prevents *fides* from lapsing into unguided revolution. It seeks to show, according to its basic conviction, that there is a positive continuity in the divine ordering of the world which can be actually found; if things are never as good as they should be, neither are they as bad as they could be. There seems to be no reason at the outset, therefore, why there could not be a perspective which is both *fides* and *caritas,* not by simple addition of the two but as the outgrowth of a new vision.

A CONCLUDING SUGGESTION

Our final question concerns the basic intuition—as it were, the vision—to which *caritas* and *fides* point. Here we are asking, not what did Thomas (and classical Roman Catholicism) and Gerhard (and classical Protestantism) *say?* but rather, what did they *see?* At this point discussion enters a stage that can properly be called a discussion of their "witness." How did Gerhard see

8. Thus, Sir Winston Churchill found it possible to soften, if only briefly, the hardened positions of opposing political ideologies by referring to the Soviet peoples as "our fellow mortals."

man differently from Thomas, and (since our own witness is also involved) how do we see man differently from, or similarly to, either or both of them?

Perhaps the different quality of the two visions can be summarily expressed in the words, man's "richness" and man's "inner contradictoriness." The former characterizes Thomas, the latter Gerhard. It is surely clear from an analysis of *caritas* that Thomas sees the whole complexity and manifoldness of the created world as reflecting the abundance of God's resourcefulness and ordering love. His ordering love is reflected in the endlessness, the inexhaustibility of the created world. Man is richly endowed. There are many and various aspects to his being, and what is partially seen in each of them is cumulative in the whole vision. Put everything together and you approach a conception of the richness of God's own life. It was as true of Thomas as of Aristotle that "there is nothing in nature, were it even the most despised and lowly thing, which does not contain something wonderful in itself."[9] The scars of sin could not hide that basic character of the created world.

By contrast Gerhard sees less of creation's richness and more of its inner contradictions: man trying to save himself though unable to do so—a sinner before the judgment of an angry and righteous God. In this vision of the creature-Creator relationship, which Gerhard witnesses, the whole appears not so much summatively as the richness of creation reflecting the largesse of God; it appears rather in a dimensionless point or critical moment as the possible impossibility, reflecting the omnipotent compassion of the One who is able to overcome the manifestly self-destructive conflicts in creation. Gerhard saw the scars on all created things—even on the most holy among them, the church in its concrete representation. The universal presence of sin and its conquest through Christ was the overpowering fact. He saw

9. W. Jaeger, *Aristoteles*, p. 365.

something which Thomas lived too early in history to see. Thomas never had to "give up" the most holy thing, the church and its depository of revelation. In the church God was always immediately and unambiguously present. For practical purposes he did not need to distinguish between what the temporal church said and what God said. It was otherwise with the Reformers, who sensed the ambiguity, even the idolatry, of the church which they knew, the spurious paradoxicality of the decision not to decide for oneself. The church had lost its equivalence to the divine; it showed the scars of sin as did every other creature, and yet it denied that they were there.

For Gerhard this meant, as it had for the earlier Reformers, that true holiness lies not in any unambiguously good works, even when performed according to the ordinance of the church, but rather in the sacrifice of every claim to a goodness that can stand against the judgment of God. The holy man is not man in the fullness of his endowment, but he is the man who forgoes any claim to absolute goodness; and the church is not that institution into whose authority and discipline sin has not penetrated, but it is that institution which lives by the *fides* it proclaims—that holiness is found only in the total acceptance of God's judgment.

In other words, God reveals Himself finally not in the multitude of things and the accumulated truths of the Scriptures and the church's tradition, but pre-eminently in that single radical sacrifice to which the Scriptures bear testimony. The most significant thing that can be said of man and his works when viewed in their fullness as good creatures of God is the judgment, "You are not good."

Multitude, manifoldness, richness on the one hand; contradictoriness, radical sacrifice on the other hand—these are two visions of man in his nature and ultimate destiny. Are they irreconcilably opposed? Perhaps it is only a matter of sobriety to acknowledge that from the viewpoint of the first the second must, at least initially, appear as poverty-stricken and "pessimistic," a system of "unbearable monotony" and "loathsome narrowness."[10] And from the viewpoint of the second the first must appear as unrealistically "optimistic" or humanistic, uncognizant of the dark aspects of life.

Yet I should like to suggest that the two visions do approximate each other so that they are at least mutually intelligible (or, more precisely, mutually viewable). For I believe that anyone who has learned to appreciate, as did Thomas, the full complexity of creation, the balances and counterbalances, the limitations of parts on other parts, and the inexhaustibility of the whole —that such a one comes close to knowing what the Reformers saw in their insistence that nothing, not even the church itself, can claim unconditional validity. On the other hand, anyone who through a single shattering experience—a *Turmelebnis* or mystical vision—or through the dawning conviction that the decisive factor of man's condition is ultimately not his nature and creaturehood but his sin and misery, has given up what is most holy and sacred in this world, does find that in the very losing of his gods he is opened in principle to regain everything in all of its richness —to have all things as though he had them not, to see God beyond the shattered gods, to see man in his holiness through the fragments of his broken goodness. Such a one comes close to beholding the richness of Thomas' vision.

Even though, therefore, these two visions are not simple complements of each other, nor identical with each other, it is possible to approximate a view of the one from within the other and to see, in the words of I Corinthians 13:12, "through a glass darkly." Surely, one can then hope that *fides* and *caritas* can be united without being destroyed.

10. "Unerträgliche Monotonie" and "Ekel erregende Enge." See Troeltsch, *Vernunft und Offenbarung*, p. 205.

Bibliography

PRIMARY SOURCES

Gerhard, Johann, *Loci Theologici*, 10 vols. Leipzig, J. C. Hinrichs, 1885.

————, *Meditationes sacrae*, London, 1672.

Pseudo-Dionysius, *De divinis nominibus,* cited according to the text in Thomas' commentary (see below).

Peter the Lombard, *Libri quattuor sententiarum*, Quaracchi, 1916.

Thomas Aquinas, *Summa Theologiae*, 3 vols. Turin and Rome, Marietti, 1952–56.

————, *Commentaria in Evangelia S. Matthaei et S. Joannis*, 4th ed. 2 vols. Turin, Marietti, 1925.

————, *Commentaria in omnes epistolas S. Pauli apostoli*, 2 vols. Turin, Marietti, 1924.

————, *In librum beati Dionysii De divinis nominibus expositio*, ed. C. Pera, Turin, Marietti, 1950.

————, *Quaestiones disputatae*, ed. Raymund Spiazzi, 8th ed. Turin, Marietti, 1949.

————, *Scriptum super libros sententiarum Magistri Petri Lombardi episcopi Parisiensis*, ed. Pierre Mandonnet and M. F. Moos, 4 vols. Paris, Lethielleux, 1929–33.

————, *Super epistolas S. Pauli lectura*, cura P. Raphaelis, ed. viii revisa, Rome, Marietti, 1953. (Quotation from I Corinthians is from this edition, the first volume. Quotation from the other Pauline letters is from the 1924 Marietti edition listed above.)

BIBLIOGRAPHY

SECONDARY SOURCES

Alszeghy, Z., *Grundformen der Liebe, die Theorie der Gottesliebe bei dem hl. Bonaventura*, Rome, 1946.

Althaus, Paul, *Die Prinzipien der deutschen reformierten Dogmatik im Zeitalter der aristotelischen Scholastik*, Leipzig, 1914.

Aubert, Roger, *Le problème de l'acte de foi, données traditionelles et résultats des controverses récentes*, 2d ed. Louvain, Warny, 1950.

Auer, Johann, *Die Entwicklung der Gnadenlehre in der Hochscholastik, I. Teil: Das Wesen der Gnade*, Freiburg, 1942.

———, *Die Entwicklung der Gnadenlehre in der Hochscholastik, II. Teil: Das Wirken der Gnade*, Freiburg, 1951.

Berkouwer, G. C., *Recent Developments in Roman Catholic Thought*, trans. J. J. Lamberts, Grand Rapids, Eerdmans, 1958.

Boettcher, Carl Julius, *Das Leben Dr. Johann Gerhards*, Leipzig, 1858.

Bouillard, Henri, *Conversion et grâce chez s. Thomas d'Aquin, étude historique*, Paris, Aubier, 1944.

Brunner, Emil, *Der Mensch im Widerspruch, die christliche Lehre vom wahren und vom wirklichen Menschen*, 3d ed. Zürich, Zwingli Verlag, 1941.

Burnaby, J., *Amor Dei, A Study of the Religion of St. Augustine*, London, 1938.

Davies, Rupert E., *The Problem of Authority in the Continental Reformers, A Study in Luther, Zwingli, and Calvin*, London, 1946.

D'Arcy, Martin C., *The Mind and Heart of Love, A Study in Eros and Agape*, London, 1945.

Dorner, J. A., *History of Protestant Theology*, trans. George Robson (vol. 1) and Sophia Taylor (vol. 2), 2 vols. Edinburgh, 1871.

Drummond, Andrew Landale, *German Protestantism since Luther*, London, Epworth, 1951.

Dublanchy, E., "Charité," *Dictionnaire de théologie catholique*, 2d ed. 2, 2217–65, Paris, 1902.

Duméry, Henry, *Critique et religion, problèmes de méthode en philosophie de la religion*, Paris, 1957.

Egenter, Richard, *Gottesfreundschaft, die Lehre von der Gottesfreundschaft in der Scholastik und Mystik des 12. und 13. Jahrhunderts*, Augsburg, 1928.

BIBLIOGRAPHY

Elert, Werner, *Der christliche Glaube*, 3d ed. Hamburg, Furche Verlag, 1956.

Eschweiler, Karl, *Die Philosophie der spanischen Spätscholastik auf den deutschen Universitäten des 17. Jahrhunderts*, Spanische Forschungen der Görresgesellschaft, vol. 1.

Fabro, Cornelio, *La nozione metafisica di partecipazione secondo Tomaso d'Aquino*, Milan, 1939.

Feder, Alfred, "Des Aquinaten Kommentar zu Pseudo-Dionysius De divinis nominibus," *Scholastik*, 1 (1926), 321–51.

Fehr, J., *Das Offenbarungsproblem in dialektischer und thomistischer Theologie*, Freiburg, 1939.

Fischer, Erdmann, *Vita Ioannis Gerhardi*, Leipzig, 1723.

Friethoff, C., "Die Prädestinationslehre bei Thomas von Aquin und Calvin," *Divus Thomas*, 4 (1926), 195–206; 280–302; 445–66.

Geiger, Louis B., *La participation dans la philosophie de s. Thomas d'Aquin*, Paris, 1942.

———, *Le problème de l'amour chez saint Thomas d'Aquin*, Montreal and Paris, 1952.

Gerrish, B. A., *Grace and Reason, A Study in the Theology of Luther*, Oxford, 1962.

Gilbert, Neal Ward, *Renaissance Concepts of Method*, New York, 1960.

Gilson, Étienne, *The Spirit of Medieval Philosophy*, trans. A. H. C. Downes, New York, 1940.

Grabmann, Martin, *Einführung in die Summa Theologiae des heiligen Thomas von Aquin*, Freiburg/Breisgau, 1928.

———, *Thomas von Aquin, eine Einführung in seine Persönlichkeit und Gedankenwelt*, 4th ed. Kempten and München, 1920.

Grünhut, L., *Eros und Agape, eine metaphysisch-religionsphilosophische Untersuchung*, Leipzig, 1931.

Guardini, Romano, *Freiheit, Gnade, Schicksal*, München, 1948.

Hägglund, Bengt, *Die heilige Schrift und ihre Deutung in der Theologie Johann Gerhards, eine Untersuchung über das altlutherische Schriftverständnis*, Lund, 1951.

———, *Theologie und Philosophie bei Luther und in der occamistischen Tradition*, Lund, 1955.

BIBLIOGRAPHY

Harnack, Adolf von, *Lehrbuch der Dogmengeschichte*, 4th ed. 3 vols. Tübingen, 1909–10.

Hazard, Paul, *The European Mind, The Critical Years 1680–1715*, New Haven, 1953.

Heim, Karl, *Das Gewissheitsproblem in der systematischen Theologie bis zu Schleiermacher*, Leipzig, 1911.

Henle, R. J., *Saint Thomas and Platonism: A Study of the Plato and Platonici Texts in the Writings of St. Thomas*, The Hague, 1956.

Heussi, Karl, *Geschichte der theologischen Fakultät zu Jena*, Weimar, 1954.

Huit, C., "Les éléments platoniciens de la doctrine de s. Thomas," *Revue Thomiste*, 19 (1911), 724–66.

Jaeger, Werner, *Aristoteles, Grundlegung einer Geschichte seiner Entwicklung*, 2d ed. Berlin, 1955.

Klaiber, (Pfarrer), "Die Lehre der altprotestantischen Dogmatiker von dem testimonium Spiritus Sancti und ihre dogmatische Bedeutung," *Jahrbücher für deutsche Theologie*, 2 (1857), 1–54.

Küng, Hans, *Rechtfertigung, die Lehre Karl Barths und eine katholische Besinnung*, Einsiedeln, 1957.

Landgraf, Artur Michael, *Dogmengeschichte der Frühscholastik*, Bd. I/1 and I/2, Regensburg, 1952–53.

Lang, Hugo, *Gottes gute Welt, die kirchliche Schöpfungslehre*, Speyer, Pilger Verlag, 1950.

Lewalter, Ernst, *Spanisch-jesuitische und deutsch-lutherische Metaphysik des 17. Jahrhunderts*, Ibero-amerikanische Studien, 4, Hamburg, 1935.

Little, Arthur, *The Platonic Heritage of Thomism*, Dublin, 1950.

Lottin, Odon, "Les dons du Saint-Esprit chez les théologiens depuis P. Lombard jusqu'à s. Thomas d'Aquin," *Rech. Théol. Anc. Méd.*, 1 (1929), 41–61.

Lubac, Henri de, *Surnaturel, études historiques*, Aubier, 1946.

Manser, Gallus M., *Das Wesen des Thomismus*, 3d ed. Freiburg, 1949.

Markovics, Robert, *Grundsätzliche Vorfragen einer methodischen Thomasdeutung*, Rome, 1956.

Monda, Antonio M. di, *La legge nuova della libertà secondo s. Tommaso*, Naples, 1954.

BIBLIOGRAPHY

Niebuhr, H. Richard, *Christ and Culture*, New York, 1951.

Nygren, Anders, *Agape and Eros*, trans. Philip Watson, London, SPCK, 1953.

Petersen, Peter, *Geschichte der aristotelischen Philosophie im protestantischen Deutschland*, Leipzig, 1921.

Preus, Herman, and Edmund Smits, ed., *The Doctrine of Man in Classical Lutheran Theology*, trans. from the works of Martin Chemnitz and Johann Gerhard, Minneapolis, 1962.

Radecke, Waldemar, *Der Rechtfertigungsbegriff in Johann Gerhards Loci theologici*, Bonn, 1900.

Reinhard, J., *Die Prinzipienlehre der lutherischen Dogmatik von 1700 bis 1750 (Hollatz, Buddeus, Mosheim)*, Leipzig dissertation, Naumburg, 1906.

Reid, John K. S., *The Authority of Scripture, A Study of the Reformation and Post-Reformation Understanding of the Bible*, London, Methuen, 1957.

Ritschl, Albrecht, *A Critical History of the Christian Doctrine of Justification and Reconciliation*, trans. John S. Black, Edinburgh, Edmonston and Douglas, 1872.

Ritschl, Otto, *Dogmengeschichte des Protestantismus*, vol. 4, Göttingen, 1927.

Robin, Léon, *La théorie platonicienne de l'amour*, Paris, 1908.

Rousselot, P., *Pour l'histoire du problème de l'amour au moyen âge*, Münster, 1908.

Schenke, Friedrich, *Der Kirchengedanke J. Gerhards und seiner Zeit*, Gütersloh, 1931.

Schlink, Edmund, "Gesetz und Evangelium als kontroverstheologisches Problem," *Kerygma und Dogma*, 7 (1961), 31–35.

Schmid, Heinrich, *The Doctrinal Theology of the Evangelical Lutheran Church*, trans. from 3d ed. by Hay and Jacobs, Minneapolis, 1961 (c 1899).

Schupp, Johann, *Die Gnadenlehre des Petrus Lombardus*, Pfullendorf, 1932.

Schwarzenau, Paul, *Der Wandel im theologischen Ansatz bei Melanchthon von 1525–1535*, Gütersloh, Bertelsmann, 1956.

Simonin, H. D., "Autour de la solution thomiste du problème de l'amour," *Archives d'histoire doctrinale et littéraire du moyen âge,* 6 (1932), 174–276.

Stévaux, A., "La doctrine de la charité dans les commentaires des Sentences de s. Albert, s. Bonaventure et s. Thomas," *Ephemerides theologiae Lovanienses,* 24 (1948), 59–97.

Troeltsch, Ernst, *Vernunft und Offenbarung bei Johann Gerhard und Melanchthon,* Göttingen, Vandenhoeck und Ruprecht, 1891.

Unamuno, Miguel de, *Tragic Sense of Life,* trans. J. E. Crawford, Dover Publications, 1954.

Völkl, Richard, *Die Selbstliebe in der Hl. Schrift und bei Thomas von Aquin,* München, Carl Zink Verlag, 1956.

Vanier, Paul, *Théologie trinitaire chez s. Thomas d'Aquin, évolution du concept d'action notionelle,* Montreal and Paris, 1953.

Vignaux, Paul, *Justification et prédestination au xive siècle,* Paris, 1934.

Warnach, Viktor, *Agape, die Liebe als Grundmotiv der neutestamentlichen Theologie,* Düsseldorf, 1951.

Weber, Emil, *Die analytische Methode der luth. Orthodoxie,* Naumburg, 1907.

———, *Der Einfluss der protestantischen Schulphilosophie auf die orthodox-lutherische Dogmatik,* Leipzig, 1908.

———, *Die philosophische Scholastik des deutschen Protestantismus im Zeitalter der Orthodoxie,* Leipzig, 1907.

Winkler, Martin, *Die Tugendlehre des hl. Thomas von Aquin nach ihren aristotelischen, plotinischen und christlichen Bestandteilen,* Bamberg, 1913.

Wundt, Max, *Die deutsche Schulmetaphysik des 17. Jahrhunderts,* Heidelberger Abhandlungen zur Philosophie und ihrer Geschichte, 22, Tübingen, 1939.

Index of References
to Loci Theologici and Summa Theologiae

LOCI THEOLOGICI

INDEX OF REFERENCES

SUMMA THEOLOGIAE

INDEX OF REFERENCES

General Index

GENERAL INDEX

Augsburg Confession, 42
Augustine, Saint, 46, 60, 64, 73, 114, 119, 121, 156, 162, 212
Austria, 41
Authority: 4, 72; double origin of, 71–75; hierarchical, 80; in new creation, 137; relation to culpable ignorance, 75; of Scripture, 112 f.
Auxilium Dei, 117, 119, 121, 230

Balthasar, H. Urs von, 245
Baroque era, 17
Barth, Karl, 1; doctrines of, 55, 238
Barzun, Jacques, 221
Beatitude: natural, 50, 54 f., 68; object of, 55; supernatural, 54 f., 137
Beatitudes, Matthean, 140
Bellarmine, Robert, 33, 84, 87, 95, 98, 154, 156, 166, 173 ff., 178, 180 n.
Berkouwer, G. C., 237 f.
Bernard of Clairvaux, 215 n.
Bernd, Margareta, 38
Bible, 4. *See also* Scripture
Birth, virgin, 31
Blasphemy, 217
Body, in relation to soul, 99
Boettcher, Carl Julius, 38 n.
Bonaventure, Saint, 212
Bonum in communi, 67–68
Bossuet, Jacques, 2, 3, 245
Bouillard, Henri, 49, 54 n., 55 n., 117 n., 172 n.
Bradley, Francis Herbert, 56
Bultmann, Rudolf, 37 n.

Calamitates, 25
Calvin and Calvinism, 3, 4, 8, 16, 18, 22, 40, 54, 113 n., 246
Caritas: acquisitive, 248; comparison of Thomas and Gerhard on, 194–95, 197; criterion implied in, 241; self-expanding, 248. *See also* Faith; Holy Spirit; Love
Caritas creata, 210
Cartesian, 22
Caselius, Johann, 15
Casimir, Johann, 40 f.
Catholic, Roman, 3, 9, 18, 37, 172, 236, 249

Causa agens, 59
Causality, divine, 56
Causes, God and, 120
Certainty, of salvation, 178
Charisma, 125
Christ: 99, 112, 175, 180, 182, 184, 193, 196, 200 ff., 216, 227, 237, 245, 247; as Mediator, 181; as Way to God, 102
Christianity, 225, 227
Christology, duality of, 53
Church: and Bible, 4; as sinful, 251
Coburg, 40 f.
Coconnier, M., 216 n.
Colomesius, Paul, 43
Command, divine, 107, 167
Commitment, to God, 197
Communication, of nature and grace, 210, 223, 226
Complacency, 188–89
Complacentia impressa, 147
Complementum, 161
Conceptualization, 36; modes of, 11, 229, 238 ff.
Concupiscence, 67 n.
Contemplation, 36
Continuity of creations, 207 f., 228
Contradiction, law of, 30
Contraries, harmony of, 99
Controversy, interconfessional, 26
Conversion, 152, 155, 230
Cooperation, with God, 137, 150
Corruption, of nature and man, 65–66, 70, 74, 101, 111, 118, 166, 236. *See also* Fallenness
Counsel, theological gift of, 133
Courage, gift of, 136
Cramer, Daniel, 19
Creation: 44, 45 n.; continuity and discontinuity of, 226; contradictions in, 250; goodness of, 49; harmony of, 82, 221; largesse of, 250; new, 10, 45, 114, 147; and restoration, 149; Trinitarian view of, 117; and Word of God, 51; wounds of, 63–69. *See also* Nature
Creations, discontinuity of, 125, 209
Creed, apostolic, 113; need and role of, 72 f.

264

GENERAL INDEX

Friendship, with God, 222
Friethoff, C., 54

Gass, Wilhelm, 15
Geiger, Louis B., 216 n.
Geneva, 16
Genus, and species, 140, 209
Georg, Johann, 41
Gerhard, Andreas (John's grandfather), 38
Gerhard, Bartholomaeus (John's father), 38
Gerhard, Johann (John's son), 43
Gerhard, Johann Andreas (John's son), 43
Gerhard, Johann Ernst (John's son), 43
Gerhard, Johann Friedrich (John's son), 43
Gerhard, John (1582–1637): "archtheologian," 3; Aristotelianism, 8, 83; children, 43; on despair, 110, 236, 240; dialectic-personal rationale, 11, 229 ff.; on *donum supernaturale*, 91–96; education and background, 38–40; on faith alone, 187; family, 38–43; on *fides*, 9, 225–28, 236–38, 241–52; as focus of the seventeenth century, 3; on free will, 153–68, 235; on God's judgment, 173; illnesses, 38, 39–40; at Jena, 39 ff.; on justification, 151–52, 168 ff.; on law, 105–07, 199–205; life of, 38–43; on man, 84; marriages, 43; Melanchthonian heritage, 22, 27–28; on merit, 187 ff.; and new metaphysics, 19–20, 22, 29; on penitence, 178–79; rationale of creation, 83–113, 123, 226, 232–35; rationale of new creation, 149–205, 232–35; on Scripture, 7–8, 30–36; Testament of, 39; and Thomas, 9, 83–88, 91–96, 105–07, 151–52, 169, 187 f., 199–205, 225–32, 236, 241–52. WORKS: *Confessio catholica* (1633–37), 42–43; *Harmoniae evangelicae Chemnitio-Lyserianae continuatio* (1626–27), 43; *Loci Theologici* (1610–

21), 42, 102–04; *Meditationes sacrae* (1606), 43; *De necessitate et contingentia* (1607), 42; *Patrologia* (1653), 43; *De vero* (1606), 42. *See also* Index of References
Germany, 8, 40
Gessner, Solomon, 19, 39
Giessen, 18, 21, 40
Gifts, of the Holy Spirit, 133 ff.
Gilbert, Neal Ward, 6 n.
Gilson, Etienne, 47, 216 n.
Glory, state of, 115–16, 137
God: agent in conversion, 230, 232, 235; creator of forms, 57; *finis* and form, 105; and gods, 252; life of man, 211; natural knowledge of, 94; object of beatitude, 55, 135, 222; openness to, 137; personal, 106; practical definition of, 255
Good: civil or natural, 111; conflict of public and private, 66–67; formal conception, 67–68; natural and lost, 118; natural and spiritual, 62, 159–60, 165; public and private, 215; self-diffusive, 59; spiritual and civic, 112; temporal and eternal, 80
Gospel: 184, 202; distinguished from law, 199–200; as proclamation, 189–90
Grace: 10; alone, 135; facility, 125; freely given, 125; habitual, 119, 180; healing and elevating, 124; infusion of, 114–15, 177, 180; loss of, 118; perfecting of nature, 126; preparation for, 117; rejection of, as superstructure, 149–50; relation to nature, 122, 125–26; state of, 115; tension in meaning, 147; uncreated, 198; underivability, 126. *See also Gratia*
Gratia: conservans, 46; *gratum faciens*, 45, 125, 174, 180; *praesupponit naturam*, 126
Groningen, 16
Grünhut, L., 216 n.
Guardini, Romano, 48

Habit, as a principle of action, 119
Hägglund, Bengt, 18, 25 n., 30 n.